My
Excel® 2016

Tracy Syrstad

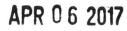

800 East 96th Street,
Indianapolis, Indiana 46240 USA

My Excel® 2016

Copyright © 2016 by Pearson Education

ISBN-13: 978-0-7897-5542-1
ISBN-10: 0-7897-5542-4

Library of Congress Control Number: 2015944607

Printed in the United States of America

First Printing: October 2015

Trademarks

Warning and Disclaimer

Special Sales

For information about buying this title in bulk quantities, or for special sales opportunities (which may include electronic versions; custom cover designs; and content particular to your business, training goals, marketing focus, or branding interests), please contact our corporate sales department at corpsales@pearsoned.com or (800) 382-3419.

For government sales inquiries, please contact governmentsales@pearsoned.com.

For questions about sales outside the U.S., please contact international@pearsoned.com.

Editor-in-Chief
Greg Wiegand

Acquisitions Editor
Michelle Newcomb

Development Editor
Charlotte Kughen

Managing Editor
Kristy Hart

Senior Project Editor
Betsy Gratner

Copy Editor
Bart Reed

Senior Indexer
Cheryl Lenser

Proofreader
Laura Hernandez

Technical Editor
Faithe Wempen

Editorial Assistant
Cindy Teeters

Cover Designer
Mark Shirar

Compositor
Bumpy Design

Contents at a Glance

Table of Contents

8 Using Formulas   **175**

About the Author

Tracy Syrstad is a Microsoft Excel developer and author of eight Excel books. She has been helping people with Microsoft Office issues since 1997 when she discovered free online forums where anyone could ask and answer questions. Tracy discovered she enjoyed teaching others new skills, and when she began working as a developer, she was able to integrate the fun of teaching with one-on-one online desktop sharing sessions. Tracy lives on an acreage in eastern South Dakota with her husband, one dog, two cats, one horse (two soon), and a variety of wild foxes, squirrels, and rabbits.

Dedication

To Eric and Galen, who taught me I'm stronger than I thought.

Acknowledgments

I've always wanted to do a full-color, step-by-step help book, and thanks to Michelle Newcomb, I finally got my chance. Zack Barresse has written *the* book on Excel Tables, and if I had a print copy, it would be rather dog-eared. Last but not least, thank you to my husband, John, who reminded me to eat and get outside when I was obsessing over deadlines.

We Want to Hear from You!

As the reader of this book, *you* are our most important critic and commentator. We value your opinion and want to know what we're doing right, what we could do better, what areas you'd like to see us publish in, and any other words of wisdom you're willing to pass our way.

We welcome your comments. You can email or write to let us know what you did or didn't like about this book—as well as what we can do to make our books better.

Please note that we cannot help you with technical problems related to the topic of this book.

When you write, please be sure to include this book's title and author as well as your name and email address. We will carefully review your comments and share them with the author and editors who worked on the book.

Email: feedback@quepublishing.com

Mail: Que Publishing
         ATTN: Reader Feedback
         800 East 96th Street
         Indianapolis, IN 46240 USA

Reader Services

Visit our website and register this book at quepublishing.com/register for convenient access to any updates, downloads, or errata that might be available for this book.

Introduction

Familiarity with Microsoft Excel is a requirement for most jobs today. Workers in every office use Excel to track and report information. Sales reps track leads, prospects, commissions, and travel expenses in Excel. Workers on the factory floor log schedules and quality data in Excel.

Excel is an amazingly flexible program. A new Excel worksheet offers a seemingly endless blank canvas of rows and columns where you can enter, summarize, and report data of any type. Charts and other data visualization tools can convert a page full of numbers to a visual snapshot. Pivot tables can summarize thousands of detailed records into a one-page summary with just a few mouse clicks.

If you've never opened Excel, or if you've used Excel only to neatly arrange lists in columns, this book will get you up to speed with the real-life skills needed to survive in a job that requires familiarity with Excel.

What's in This Book

Chapter 1, "Understanding the Microsoft Excel Interface," starts off by exploring the user interface. If you're new to Excel or last used a legacy version (Excel 2003 and earlier), you should review this chapter so that you understand the instructions given later in the book. Afterward, you'll learn the basics of managing workbooks and sheets.

Because this book is meant to be a quick reference, you don't have to go through and read the chapters in order. But if you do plan on reading them in order, you'll notice that each chapter builds on skills learned in previous chapters. These skills range from various methods of entering information on a sheet and formatting it to make it more readable, to entering formulas and functions that can calculate data or retrieve information.

But what's Excel without charts and pivot tables? You learn how to insert and format charts, including Sparklines, which are charts that fit in a single cell. You'll be introduced to PivotTables, a powerful tool for quickly summarizing numbers.

Excel also has tools to make it easier to sort data, filter data, consolidate multiple sources, and remove duplicates. It can also quickly subtotal and group your data. What's more, you can add a splash of distinctiveness to a sheet using SmartArt or your own pictures.

Excel even has an online version of itself, the Excel Web App, allowing you to work on a workbook wherever you have Internet access. It's a limited version of Excel, but more functionality is being added all the time. Although this book doesn't cover the app in detail, it will show you how to set up an account and upload a workbook. The functionality it has is similar to the desktop version, so once you know how to perform a certain task on the desktop, you should know how to do it online.

Guidance for Beginners

Most steps in this book require the use of the mouse. All mouse instructions are based on a right-handed mouse. *Click* refers to a single click using the left mouse button. *Double-click* refers to two quick, successive clicks using the left mouse button. *Click and drag* refers to holding down the mouse button while you move the mouse, then releasing the mouse button at the end of the movement. *Right-click* refers to a single click using the right mouse button.

If a keyboard shortcut is provided, you have to press two or more keys on the keyboard at the same time. The keys two are shown with the key names joined with a plus (+) sign. For example, Ctrl+V would require you to hold down the Ctrl key, press the V key once, and then let go of both keys.

Quick Access Toolbar (QAT)

Built-in help

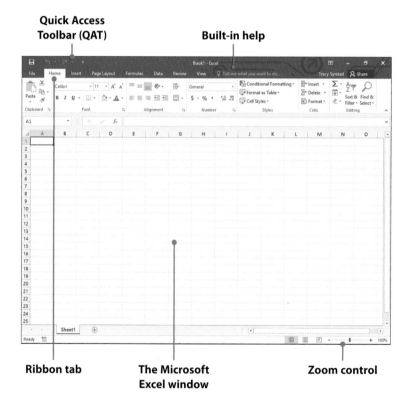

Ribbon tab

The Microsoft Excel window

Zoom control

In this chapter, you'll learn some basic Excel terminology and functionality. The topics in this chapter include the following:

→ Identifying parts of the Excel window

→ Customizing the ribbon and QAT

→ Viewing sheets

→ Selecting a range of cells

Understanding the Microsoft Excel Interface

If you already know how to add a custom tab to the ribbon or select cell D28, then you've probably spent some time using Excel. However, if what you've just read makes little sense to you, then this chapter is especially for you. This chapter explains the basic parts of the Microsoft Excel window, how to use them, and the terminology used to refer to them. It also shows you how to customize the interface, navigate around a sheet, and select a range of cells.

Identifying Parts of the Excel Window

When you open Excel 2016 the first time, you see icons for various templates. Chapter 2, "Working with Workbooks and Templates," covers templates in more depth. For now, click the Blank workbook icon to open a blank sheet.

Not Seeing the Templates Window

If you don't see the templates window, a previous user changed the settings to turn off the Start screen. Instead, when you open Excel, you'll go straight to a blank workbook.

**Select the Blank workbook icon
to open a blank sheet**

The Excel application window has many parts to it, such as the ribbon, row headings, column headings, and cells. Following are descriptions of the various parts we'll be interacting with in this book:

- The big grid taking up most of the Excel window is the sheet, also known as a worksheet or spreadsheet.

- Right above the grid are letters known as column headings. Down the left side of the grid are numbers, also known as row headings.

- An intersection of a column and row is a cell. Each cell has an address made up of the column letter then the row number that intersect at the cell. Multiple cells selected together are commonly known as a range.

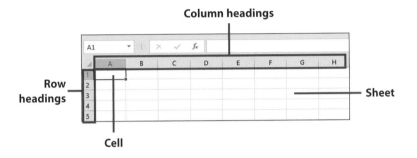

Column headings

Row headings

Cell

Sheet

- The ribbon is where you choose what you want to do on your sheet, such as formatting text or inserting a chart. See the section "Making Selections from the Ribbon" for information on the different types of controls on the ribbon. As you use Excel, you'll notice new tabs in the ribbon appearing, depending on what you're doing in the sheet area, such as working with a pivot table. These tabs are "context sensitive"—that is, they appear only when they are useful. Other times, they stay out of your way.

It's Not All Good

My Ribbon Doesn't Match Yours

The ribbon has nice big buttons on it, but it doesn't fit well on small screens or low-resolution monitors. To compensate, the ribbon will automatically resize the buttons, but this also gets rid of the labels, leaving only the icons. When the screen is very narrow, entire groups of commands collapse, so you might need to click a group button to see the icons. Throughout this book, you might notice the ribbon in the images doesn't match yours. In those cases, look for a matching icon.

- The Quick Access Toolbar, also known as the QAT, is always visible, even when the ribbon is minimized. However, unlike in the ribbon, the commands that display in the QAT don't depend on what you are doing in Excel.

QAT   **Ribbon tab**

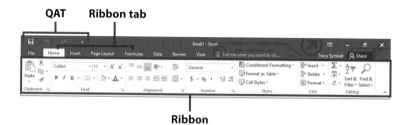

Ribbon

- The status bar has many uses. It holds zoom and page view controls, it lets you know if calculations need to be updated, and it can provide information, such as the sum or average, on a selected range.

- Every sheet in a workbook has a sheet tab. Clicking the tab is how you move between sheets.

Sheet tab

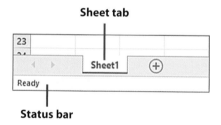

Status bar

Using the Built-in Help

The help interface in Excel provides assistance in three ways. You can use it to jump to a specific command or search Microsoft's online help system. It can also return more information on any topic from the Internet.

Perform a Search

As you enter your search criteria, Excel updates a drop-down of possible matches. The drop-down list is broken into three parts: Excel commands, a Get Help link, and Smart Lookup to run an online search.

1. Click the Tell Me search box and type the search phrase.

2. Select an Excel command. A dialog box might open, a formula might be inserted into a cell, cell formatting changed, or something else, depending on what the command is.

   Or

3. Select Get Help to open a new window with information from Microsoft's online help files.

   Or

4. Select Smart Lookup to open the Insights task pane to view web-based information on the search term.

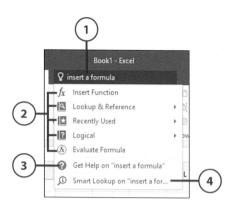

Detailed help

Insights task pane

Making Selections from the Ribbon

Along the top of the ribbon are tabs (labeled File, Home, Insert, Page Layout, Formulas, Data, Review, and View) that you can select to show options in the ribbon area below the tabs.

- Each tab consists of multiple groups containing buttons and drop-down menus.

- Clicking a button performs a function right away, such as bolding a cell or opening the Name Manager.

- Some buttons include arrows in the design. Clicking the main button area will perform the button's default function, but clicking the arrow opens a drop-down with other options to choose from.

- Clicking a dialog box launcher opens up a dialog box with all the options of that group and more. If you can't find the option you want on the group or you want to use multiple commands (for example, changing the font type and alignment of a cell's contents), you might want to use the dialog box.

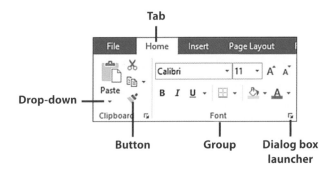

Customizing the Ribbon

If you're working on a system with a small screen, the ribbon probably takes up too much space on the screen. You can minimize it or hide some tabs. Alternatively, perhaps you want a quicker way of getting to the ribbon options you use the most. In any case, Excel offers multiple customizations to make the interface handier for the way you use it.

Minimize the Ribbon Size

The ribbon can be minimized so that only the tabs are shown. When minimized, you can click the tab to temporarily view the tab's controls.

1. Minimize the ribbon area by clicking the arrow in the lower-right corner of the ribbon.

2. Open the ribbon back up by clicking any tab.

3. Lock the ribbon open by clicking the pin that now appears where the arrow used to be.

Toggling the Ribbon

To quickly toggle the ribbon between being minimized and normal (and locked), press Ctrl+F1 on the keyboard.

>>>*Go Further*

RIBBON DISPLAY OPTIONS

The Ribbon Display Options menu offers additional controls for showing and hiding the ribbon:

Ribbon display options

- **Auto-hide Ribbon:** This option completely hides the ribbon and the QAT, maximizing the sheet on your display. The Name box and Formula bar are still visible. When in this view, you can temporarily open the ribbon by clicking the three small dots in the top right corner of the screen. To hide the ribbon again, just click on the sheet.

- **Show Tabs:** This option minimizes the ribbon in the same way as the steps outlined previously.

- **Show Tabs and Commands:** This option returns Excel to the default view showing all commands.

Add More Commands to the Ribbon

The default tabs and groups in Excel might not be the best ones for you or for a particular situation. You can insert a custom tab into the Main Tabs group or the Tool Tabs group. Once the tab has been added, you can add the commands most useful to you.

1. Right-click any tab and select Customize the Ribbon.

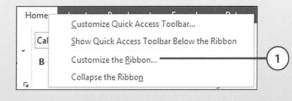

2. From the list on the right side of the dialog box, select where you want your tab to be. The new tab will be placed below and to the right of your selection.

3. Click New Tab. Excel creates a new tab with a new group, both with (Custom) after the name.

4. Click New Tab (Custom) and click Rename.

5. Type a new name in the Display Name field and click OK.

6. Highlight New Group (Custom) and click Rename.

7. Type a new name in the Display Name field and click OK.

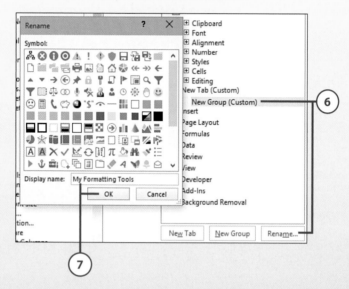

8. With the group to which you want to add a command selected, select the command you want to add.

9. Click Add.

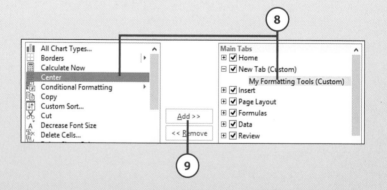

Customize an Existing Tab

Excel won't let you add a command to its existing groups. You can get around this by adding a custom group to an existing tab. Click the tab and add a new group by clicking the New Group button.

Customizing the QAT

The Quick Access Toolbar (QAT) is useful in that it doesn't take up as much space as the ribbon, the commands don't change based on what you're doing, and you can customize it for a specific workbook.

Move the QAT to a New Location

By default, the QAT appears above the ribbon, but you can move it to below the ribbon.

1. Click the arrow on the right end of the Quick Access Toolbar.

2. Select Show Below the Ribbon. If the toolbar is already below the ribbon, the option appears as Show Above the Ribbon.

Add More Commands to the QAT

Clicking the arrow on the right end of the QAT opens a list of commonly used commands. Click one of the options to add it to the QAT. If the command you want isn't listed, you can select from the full list.

1. Right-click an existing command on the toolbar and select Customize Quick Access Toolbar.

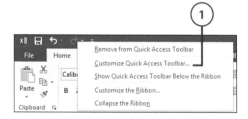

2. Select the desired command from the list and click Add.

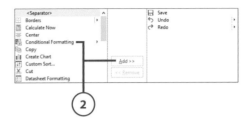

Remove a Command

To remove a command from the QAT, right-click the command button you want to remove. Then, from the menu, select Remove from Quick Access Toolbar.

>>>Go Further

CUSTOMIZE THE QAT FOR JUST THE CURRENT WORKBOOK

You can add commands to the QAT that will appear only when a specific workbook is open. To do this, select the workbook from the Customize Quick Access Toolbar drop-down on the right side of the dialog box.

Viewing Multiple Sheets at the Same Time

It's easier to work on two sheets at the same time if you can view them simultaneously. If you have multiple monitors, you can drag one Excel window to another monitor. However, if you only have a single screen, you need to rearrange the windows to see them both.

Arrange Multiple Sheets

If you have multiple workbooks open, you can arrange the sheets so you can view them at the same time.

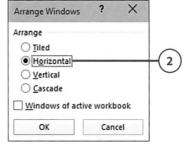

Compare Sheets of the Same Workbook

If you want to view multiple sheets of the active workbook at the same time, select View, New Window to create a duplicate window of the active workbook.

1. Click the View tab and then click the Arrange All button.

2. Select how you want to position the sheets (such as Horizontal) and then click OK.

3. Excel will rearrange the windows of all open workbooks. To work in a specific window, click once anywhere on the sheet to activate it.

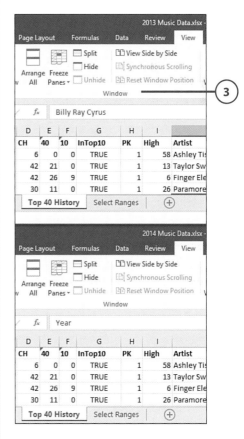

Scroll Two Sheets Side by Side

You can compare data row by row in two sheets by turning on Synchronous Scrolling.

1. Click the View tab and then click the View Side by Side button.

Change Window Layout

If you don't like the window positions after clicking the View Side by Side button, you can change them through the Arrange All tool. See the section "Arrange Multiple Sheets" for more information.

2. If you have only two workbooks open, Excel will arrange the two windows side by side. If you have more than two workbooks open, Excel will prompt for which window you want to use as the second one. Select the window and click OK.

3. Click the View tab and then click the Synchronous Scrolling button. As you scroll in one window, the other window will also scroll.

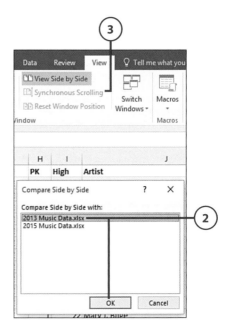

Changing the Zoom on a Sheet

The ability to zoom in and out on a sheet is an often-forgotten functionality in Excel. Instead, large fonts are used when a sheet is being designed, and then the designer later wonders why there are problems, such as the validation text being too small to see. Instead of relying on font size to make the text on the sheet larger, zoom in on the sheet. Excel offers several ways of changing the zoom on a sheet.

Use Excel's Zoom Controls

Excel offers multiple methods for changing the zoom level of the active sheet.

1. In the lower-right corner of the Excel window is the Zoom slider. Use the slider or the – and + buttons to change the zoom of the active sheet.

    Or

2. Click the View tab and then click Zoom. Select the desired magnification from the dialog box and then click OK.

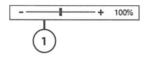

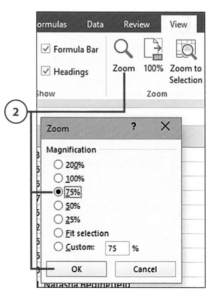

Or

3. Select the range you want to zoom in on and then click View, Zoom to Selection.

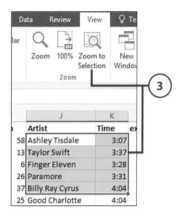

Zooming with the Mouse

If your mouse has a wheel, you can use it to quickly zoom in and out on a sheet. While holding down the Ctrl key, spin the wheel on your mouse to change the magnification.

The magnification will focus on the active cell, keeping it always in view. So if there is a certain area you want to zoom in on, select a cell in that area first.

Moving Around on a Sheet

You can move around on a sheet using the mouse or the keyboard, depending on which method is most comfortable for you. To select a cell using the mouse, click the desired cell. To select a cell using the keyboard, use the navigation arrows on the keyboard. You can also use the number keypad arrows if the NumLock feature is turned off.

Keyboard Shortcuts for Quicker Navigation

Using the navigation arrows on the keyboard can be a little slow, especially if you have a lot of cells between your currently selected cells and the one you want to select. Even using the mouse can take some time to navigate from the top of your data to the bottom. The following list details a few keyboard shortcuts to make navigation a little easier:

- Ctrl+Home jumps to cell A1, located at the upper-left corner of the sheet.

- Ctrl+End jumps to the last row and column in use.

- Ctrl+Left Arrow jumps to the first column with data to the left of the currently selected cell. If there is no data to the left, a cell in the first column (A) will be selected.

- Ctrl+Right Arrow jumps to the first column with data to the right of the currently selected cell. If there is no data to the right, a cell in the last column (XFD) will be selected.

- Ctrl+Down Arrow jumps to the first row with data below the currently selected cell. If there is no data below the selected cell, a cell in the last row will be selected.

- Ctrl+Up Arrow jumps to the first row with data above the currently selected cell. If there is no data above the selected cell, a cell in row 1 will be selected.

Selecting a Range of Cells

To select a single cell, you click it once. However, you'll often find yourself needing to select more than a single cell. For example, if you have text on a sheet you want to apply a new font to, instead of selecting one cell at a time and applying the font, you can select all the cells and then apply the font. When you have more than one cell selected, it's called a range.

Where to Start

When you're selecting a range, it doesn't matter if you start at the top or bottom or the far left or far right of the range.

Select a Range Using the Mouse

Use the mouse to click and drag to select multiple cells.

1. Select a cell that will be in the corner of your selection, such as B2.

⊿	A	B	C	D	E	F
1	Year	Decade	Yearly Rank	CH	40	10
2	2008	2000	50	6	0	0
3	2008	2000	123	42	21	0
4	2008	2000	233	42	26	9
5	2008	2000	258	30	11	0
6	2008	2000	264	23	4	0
7	2008	2000	310	21	12	0

2. Hold down the mouse button as you drag the mouse to cover the desired cells.

3. When you get to the last cell, such as E5, let go of the mouse button. As long as you don't click else-where on the sheet, the range will remain selected.

◢	A	B	C	D	E	F
1	Year	Decade	Yearly Rank	CH	40	10
2	2008	2000	50	6	0	0
3	2008	2000	123	42	21	0
4	2008	2000	233	42	26	9
5	2008	2000	258	30	11	0
6	2008	2000	264	23	4	0
7	2008	2000	310	21	12	0

Selected range

>>>Go Further
USE THE KEYBOARD

You can use the keyboard to select a range by turning Extend Selection mode on and off as needed. After selecting your starting cell, press F8 on the keyboard. The left side of the status bar shows Extend Selection mode is on. Use the keyboard to create your range and then press F8 again to stop the selection from extending. As long as you don't select another cell, the range will remain selected. Refer to the previous section, "Keyboard Shortcuts for Quicker Navigation," for shortcuts you can use to quickly select a range.

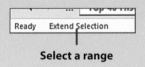

Ready	Extend Selection

Select a range

Select File to go into Backstage view

Info

New

Open

Save

Save As

Print

Share

Export

Close

Account

Options

Use the commands in Backstage view to open, save, and close your workbook

In this chapter, you'll learn how to interact with workbooks and create your own custom templates. Topics in this chapter include the following:

→ Opening, saving, and closing workbooks

→ Using templates

→ Creating your own template

Working with Workbooks and Templates

Most of the commands for working with workbooks, including templates, are found on Backstage view, accessed by clicking the File tab. You don't always have to start from scratch when creating a workbook—you can use templates offered online from Microsoft or create your own.

Managing Workbooks

Workbook is another name for an Excel file. It's the workbook you open, save, and close. This section shows you how to create a new workbook, open an existing workbook, and save and close a workbook.

Create a New Workbook

When you open Excel, it already makes a new workbook available, but you can always create another.

1. Click File to open Backstage view.

2. Select New and then click Blank Workbook.

Do It Quicker

Use the keyboard shortcut Ctrl+N to create a new workbook.

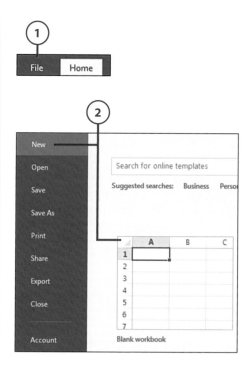

Open an Existing Workbook

If you need to open an existing workbook, you have to tell Excel where it is so it can open the workbook.

1. Click File to open Backstage view.

2. Select Open.

3. Select where the file is located, such as This PC.

4. If the desired folder appears in the list to right, select it then click on the file to open. If it is not listed, choose Browse.

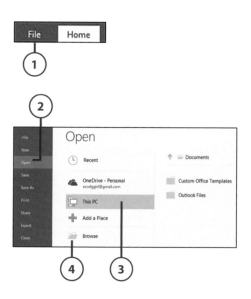

5. Navigate in the Open dialog box to the file and select it.

6. Select Open.

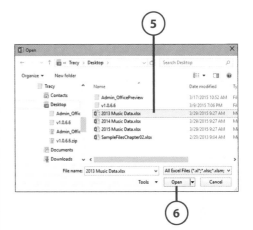

Use the Recent Workbooks List

The Recent Workbooks list makes it easy to open files you've recently worked on.

1. Click File to open Backstage view.

2. Select Open then Recent.

3. Select the desired file from the list.

Remove a Workbook from the List

To remove a workbook from the list, right-click it and select Remove from List.

Change the Number of Recent Workbooks

By default, the Recent list shows the most recent 25 workbooks you opened. You can change this by clicking File, Options, Advanced. Then under Display, change the value for Show This Number of Recent Workbooks.

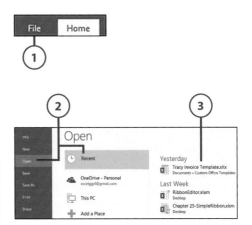

>>>Go Further
PIN A WORKBOOK TO THE LIST

The most recently opened workbook is always at the top of the list, but it will move down the list and eventually off of it unless you pin it.

A pushpin appears when you place your cursor over a workbook on the Recent list. The pushpin points to the left when not in use. If you place your cursor over the pushpin and click, the pushpin will face downward. The workbook will be moved to the top section of the list. A workbook with a pin facing down is stuck—that is, the workbook will not be removed from the list of recent workbooks until you unstick it by clicking the pushpin again.

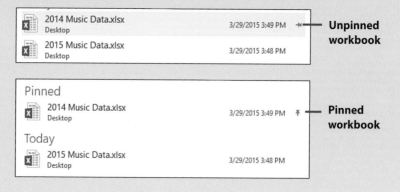

Save a Workbook

When you click the File tab, you see two options for saving your workbook: Save and Save As. Selecting Save saves the workbook with the current name, overwriting the existing file. If the workbook is new and doesn't have a filename yet, clicking Save opens the Save As dialog box. The Save As dialog box allows you to save the active workbook with a new name in a different location.

1. Click File to open Backstage view.

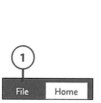

2. Select Save As.

3. Select where the file will be saved, such as This PC.

4. If the desired folder is listed, such as Documents, select it. Otherwise, choose Browse.

5. Navigate in the Save As dialog box to the folder you want to save in.

6. Enter the filename.

7. Select Save.

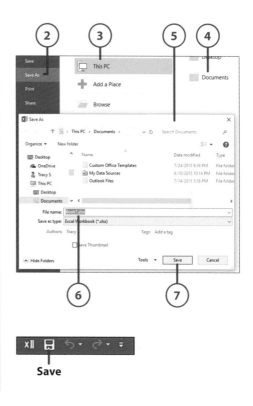

Quick Saves

If the workbook already has been saved and you just want to save your work without renaming the file or creating a copy, you can use the Save icon on the QAT.

Save

>>>Go Further
CHOOSING A DIFFERENT FILE TYPE

By default, Excel saves your workbook with an .xlsx extension. However, if you have macros in your workbook or want to create a PDF, you must choose another Save As file type. Commonly used extensions are as follows:

- **Excel Workbook (.xlsx)**—A workbook without macros.

- **Excel Macro-Enabled Workbook (.xlsm)**—A workbook with macros.

- **PDF**—The Portable Document Format can be used to distribute your report while still preventing users from making changes (because you retain the original, editable file).

| File name: | 2015 Music Data (updated).xlsx | ⌄ |
| Save as type: | Excel Workbook (*.xlsx) | ⌄ |

Choose a different file type

If you find yourself often changing the Save As file type to something else, such as Macro-Enabled Workbook, you can change the default setting by clicking File, Options, Save and changing the Save Files in This Format value. You will still have the ability to select another file type when saving.

Close a Workbook

When you're done working with a workbook, you need to close it. If changes have been made (including recalculating formulas) since the last save, Excel will prompt you to save the file. When the final workbook is closed, Excel shuts down.

1. Click File to open Backstage view.

2. Select Close.

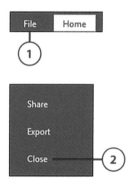

Using Templates to Quickly Create New Workbooks

Templates are a great way for keeping data in a uniform design. You could simply design your workbook and reuse it as needed, but if you accidentally save data before you have renamed the file, your blank workbook is no longer clean. When using a template, there's no risk of saving data in the template because you are working with a copy of the original workbook, not the workbook itself.

Use Microsoft's Online Templates

Microsoft offers a variety of templates, such as budgets, invoices, and calendars, to help you get a start on a project.

1. Click File to open Backstage view.

2. Select New.

3. Type keywords in the search field and press Enter, or choose one of the recommended templates.

4. A preview of the selected template is shown. If you want to create a workbook based on this template, click Create. Excel will download the file (the first time) and then open it.

5. If you don't want to use the previewed template, click the X in the top-right corner to close it.

Pinning Templates

When you place your cursor over a template icon, a pushpin appears in its lower-right corner, giving you the option to pin it so that it always appears in the list. If you found your template by searching for it, this is a way to make the template easily accessible the next time you need it.

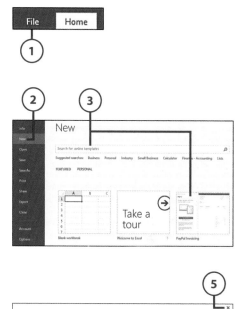

Save a Template

You can create your own templates by starting a new workbook, setting it up as you like it, and then saving it as a template. The important thing here is to save it with the correct extension—either as *.xltx, if it doesn't have any macros, or as *.xltm if it does include macros.

1. Click File to open Backstage view.

2. Select Save As.

3. Select where the file will be saved, such as This PC.

4. Select Browse.

5. Select the extension for your file. If the workbook doesn't have any macros, choose Excel Template (*.xltx); if it does include macros, choose Excel Macro-Enabled Template (*.xltm).

Undoing Excel's Location Change

When you choose a template file type, Excel automatically changes the Save As location to the default personal template location. If that's not where you want to save the file, but you had the desired location selected before choosing the file type, click the Back arrow.

6. Type the filename.

7. Click Save.

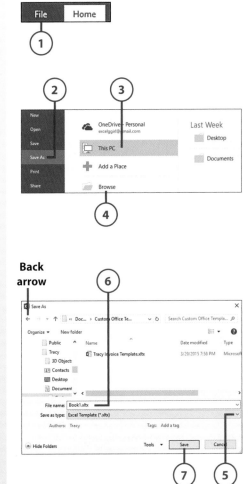

If You Want to Save in Another Location

You do not have to save templates to the configured templates location if you plan to use the double-click or right-click method to open a copy of the file.

Open a Locally Saved Template to Enter Data

You aren't limited to the templates available online. You can use templates saved on your computer.

1. Click File to open Backstage view.

2. Select New.

3. Select Personal. The Personal option is not available unless a personal template location has been specified. See "Change Personal Templates Location" later in this chapter to define this location if needed.

4. Click the template you want to work with to open a copy of it.

Other Ways to Open Templates

If you have easy access to a template (for example, on your desktop), you have two other options for opening a template to work with: double-click the file from its saved location or right-click the file and select New.

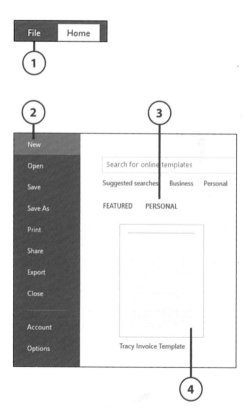

It's Not All Good

Can't Browse for Personal Templates

The personal templates list shows only templates stored in a configured location. There is no way to browse to another location when trying to open a template. Instead, you have to change the configured location where Excel looks for your personal templates. See the "Change Personal Templates Location" section for instructions on how to set up a new location.

Edit the Design of a Locally Saved Template

If you do open a template using one of the previous methods and make changes, you must use the Save As option and save it as a new template. If you want to edit the original file, you'll need to open the actual file, not create a copy of it.

1. Click File to open Backstage view.

2. Select Open.

3. Select where the file is located, such as This PC.

4. If the desired folder is listed, select it. Otherwise, click Browse.

5. Navigate in the Open dialog box to the template and select it.

6. Select Open.

Open It Faster

If you have easy access to a template (for example, on your desktop), you can edit it by right-clicking the file and selecting Open.

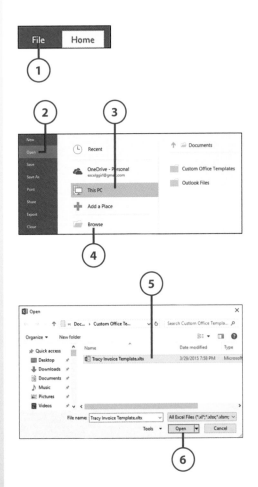

Change Personal Templates Location

The first time you save a template, Excel take you to the default personal templates location, C:\Users*username*\Documents\Custom Office Templates\). You can change this location to something more convenient for you.

1. Click File to open Backstage view.

2. Select Options.

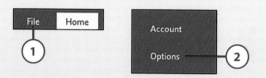

3. Select Save.

4. Enter your preferred path in the Default Personal Templates Location field.

5. Click OK.

Ensure the Path Exists

The location must exist before you enter it in the field. To make sure you get the path correct, navigate to the folder in File Explorer, copy the full path from the address bar, and then paste it in the Excel field.

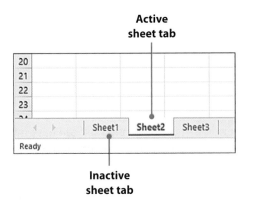

In this chapter, you'll discover what you can do with sheets, including the following:

→ Inserting additional sheets

→ Deleting sheets

→ Moving sheets to other workbooks

→ Selecting multiple sheets

3

Working with Sheets

A sheet, also known as a spreadsheet or worksheet, is where you enter all your data in Excel. A workbook can have multiple sheets— the number is limited only by the power of the computer opening the workbook.

Each sheet has a tab, visible above the status bar. The sheet with data that you're looking at is considered the active sheet. To select another sheet, click its tab.

Adding and Deleting Sheets

You can add and delete sheets as needed, allowing you to separate your data, lookup tables, and reports on different sheets.

Add a New Sheet

By default, a new workbook has a single sheet, but you aren't limited to using just that one sheet. When you add a new sheet, it becomes the active sheet.

1. Click the New Sheet icon to the right of the rightmost sheet tab. This inserts a new sheet to the right of the active sheet.

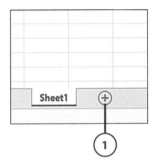

Delete a Sheet

If you no longer need a sheet, you can delete it, thus getting it out of your way and reducing the size of your workbook.

1. Right-click the sheet tab you want to delete and select Delete.

2. If data is on the sheet, a prompt appears to verify that this is the action you want to take. Click Delete to continue with the deletion.

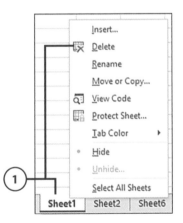

It's Not All Good

Deletion Is Permanent!

Be very careful when deleting a sheet because the Undo function will not work to recover it. Once you delete a sheet, it is gone.

Navigating and Selecting Sheets

Excel has a few tools to help navigate between sheets, which is useful if your workbook has a lot of sheets. And sometimes you might need to select multiple sheets at the same time—for example, if you want to print multiple sheets together.

Activate Another Sheet

To activate another sheet, click its tab along the bottom of the Excel window. You can also navigate from sheet to sheet using the keyboard. Ctrl+Page Up selects the sheet to the left; Ctrl+Page Down selects the sheet to the right.

If you have more sheets than can fit in the tab area, an ellipsis (three small dots) will appear on the left and right sides of the area, to show there are more sheets available to view in that direction. Clicking the three dots jumps you to the sheet closest to the dots. If you need to scroll one sheet at a time, click the left or right arrow located to the left of the tab area.

To scroll to the leftmost sheet, hold down Ctrl while clicking the left arrow. To scroll to the rightmost sheet, hold down Ctrl while clicking the right arrow. Note that scrolling the tab area doesn't activate a different sheet; it just makes different sheet tabs visible.

If you right-click the left or right arrow instead, a list of all visible sheets in the workbook appears. You can then select a sheet, click OK, and you'll go straight to that sheet.

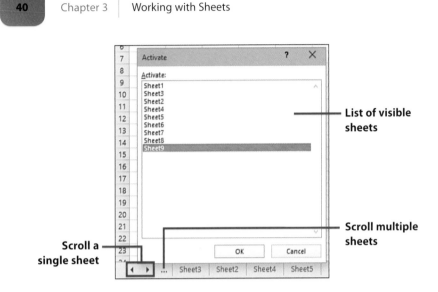

Select Multiple Sheets

You can select multiple sheets at one time. This doesn't activate them all at once. Instead, it groups them together so that an action on one, such as changing the tab color or typing in a cell, affects all of them.

To select multiple sheets, select the first one; then, while holding down the Ctrl key, select the tabs for the others. You can also hold down the Shift key and click on the first tab you want and the last one in a set, and Excel will select the entire contiguous range for you. As you select each sheet tab, the sheet name will become bold.

To ungroup the sheets, you can either select any sheet not in the group or right-click any tab and select Ungroup Sheets.

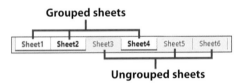

Moving or Copying Sheets

You might want to reorganize sheets in the current workbook to place similar sheets together. Or you might need to copy a sheet to run tests on the data but don't want to change the original.

Move or Copy a Sheet in the Same Workbook

Copying or moving a sheet duplicates everything on the sheet, including formatting, links, and charts.

1. Right-click the sheet tab you want to move or copy.

2. Select Move or Copy.

Alternative Method

You can also open the Move or Copy dialog box by going to the Home tab, opening the Format drop-down and selecting Move or Copy Sheet.

3. Make sure the To Book field is the name of the current workbook.

4. If you're making a copy of the sheet, select the Create a Copy box.

5. Select the sheet you want the active sheet to be placed in front of (that is, to the left of). You can also just move it to the end by selecting (Move to End).

6. Click OK.

Do It Quicker

You can also reorganize the sheets in a workbook by holding the mouse button down and dragging a sheet's tab to a new location. If you want to copy the sheet, hold down the Ctrl key as you drag the sheet tab.

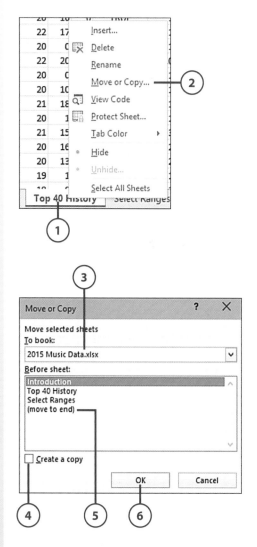

Move or Copy a Sheet Between Workbooks

Many database programs will export data to an Excel workbook or compatible file, but might not let you choose an existing workbook to export to. You can move sheets from one workbook to another. This is also useful when you need to combine the content from two or more workbooks.

1. Make sure the workbook into which you want to move or copy the sheet is open. Alternatively, you can transfer the sheet to a new, blank workbook by choosing it in step 5.

2. Right-click the sheet tab you want to move or copy.

3. Select Move or Copy.

4. Select the workbook to which you want to move or copy the sheet.

5. If you're making a copy of the sheet, select the Create a Copy box.

6. Select the sheet you want the moved or copied sheet to be placed in front of (that is, to the left of) in the other workbook. You can place it at the end by selecting (Move to End).

7. Click OK.

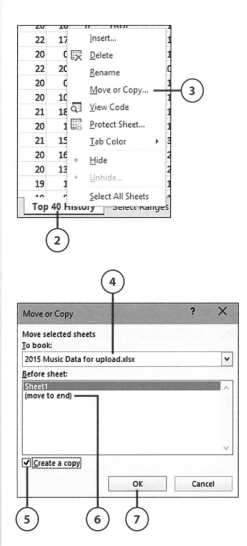

Linked Formulas

When you move or copy a sheet from one workbook to another, any formulas on that sheet linked to another sheet in the original workbook will remain linked to the sheet in the original workbook unless you also include the linked sheet(s) in the move or copy procedure.

Sheet Names Are Unique

Sheet names must be unique. If you copy or move a sheet into a workbook that already has a sheet by that name, Excel will append a number to the end of the copied sheet's name. For example, if you copy (or move) Sheet1 and there is already a Sheet1, Excel renames the new sheet to Sheet1 (2).

Renaming a Sheet

Excel's sheet names (Sheet1, Sheet2, and so on) aren't very descriptive. Sheets are easier to find when they have meaningful names.

Change a Sheet's Name

1. Right-click the sheet tab you want to rename.

2. Select Rename.

3. Type a new name and press Enter.

Sheet Name Limitations

A sheet name is limited to 31 characters, and you can't use some symbols, such as asterisks and slashes. Also, the renaming of a sheet cannot be undone.

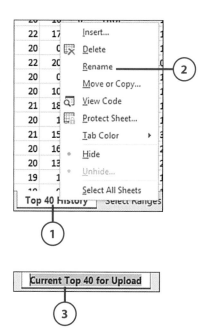

	A	B	C	D	E	F	G	
1	Region	Product	Date	Customer	Quantity	Revenue	COGS	
2	East	Tools	1/1/2015	Exclusive Shovel Traders	1000	22810	10220	
3	Central	Accessories	1/2/2015	Bright Hairpin Company	100	2257	984	
4	East	Jewelry	1/4/2015	Cool Jewelry Corporation	800	18552	7872	
5	East	Food	1/4/2015	Tasty Kettle Inc.	400	9152	4088	
6	East	Tools	1/7/2015	Remarkable Meter Corporation	400	8456	3388	— Data range
7	East	Jewelry	1/7/2015	Wonderful Jewelry Inc.	1000	21730	9840	
8	Central	Tools	1/9/2015	Remarkable Meter Corporation	800	16416	6776	
9	Central	Tools	1/10/2015	Safe Flagpole Supply	900	21438	9198	
10	Central	Tools	1/12/2015	Reliable Tripod Company	300	6267	2541	
11	East	Tools	1/14/2015	Matchless Vise Inc.	100	2401	1022	
12	East	Accessories	1/15/2015	Bright Hairpin Company	500	9345	4235	
13	East	Tools	1/16/2015	Appealing Calculator Corporation	600	11628	5082	
14	West	Accessories	1/19/2015	Bright Hairpin Company	100	2042	984	
15	East	Food	1/21/2015	Best Vegetable Company	800	14440	6776	
16	Total						73006	

Table Tools

Tables.xlsx - Excel

File Home Insert Page Layout Formulas Data Review View Design

Table Name: Summarize with PivotTable Properties Header Row F
Table2 Remove Duplicates Open in Browser Total Row L
Resize Table Convert to Range Insert Export Refresh Unlink Banded Rows B
Properties Tools Slicer External Table Data Tabl

A2 | fx | East

	A	B	C	D	E	F	G	
1	Region	Product	Date	Customer	Quantity	Revenue	COGS	— Header row
2	East	Tools	1/1/2015	Exclusive Shovel Traders	1000	22810	10220	
3	Central	Accessories	1/2/2015	Bright Hairpin Company	100	2257	984	
4	East	Jewelry	1/4/2015	Cool Jewelry Corporation	800	18552	7872	
5	East	Food	1/4/2015	Tasty Kettle Inc.	400	9152	4088	
6	East	Tools	1/7/2015	Remarkable Meter Corporation	400	8456	3388	
7	East	Jewelry	1/7/2015	Wonderful Jewelry Inc.	1000	21730	9840	
8	Central	Tools	1/9/2015	Remarkable Meter Corporation	800	16416	6776	
9	Central	Tools	1/10/2015	Safe Flagpole Supply	900	21438	9198	
10	Central	Tools	1/12/2015	Reliable Tripod Company	300	6267	2541	
11	East	Tools	1/14/2015	Matchless Vise Inc.	100	2401	1022	
12	East	Accessories	1/15/2015	Bright Hairpin Company	500	9345	4235	
13	East	Tools	1/16/2015	Appealing Calculator Corporation	600	11628	5082	
14	West	Accessories	1/19/2015	Bright Hairpin Company	100	2042	984	
15	East	Food	1/21/2015	Best Vegetable Company	800	14440	6776	
16	Total						73006	— Total row

Table

You never know where your data is going to come from—manually typed in, imported or copied from another file, or from the Web. Because of this, Excel offers a multitude of ways to enter data. In this chapter, you'll learn those ways and also the following:

4

→ Entering different types of data

→ Quickly copying data using the fill handle

→ Working with lists

→ Using Text to Columns

→ Controlling user entry with Data Validation

→ Spell checking a sheet

→ Finding data on a sheet

→ Fixing numbers stored as text

Getting Data onto a Sheet

Data entry is one of the most important functions in Excel—and one of the most tedious, especially when the data is repetitive. This chapter includes tricks for copying down data, fixing entered data, and helping your users enter data correctly by providing a pre-defined list of entries.

Entering Different Types of Data into a Cell

Excel treats different types of data, such as numbers and dates, differently. You tell Excel what kind of data is in a cell by how you type it into the cell or by how you format the cell. You can save yourself some time if you let Excel format your data, but it will only do so properly if it can understand what you want.

Type Numbers or Text into a Cell

If you're entering numbers or text into a cell, just select the cell and start typing.

1. Select the cell you want to enter the data into, such as A1.

2. Type a value, such as 500. The data will appear in the cell and in the formula bar.

3. Press Enter or Tab to tell Excel you're done. The active cell will move to the next cell.

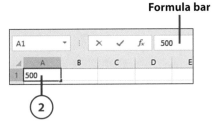

Formula bar

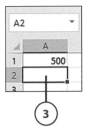

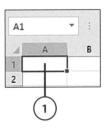

Enter Numbers as Text

Suppose you select a cell and type the ZIP code for Chester, MA, which is 01011, and then press Enter or Tab. The beginning 0 disappears, and all you see is 1011. This happens because Excel assumes you are typing in a number, and numbers do not start with zeros. Although ZIP codes are numeric, they aren't numbers—that is, you don't do any math with them. You can type an apostrophe to let Excel know the number should be treated as text. The apostrophe does not display.

1. Select the cell you want to enter the data into, such as A1.

2. Type an apostrophe, and then type the value.

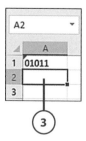

Show That Apostrophe

If you need an apostrophe shown at the beginning of a cell, then enter two apostrophes—only the second one will show when you're done.

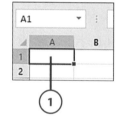

3. Press Enter or Tab to tell Excel you're done. The active cell will move to the next cell.

What's That Green Triangle For?

You'll notice a small green triangle in the upper-left corner of the cell. This is an Error Checking option. See the section "Fixing Numbers Stored as Text" for more information.

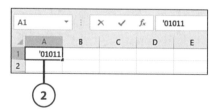

Type Dates and Times into a Cell

Excel uses the system-configured date format by default. For example, in the United States, when you enter numeric dates, the month comes first—that is, May 14, 2015 is written as 5/14/15.

Excel is smart about date and time entry, and if you simply type in dates and times, it does a good job of deciphering your data. When entering times, you must use the 24-hour clock format, also known as military time, or include a.m. or p.m.

1. Select the cell you want to enter the date into, such as A1.

2. Type a date, such as 5/14/15. The data will appear in the cell and in the formula bar.

3. Press Enter or Tab to tell Excel you're done. The active cell will move to the next cell.

For Every Date, There' a Time

When entering a date, the time (12:00 a.m.) is included. But you might not see the part you didn't type in until the cell is formatted to show it.

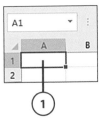

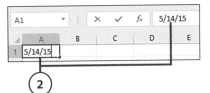

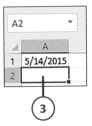

It's Not All Good

When Fractions Turn into Dates

If you enter only two parts of a date, such as the month and day, Excel will append the current year. But this also means that if you enter a fraction that could be interpreted as date, such as 3/4, Excel will convert it to a date (for example, 3/4/15). To enter a fraction, you must format the cell as Fraction before entering it.

Dates must always include a day, month, and year, even if not all three will appear when the cell is formatted.

See Chapter 6, "Formatting Sheets and Cells," for more details on applying different number formats and how formatting affects what you see, but not actually what's in the cell.

Undo an Entry

If you make a mistake, such as in formatting, data entry, or chart creation, you can undo it by click the Undo button. Located in the QAT, the Undo button will undo the most recent action each time it is clicked. If you decide you don't want to undo an action, you can click the Redo button, which will redo the most recently undone action.

Redo

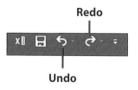

Undo

Use Keyboard Shortcuts

Press Ctrl + Z to undo the previous action; press Ctrl + Y to redo the recently undone action.

Using Lists to Quickly Fill a Range

The fill handle can speed up data entry by completing a list for you. Excel comes with several preconfigured lists. You can also add your own list, as described in the "Create Your Own List" section later in this chapter.

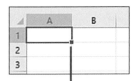

Fill handle

Extend a Series Containing Text

Excel comes with custom lists of days of the week and months of the year.

1. Enter the weekday or month you want the list to begin with. Press Ctrl+Enter so Excel accepts the entry, but keeps the cell selected.

2. Place your pointer over the fill handle until a black cross appears.

3. Hold the mouse button down as you drag the fill handle. A ScreenTip will show you the value that will be in the cell as you pass it by.

4. Release the mouse button when you're done making your list.

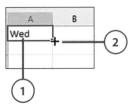

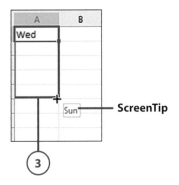

ScreenTip

The List Will Repeat

If you drag the list for more rows or columns than there are values in the list, the list will repeat. For example, if you begin a series in A1 with Wednesday and drag the fill handle to A8, Wednesday will appear again, repeating the series.

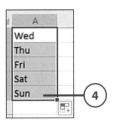

Extending Numbers Mixed with Text

If the text series contains a numerical value, Excel copies the text and extends the numerical portion. For example, if you try to extend Monday 1, you get Monday 2, not Tuesday 2. But if you type in Jan 1 and extend that text, Excel extends the numerical portion until Jan 31, then switches to Feb 1. It does this because dates are actually numbers. Seeing the date as Jan 1 is a matter of formatting.

Extend a Numerical Series

If you try to fill numerical series based off of a single cell entry, Excel just copies the value instead of filling the series. Use the following method to get around this:

1. Enter and select at least the first two values of the series.

2. Place your pointer over the fill handle so that a black cross appears.

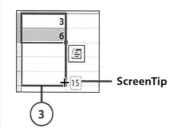

3. Hold the mouse button down as you drag the fill handle. A ScreenTip will show you the value that will appear in the cell as you pass it by.

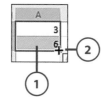

ScreenTip

4. Release the mouse button when you're done making your list.

>>>*Go Further*
ALTERNATIVE METHODS

There are a few alternative methods you can choose from to extend a series:

- Enter the first value and hold down the Ctrl key while dragging the fill handle.

- If there is a blank column to the left or right of the numerical column, include that column in your selection when dragging the fill handle down.

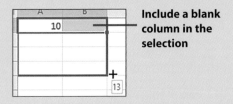

Include a blank column in the selection

- Hold the right mouse button down while dragging the fill handle and select Fill Series from the context menu that appears when you release the mouse button. This will also work on a series containing text.

Right-click as you drag to open this context menu

Create Your Own List

You can teach Excel the lists that are important to you so that you can take advantage of its list capabilities. You can take almost any list of items on a sheet and create a custom list for use in filtering or sorting.

1. Create your list on the sheet and select the range.

2. Click File to enter Backstage view.

3. Select Options.

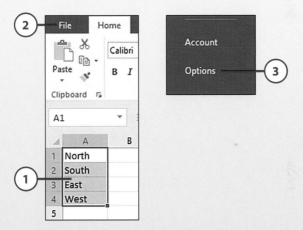

4. Select Advanced, scroll down to General, and click Edit Custom Lists.

5. If your range is not showing in the Import List from Cells field, click the range selector button. Otherwise, skip to step 8.

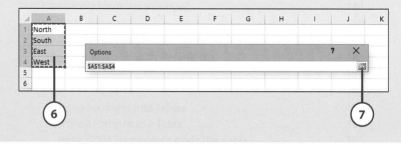

6. Select the list on the sheet.

7. Click the range selector button to return to the dialog box.

8. Click Import. The list is added to both the Custom Lists and List Entries list boxes and will be available for creating custom lists or doing a custom sort or filter.

9. Click OK.

Using Paste Special

The Paste Special dialog box gives you control over how a range is pasted. For example, you can paste values only, formatting only, or a combination of the two. You can also use Paste Special to change the numeric value of a cell.

Paste Values Only

The Values option of the Paste Special dialog box allows you to copy a range containing formulas and paste just the calculated values, replacing the formulas. You can also paste the values to a new location, leaving the original formatting behind.

1. Select the range to copy.

2. On the Home tab, click Copy.

3. Select the top-left cell of the area into which you want to paste.

4. On the Home tab, open the Paste drop-down.

5. Select the Values option. The range will be pasted without any of the original formatting.

Paste Preview

You can preview what your pasted range will look like as you move your cursor over the Paste Special options. When you find the one you want, click it.

Combine Multiple Paste Special Options

The Paste drop-down has many different options, but sometimes you may need a combination of data and formatting that isn't available in the drop-down. The Paste Special dialog box allows you to choose individual properties of the copied range that you want pasted, and by using the dialog box multiple times in succession, you can stack the properties. For example, you might want to paste values and also retain the column widths. In that case, use the Paste Special dialog box twice in succession, as described in the following steps.

1. Select the range to copy.

2. On the Home tab, click Copy.

3. Select the top-left cell of the area into which you want to paste.

4. On the Home tab, open the Paste drop-down.

5. Select the Paste Special option.

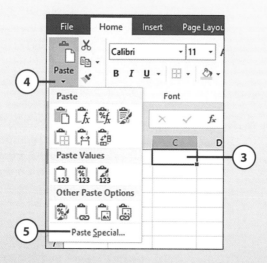

6. Select Values.

7. Click OK.

8. Only the values will be pasted into the cells.

9. Reopen the dialog box and select Column Widths.

10. Click OK.

	C	D	E	F	G	H	I	J	K
	Region	Product	Date	Customer	Quantity	Revenue	COGS		
	East	Tools		42005 Exclusive	1000	22810	10220		
	Central	Accessorie							
	East	Jewelry							
	East	Food							
	East	Tools							
	East	Jewelry							
	Central	Tools							
	Central	Tools							
	Central	Tools							
	East	Tools							
	East	Accessorie							
	East	Tools							
	West	Accessorie							
	East	Food							
	Total								

Paste Special   ?   ✕

Paste

- ○ All
- ○ Formulas
- ○ Values
- ○ Formats
- ○ Comments
- ○ Validation

- ○ All using Source theme
- ○ All except borders
- ● Column widths
- ○ Formulas and number formats
- ○ Values and number formats
- ○ All merging conditional formats

Operation

- ● None
- ○ Add
- ○ Subtract

- ○ Multiply
- ○ Divide

☐ Skip blanks   ☐ Transpose

Paste Link   OK   Cancel

11. The column widths used by the copied range will be duplicated onto the pasted range.

C	D	E	F	G	H	I
Region	Product	Date	Customer	Quantity	Revenue	COGS
East	Tools	42005	Exclusive Shovel Traders	1000	22810	10220
Central	Accessories	42006	Bright Hairpin Company	100	2257	984

Multiply the Range by a Specific Value

The Operation area in the Paste Special dialog box allows you to perform simple math on a selected range, such as increasing all prices by 15%.

1. In any blank cell on the sheet, enter the value by which you want to change the range. For example, to increase by 15%, enter 1.15.

2. Copy the cell by clicking the Copy button on the Home tab.

3. Select the range you want to update.

4. Right-click over the selected range and select Paste Special, Paste Special.

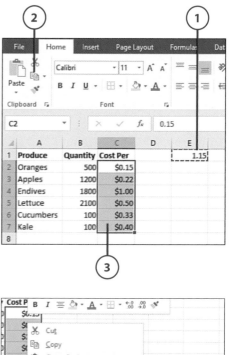

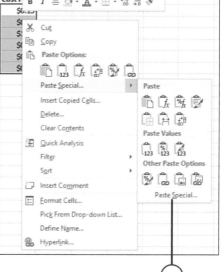

5. Select Values, so you don't replace the formatting of the range, and then select Multiply, the mathematical operation you want to perform on the range.

6. Click OK.

7. Excel will update the values in the selected range.

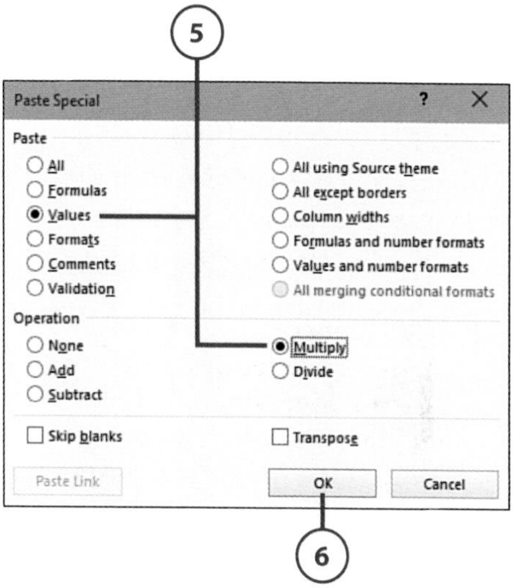

⑤

Paste Special	? ✕
Paste	
○ All	○ All using Source theme
○ Formulas	○ All except borders
● Values	○ Column widths
○ Formats	○ Formulas and number formats
○ Comments	○ Values and number formats
○ Validation	○ All merging conditional formats
Operation	
○ None	● Multiply
○ Add	○ Divide
○ Subtract	
☐ Skip blanks	☐ Transpose
Paste Link	OK Cancel

⑥

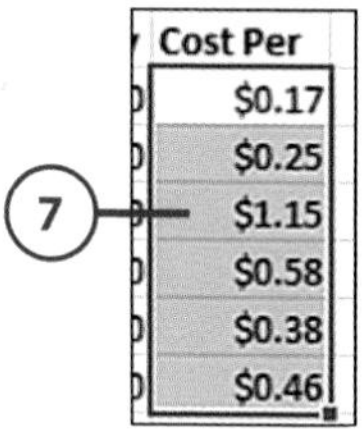

Cost Per
$0.17
$0.25
$1.15
$0.58
$0.38
$0.46

⑦

>>>Go Further

PASTE SPECIAL WITH NON-RANGE OR NON-EXCEL SOURCES

If you copy or cut data within a cell (versus the entire cell), from a chart, or from a non-Excel source, such as a Word document or web page, the Paste Special options are limited, depending on the original source.

Paste Link option **As list box** **Display as Icon option**

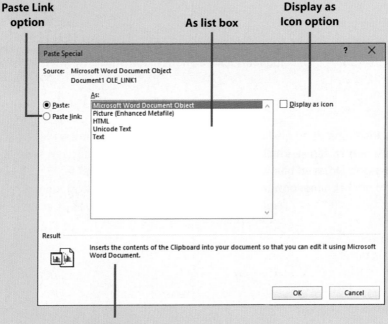

Result area

As you select an option in the As list box, an explanation appears in the Result area at the bottom of the dialog box. Selecting the Paste Link option also links the pasted data to its original source.

If available, the Display as Icon option lets you paste an icon instead of the text. Double-clicking the resulting icon in the worksheet opens the text in an editing application. (For example, if you're pasting text from a Word document, you can edit the text in Word.)

Use Paste to Merge a Noncontiguous Selection

If you try to copy/paste a noncontiguous selection from different rows and columns, an error message appears. But if the selection is in the same row or column, Excel allows you to copy and paste the data. When the data is pasted, though, it is no longer separated by other cells. You can use this method to create a range of specific values copied from another dataset.

1. Select the first range you want to copy.

2. While holding down the Ctrl key, select the other ranges.

3. On the Home tab, select Copy.

4. Select the top-left cell where you want the new range to go.

5. On the Home tab, select Paste. The data will be pasted together.

This Action Won't Work on Multiple Selections

For Excel to see the selection as a single selection, it must be stacked—that is, it must start and end in the same columns or rows.

	A	B	C
1	Produce	Quantity	Cost Per
2	Oranges	500	$0.15
3		Total	$75.00
4	Apples	1200	$0.22
5		Total	$264.00
6	Endives	1800	$1.00
7		Total	$1,800.00
8	Lettuce	2100	$0.50
9		Total	$1,050.00
10	Cucumbers	100	$0.33
11		Total	$33.00
12	Kale	100	$0.40
13		Total	$40.00

	A	B	C	D		E	F	G
1	Produce	Quantity	Cost Per			Produce	Quantity	Cost Per
2	Oranges	500	$0.15			Oranges	500	$0.15
3		Total	$75.00			Apples	1200	$0.22
4	Apples	1200	$0.22			Endives	1800	$1.00
5		Total	$264.00			Lettuce	2100	$0.50
6	Endives	1800	$1.00			Cucumber	100	$0.33
7		Total	$1,800.00			Kale	100	$0.40
8	Lettuce	2100	$0.50					
9		Total	$1,050.00					
10	Cucumbers	100	$0.33					
11		Total	$33.00					
12	Kale	100	$0.40					
13		Total	$40.00					

Microsoft Excel

This action won't work on multiple selections.

OK

Invalid selection

Using Text to Columns to Separate Data in a Single Column

Importing data from other sources, such as databases, is a common use of Excel. Often, the files generated by these other sources are delimited by a common character, such as a comma, or are fixed width, where each field is a specific number of characters, including spaces.

If you open a file like this in Excel, you can use Text to Columns to parse the data out from one column into individual columns for each field.

Parsing a Column in the Middle of an Existing Dataset

If you need to parse a column in the middle of an existing dataset, you first need to insert enough columns to cover the number of columns the parsed data will use. Otherwise, it will overwrite any data to the right of the original column.

Work with Delimited Text

Delimited text is data that has some character, such as a comma, tab, or space, separating each value that you want placed into its own column.

1. Highlight the range to be separated.

2. On the Data tab, select Text to Columns. The Convert Text to Columns Wizard opens.

3. Select Delimited.

4. Click Next.

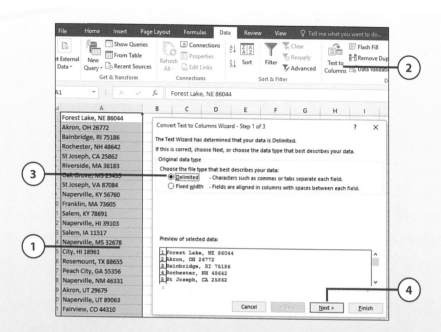

5. Select the delimiter or enter one in the Other field. If multiple delimiters may be next to each other but should be treated as one, select Treat Consecutive Delimiters as One.

6. If you have quotation marks or apostrophes around the text fields in the data, select the corresponding Text Qualifier.

7. Click Next.

Multiple Delimiters

If you need more than one delimiter but one of the delimiters is used normally in the text, such as the space between city names and the space between a state and ZIP code (Sioux Falls, SD 57101), consider running Text to Columns twice: once to separate the city (Sioux Falls) from the state ZIP code (SD 57101) and again to separate the state and ZIP code.

8. For each column of data, click on the column's header then select the data format for that column. For example, if you have a column of ZIP codes, you need to set the format as Text so any leading zeros are not lost. But be warned—setting a column to Text prevents Excel from properly identifying formulas entered into that column.

9. If you want the results placed in a different location, place your cursor in the Destination field and then select a new target cell.

10. Click Finish.

11. The data is separated.

>>>*Go Further*

WORK WITH FIXED-WIDTH TEXT

Text to columns also works with fixed-width text, which is text where each field is a set number of characters. If your text doesn't look like it's a fixed width, try changing the font to a fixed-width font, such as Courier. It's possible that it's fixed-width text in disguise.

When you select this option, instead of choosing a delimiter, Excel shows a preview with lines where it thinks the column breaks should go. You can move a break line by clicking and dragging it to where you want it. You can insert a new break by clicking where it should be, and you can remove a break by double-clicking it.

Using Data Validation to Limit Data Entry in a Cell

Data validation allows you to limit what a user can type in a cell. For example, you can limit users to whole numbers, dates, a list of selections, or a specific range of values. Custom input and error messages can be configured to guide the user entry.

Limit User Entry to a Selection from a List

A data validation list allows you to create a drop-down in a cell, thus restricting the user to selecting from a predefined list of values.

1. Create a list of the values to appear in the drop-down. For example, in A1, type **Apples**, in A2, **Oranges**, and so on.

Protect the List By Placing It on Another Sheet

You can place the list on a sheet other than the one where the drop-down will actually be placed. You can then hide that sheet, thus preventing the user from changing the list.

---

2. Select the cell in which you want the drop-down to appear.

3. On the Data tab, select Data Validation.

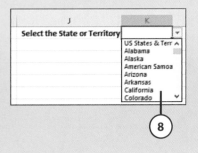

4. Select List from the Allow drop-down.

5. Place your cursor in the Source field.

6. Select the list you created in step 1.

7. Click OK.

8. The cell selected in step 2 is now a drop-down. Users will be limited to values in the list.

Skip the List

If your list is short, instead of the separate list you created in step 1, you can enter the values separated by commas directly in the Source field. For example, in the Source field you could enter **Yes, No** (no quotes, no equal sign).

Add a Prompt or Error Message

If you want to provide the user with an input prompt, go to the Input Message tab and fill in the Title and Input Message fields.

If you want to provide the user with an error message, go to the Error Alert tab and fill in the Style, Title, and Error Message fields.

>>>Go Further

OTHER VALIDATION OPTIONS

A drop-down list isn't the only way to validate data. Other available validation criteria include the following:

- **Any Value**—The default option allowing unrestricted entry.
- **Whole Number**—Requires a whole number be entered. You can select a comparison value (Between, Not Between, Equal To, and so on) and set the Minimum and Maximum value.
- **Decimal**—Requires a decimal value be entered. You can select a comparison value (Between, Not Between, Equal To, and so on) and set the Minimum and Maximum values.
- **Date**—Requires a date be entered. You can select a comparison value (Between, Not Between, Equal To, and so on) and set the minimum and maximum values.
- **Time**—Requires a time be entered. You can select a comparison value (Between, Not Between, Equal To, and so on) and set the minimum and maximum values.
- **Text Length**—Requires a text value be entered. You can select a comparison value (Between, Not Between, Equal To, and so on) and set the minimum and maximum number of characters.
- **Custom**—Uses a formula to calculate TRUE for valid entries or FALSE for invalid entries.

Using Web Queries to Get Data onto a Sheet

Excel can be used to retrieve data from a website, if the site has been designed in such a way that Excel can find the tables on it. A link is created so the data on the sheet will update as often as you wish.

Insert a Web Query

A web query allows you to link a range to data from a web page. As the web page updates, the data on the sheet also updates.

1. On the Data tab, open the Get External Data drop-down and select From Web.

No Get External Data Drop-Down

If your screen resolution is set high enough, you won't have a Get External Data drop-down. Instead, the From Web button will be directly on the Data tab.

---

2. In the New Web Query dialog box, navigate to the desired web page.

Script Errors

If you receive Script Errors while loading the web page, click Yes to allow scripts to continue and the page to load.

---

3. Resize the window if needed by clicking and dragging the lower-right corner.

4. A box with an arrow appears near the data that can be retrieved. Place your pointer over the box, and it changes color. A frame appears around the data that box is tied to.

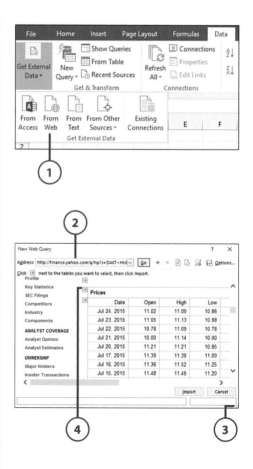

5. Click the box, and it turns into a box with a check mark.

6. Select as many sections as you need; then click Import.

7. Select the cell where you want the data to appear. To change the current cell address shown, click the correct cell. If you want the entry on a new sheet, select the New Worksheet option.

8. Click Properties.

9. Select the Refresh Every check box and enter how often (in minutes) you want the data refreshed.

10. Click OK.

11. Click OK.

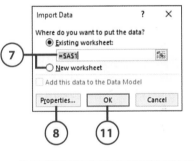

Data available for import

12. After a few seconds, depending on your Internet connection, the data appears on the sheet.

	A	B	C	D	E	F	G
1	Prices						
2							
3	Date	Open	High	Low	Close	Volume	Adj Close*
4	24-Jul-15	11.02	11.09	10.86	10.95	138,800	10.95
5	23-Jul-15	11.05	11.13	10.98	11.07	91,200	11.07
6	22-Jul-15	10.78	11.09	10.78	11.07	136,500	11.07
7	21-Jul-15	10	11.14	10	10.88	122,900	10.88

(12)

Editing Data

Now that you know how to enter data into a blank cell, how do you edit data already in a cell? If you select a cell and start typing, you'll overwrite what was originally in the cell.

Modify Cell Data

You can modify the data in a cell without retyping it.

1. Double-click a cell, and the cursor appears in that cell.

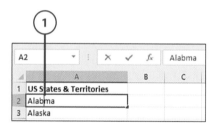

Alternative Methods

You can also enter edit mode on a cell by selecting a cell and then clicking where you want to edit in the formula bar. Or, you can select the cell and press F2. The cursor will appear at the right end of the data in the cell.

2. When you're done making changes, press Tab or Enter to exit out of the cell and save your changes. If you change your mind about the changes while you're still in the cell, press Esc and you'll exit the cell without saving your changes.

Clearing the Contents of a Cell

When you delete a cell, you remove it from the sheet and other cells move to take fill the space. If you want to delete only the data, leaving the cell intact, you have to clear it.

Clear Only Data from a Cell

Clear a cell to remove the data but retain the formatting.

1. Select the cell to clear.

2. Press Delete on the keyboard. The data in the cell is deleted.

   Or

3. Right-click over the cell and choose Clear Contents.

Don't Use the Spacebar!

You may be tempted to use the space-bar to clear a cell. *Don't!* Although you can't see the space in the cell, Excel can. That space can throw off Excel's functions because to Excel, that space is a character.

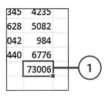

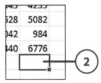

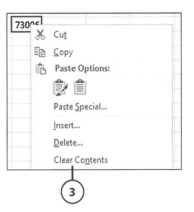

Clearing an Entire Sheet

You can clear all data from a sheet without actually deleting the sheet.

Clear an Entire Sheet

You quickly delete all cells from a sheet, or the data only, retaining the formatting.

1. Click the intersection between the headings. This will select all the cells on the sheet.

2. To clear a sheet of all data, but leave any formatting intact, press Delete on the keyboard or right-click and choose Clear Contents.

3. To clear a sheet of all data and formatting, right-click and select Delete.

   Or

4. On the Home tab, select Delete.

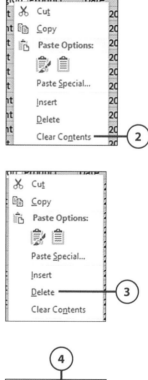

Working with Tables

Excel also has a special format, table, you can apply to a dataset, imbuing it with special abilities and rules. When your dataset is defined as a table, additional functionality in Excel is made available. For example, with Excel's intelligent tables, the following additional functionality becomes available:

- AutoFilter drop-downs are automatically added to the headers.

- You can apply predesigned formats, such as banded rows or borders.

- You can remove duplicates based on the values in one or more columns.

- You can toggle the Total Row on and off.

- Adding new rows or columns automatically extends the table.

- You can take advantage of automatically created range names.

>>>Go Further

GET THE MOST OUT OF TABLES

This section is a brief introduction to tables. To get the most out of a table, check out *Excel Tables: A Complete Guide for Creating, Using, and Automating Lists and Tables* by Zack Barresse and Kevin Jones (ISBN: 978-1615470280).

Define a Table

For a dataset to convert to a table, it must be set up properly. This means that, except for the header row, each row must be one complete record of the dataset—for example, a customer or inventory item. Column headers are not required, but if they are included, they must be in the row at the top of the dataset. If your data does not include headers, Excel inserts some for you.

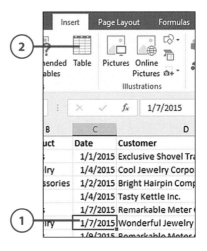

1. Select a cell in the dataset.

2. On the Insert tab, select Table.

3. Excel will determine the range of the dataset. If what is shown is incorrect, click the sheet and select the dataset.

Excel Doesn't Select Your Entire Dataset

When Excel is determining what cells belong together in a dataset, it does this by looking for empty rows and columns. If you have any empty rows or columns in the middle of your dataset, Excel will see them as the end of the table.

4. If your dataset has headers, be sure My Table Has Headers is selected.

5. Click OK.

6. Excel converts the dataset to a table and applies the default formatting and settings.

7. A new tab called Table Tools, Design appears in the ribbon. Whenever you select a cell in a table, this tab appears. It contains functionality and options specific to tables.

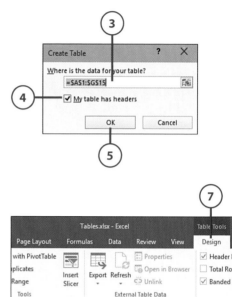

Add a Total Row to a Table

When you add a total row to your table, Excel adds the word *Total* to the first column of the table and sums the data in the rightmost column. If the rightmost column contains text, Excel returns a count instead of a sum.

1. Select a cell in the table to display the Table Tools ribbon tab.

2. On the Table Tools, Design tab, select Total Row. Excel will add a total row to the bottom of the table.

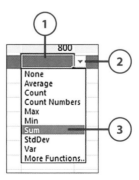

Change the Total Row Function

Each cell in the total row has a drop-down of functions that can be used to calculate the data above it.

1. Select the cell in the total row that you want add a Total function to.

2. Open the drop-down list.

3. Select the desired function.

4. Excel will insert the correct formula in the cell.

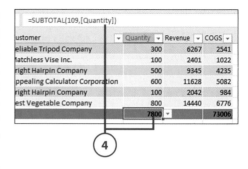

Total Rows Using the SUBTOTAL Function

The functions listed in the drop-down are calculated using variations of the SUBTOTAL function. For more information on this function, see Chapter 13, "Inserting Subtotals and Grouping Data."

Expand a Table

As you enter text in adjacent rows and columns, the table automatically expands to include them.

1. Enter data in a cell in the next available row and then press Tab or Enter.

East	Jewelry	1/7/2015	Wonderful Jewelry Inc.	1000	21730	9840
Central	Tools	1/9/2015	Remarkable Meter Corporation	800	16416	6776
Central	Tools	1/10/2015	Safe Flagpole Supply	900	21438	9198
Central	Tools	1/12/2015	Reliable Tripod Company	300	6267	2541
East	Tools	1/14/2015	Matchless Vise Inc.	100	2401	1022
East	Accessories	1/15/2015	Bright Hairpin Company	500	9345	4235
East	Tools	1/16/2015	Appealing Calculator Corporation	600	11628	5082
West	Accessories	1/19/2015	Bright Hairpin Company	100	2042	984
East	Food	1/21/2015	Best Vegetable Company	800	14440	6776
	Accessories					

Expansion When Entering Multiple Records

The table will also automatically add a new row when you enter a value in the last row and column and then press Tab.

2. The table expands to include the new row.

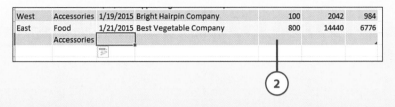

West	Accessories	1/19/2015	Bright Hairpin Company	100	2042	984
East	Food	1/21/2015	Best Vegetable Company	800	14440	6776
	Accessories					

Stop Automatic Expansion

A table automatically expands as you add adjacent rows and columns. If you don't want the new entry to be part of the table, you can tell Excel by clicking the lightning bolt icon that appears and then selecting either Undo Table AutoExpansion or Stop Automatically Expanding Tables. If you choose Stop Automatically Expanding Tables, this will stop automatic expansion for future tables as well.

Turn Off the Total Row

When adding new rows to the bottom of a table, make sure the Total row is turned off; otherwise, Excel cannot identify the new row as belonging with the existing data. The exception is if you tab from the last data row, Excel inserts a new row and moves the Total row down.

Fixing Numbers Stored as Text

Sometimes when you import data or receive data from another source, the numbers might be converted to text. When you try to sum them, nothing works. That is because Excel will not sum numbers stored as text.

When numbers in a sheet are being stored as text, Excel lets you know by placing a green triangle in the cell. When you select the cell, an information symbol appears. The following two sections show you how to convert these values to true numbers so that calculations can be performed.

	antity	Revenue	CC
Green triangle	1000	22810	
Information symbol	0	18552	
	100	2257	
	400	0152	

No Green Triangle

If you have numbers stored as text but don't see a green triangle, it's possible you have the Error Checking feature turned off. To check, and turn it on, go to File, Options, Formulas, Error Checking, Enable Background Error Checking.

Use Convert to Number on Multiple Cells

One option for converting multiple cells into numbers is to use the Convert to Number option in the information symbol.

1. Select the range you need to convert, making sure that the first cell in the range needs to be converted. The range can include text and other numerical values, as long as it doesn't include cells you do not want to be converted to numbers.

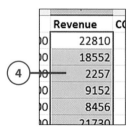

2. Click the information symbol in the first cell.

3. From the drop-down, select Convert to Number.

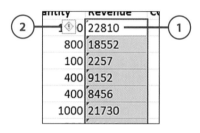

4. All cells in the selected range will be modified, turning the numbers to true numbers. The green triangles will go away.

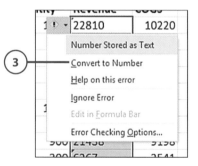

Use Paste Special to Force a Number

If you have Background Error Checking disabled or don't see the green warning triangle, try this method for converting cells to numbers.

1. Enter a 1 in a blank cell. Press Ctrl+Enter so that Excel accepts the value but the cell also remains the active cell.

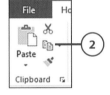

2. On the Home tab, select Copy.

3. Select the cells containing the numbers to convert.

4. On the Home tab, select Paste Special from the Paste Special drop-down.

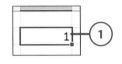

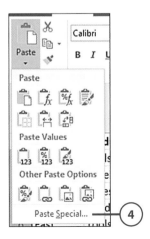

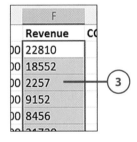

5. Select the Values and Multiply options.

6. Click OK.

7. All cells in the selected range will be modified, turning the numbers to true numbers.

The act of multiplying the values by 1 forces the contents of the cells to become their numerical values.

⑤

Paste Special		? ✕
Paste		
○ All		○ All using Source theme
○ Formulas		○ All except borders
⦿ Values		○ Column widths
○ Formats		○ Formulas and number formats
○ Comments		○ Values and number formats
○ Validation		○ All merging conditional formats
Operation		
○ None		⦿ Multiply
○ Add		○ Divide
○ Subtract		
☐ Skip blanks		☐ Transpose
Paste Link		OK Cancel

⑥

	Revenue	CC
⑦ 00	22810	
00	18552	
00	2257	
00	9152	

Spell Checking a Sheet

Just like Word, Excel has a spell checker included. It reviews all text entries on the sheet.

1. On the Review tab, select Spelling.

2. As Excel goes through the sheet, select the desired option, such as Change to correct a misspelling.

Finding Data on a Sheet

Through the Find and Replace dialog box, you can find data on any sheet in the workbook.

Perform a Search

When you perform a search, Excel will select the matching cell.

1. On the Home tab, select Find from the Find & Select drop-down.

2. Enter your search term.

3. Click Find Next. Excel will select a cell containing the term.

   Or

4. Click Find All. Excel will select a cell containing the term and also provide a list of all cells with the term.

5. You can click a row in the search results, and Excel will jump to that selection.

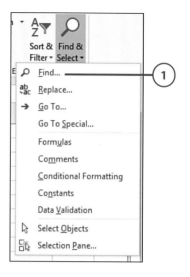

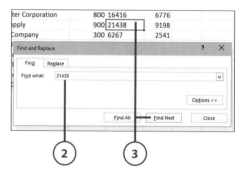

>>>*Go Further*

REFINE YOUR SEARCH

If you click the Options button on the Find and Replace dialog box, several options appear to help you refine your search:

- **Within**—You can search just the active sheet or the entire workbook. You can also narrow Excel's search by selecting the range before bringing up the dialog box.

- **Search**—To have the search go down all the rows of one column before going on to the next column, set this to By Rows. To have the search go across all columns in a row before going on to the next row, select By Columns.

- **Look In**—By default, Excel looks in formulas (that is, the true value of the data in a cell). When you've applied formulas or formatting to a sheet, what you see in a cell might not be what is actually in the cell. To search for the value, what you see in the cell, change the drop-down to Values. You can also choose to search in comments.

It's Not All Good

When Find Doesn't Work

You perform a Find operation for a value (for example, 123) you know is on the sheet, but Excel says it cannot find it. You find the value manually, and it's actually 123.18, but you know this method worked before—so why not this time?

You look at the options and notice Match Entire Cell Contents is selected. You had selected it earlier in the day when you were searching in another workbook.

The settings in the Find and Replace dialog box are stored throughout an Excel session. This means that if you change them in the morning for a search and then try a different search later in the afternoon without having closed Excel at all during the day, the settings changes you've made are still active, even if you're searching a different workbook.

Perform a Wildcard Search

What if you don't know the exact text you're looking for? Wildcards can be added to the search term, each wildcard helping in a different way.

1. Use an asterisk (*) in the search term to tell Excel there might or might not be additional characters between two known characters.

2. Use a question mark (?) to replace an unknown character.

3. If you need to include the * or ? as part of your search term, not as a wildcard, the use the tilde (~) symbol to tell Excel the character is an actual text character. If your search term character is a ~, then you would have two in the search term.

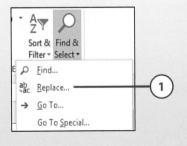

Replace Data on a Sheet

You can replace data as you find it, or replace all matches with a single click.

1. On the Home tab, select Replace from the Find & Select drop-down.

2. Enter your search term.

3. Enter the term you want to replace it with.

4. Click Find Next. Excel will select a cell containing the term. If you want to replace the term in that cell, click Replace. If you don't want to replace that instance, click Find Next. Repeat this step until all desired replacements are made.

Or

5. Click Replace All. Excel will replace all instances of the term.

Find and Replace Formatting

Through the Format buttons on the Find and Replace dialog box, you can narrow down your search by choosing the formatting the desired matches have, such as the number format or font. You can also use the Format option to apply a format to matches.

Cell

	A	B	C	D	E	F	G
1	Region	Product	Date	Customer	Quantity	Revenue	COGS
2	East	Tools	1/1/2015	Exclusive Shovel Traders	1000	22810	10220
3	Central	Accessorie	1/2/2015	Bright Hairpin Company	100	2257	984
4	East	Jewelry	1/4/2015	Cool Jewelry Corporation	800	18552	7872
5	East	Food	1/4/2015	Tasty Kettle Inc.	400	9152	4088
6	East	Tools	1/7/2015	Remarkable Meter Corporation	400	8456	3388
7	East	Jewelry	1/7/2015	Wonderful Jewelry Inc.	1000	21730	9840
8	Central	Tools	1/9/2015	Remarkable Meter Corporation	800	16416	6776
9	Central	Tools	1/10/2015	Safe Flagpole Supply	900	21438	9198
10	Central	Tools	1/12/2015	Reliable Tripod Company	300	6267	2541
11	East	Tools	1/14/2015	Matchless Vise Inc.	100	2401	1022
12	East	Accessorie	1/15/2015	Bright Hairpin Company	500	9345	4235
13	East	Tools	1/16/2015	Appealing Calculator Corporation	600	11628	5082
14	West	Accessorie	1/19/2015	Bright Hairpin Company	100	2042	984
15	East	Food	1/21/2015	Best Vegetable Company	800	14440	6776
16	Total						73006

Row

Column

The ability to move data around easily is important. Excel makes the process fairly easy by offering numerous methods. In this chapter, you'll learn about moving entire rows and columns and selected ranges. This chapter also covers the following:

→ Selecting, inserting, and deleting rows and columns

→ Selecting noncontiguous cells and ranges

→ Selecting, inserting, moving and deleting cells

Selecting and Moving Data on a Sheet

It's hard to create the perfect data table the first time around. There's always something you've forgotten, such as the date column. Or maybe you did remember the date column but put it in the wrong place. Thankfully, you don't have to start over. You can insert, delete, and move entire columns and rows, or just some cells, with a few clicks of the mouse.

Working with Rows and Columns

When working with an entire row or column, what you do affects the entire sheet, beyond what you can see on your screen. In other words, when you select an entire row or column, whatever you do to the part you can see affects the entire selection.

Select a Row or Column

A click in the right place will select an entire row or column.

1. Place your pointer on the row number so that it turns into a single black arrow. Then click. The row will be highlighted from the first column to the very last.

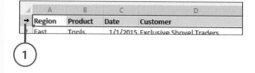

Select a Column

Selecting a column isn't that different from selecting a row. To select an entire column, click the column letter.

Turn Off a Selection

When you cut or copy data, a flashing border appears around it. If you need to cancel the selection, press Esc.

>>>Go Further

SELECT MULTIPLE ROWS OR COLUMNS

If you need to select multiple, contiguous rows, click the heading of the first row, then, as you hold down the mouse button, drag the mouse down (or up) until you have selected all the rows you need. Let go of the mouse button and perform your desired action on the selection.

You can also select multiple rows (or columns) by selecting the first row, holding the Shift key down, and selecting the last row you want.

>>>Go Further

SELECT NONCONTIGUOUS ROWS OR COLUMNS

If you need to select multiple, noncontiguous rows, click the heading of the first row, then, as you hold down the Ctrl key, carefully click the numbers of the other rows you want to select. When you are done selecting, release the Ctrl key and perform your desired action on the selection.

Once a row has been selected using the Ctrl key method, you cannot deselect it without also deselecting all other selected rows. If you make a mistake in your selection, you have to start over.

Insert a New Row or Column

You might want to insert a row if your dataset is missing titles over the data. Or, you might need to insert a column if the data table is missing a column of information and you don't want to enter the information at the end (right side) of the table. When you insert a new row, Excel shifts the existing data down. When you insert a new column, Excel shifts the existing data to the right.

1. Right-click the number of the row where you want to insert a blank row.

2. Select Insert.

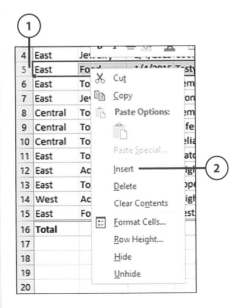

Insert Sheet Rows Ribbon Option

Rows can also be inserted using the ribbon. First, select a cell where you want the new row to go. For example, if you need to insert a new row 5, select a cell in row 5. Then, on the Home tab, select Insert Sheet Rows from the Insert drop-down.

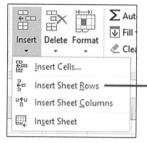

Use the option on the ribbon to insert a new row

Insert a Column

Inserting a column isn't that different from inserting a row. To insert a column, click the column heading and then right-click and choose Insert or Insert Sheet Columns from the Insert drop-down.

Insert Individual Cells

If you don't have the entire row or column selected and you try to right-click and insert, Excel displays the Insert dialog box, prompting you to specify whether you want to shift the selected cells right or down, or if you want to insert an entire row or column. See the "Insert Cells" section for more information.

Insert Multiple Rows or Columns

If you select multiple rows or columns, Excel will insert that many rows or columns. For example, if you need to insert five new rows in your data, select five rows before choosing Insert.

This also applies to deleting multiple rows or columns—Excel deletes all of what you have selected.

Delete a Row or Column

When you import data from another source, you might need to clean it up by deleting rows or columns of data you don't need. When deleting a row, Excel shifts the data below the row up. For example, after you delete row 5, what was in row 6 now appears in row 5. If you're deleting a column, Excel shifts the data that was to the right of the deleted column to the left.

1. Right-click the heading of the row you want to delete.

2. Select Delete.

Delete Sheet Rows Ribbon Option

Rows can also be deleted using the ribbon. First, select a cell in the row you want to delete. Then, on the Home tab, select Delete Sheet Rows from the Delete drop-down.

Delete Noncontiguous Rows or Columns

Your selection of rows or columns does not have to be contiguous. Excel will delete what you have selected. See the section "Select a Row or Column" for instructions on how to select the data.

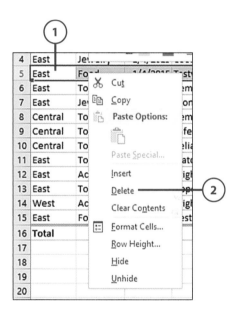

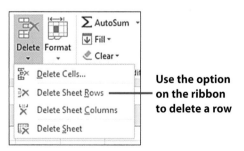

Use the option on the ribbon to delete a row

>>>*Go Further*

HIDING AND UNHIDING ROWS OR COLUMNS

You don't have to delete your rows and columns to get them out of your way. Instead, you can choose to hide them—and you can unhide them at a later time. To do this, select the heading and, from the Format drop-down on the Home tab, open the Hide & Unhide menu and choose what you want to hide—either Hide Rows or Hide Columns.

To unhide data, select the visible headings on both sides of the hidden data and select Unhide Rows or Unhide Columns from the Hide & Unhide menu in the Format drop-down.

Move Rows or Columns by Dragging

You have to be careful when moving rows and columns. Depending on the method you use, you could end up over-writing other cells. Use this method to move rows or columns when you aren't worried about overwriting existing data. If you don't want to overwrite existing data, see the section "Move Rows or Columns by Cutting."

1. Select the row you want to move.

2. Place the pointer over the selection's border so that a four-headed arrow appears.

3. Click the border and hold the mouse button down.

5	East	Food	1/4/2015	Tasty Kettle I
6	East	Tools	1/7/2015	Remarkable N
7	East	Jewelry	1/7/2015	Wonderful Je
8	Central	Tools	1/9/2015	Remarkable N

4. Drag the selection to a new location and let go of the mouse button.

5. If there is any data in the new location, Excel asks if you want to overwrite it. If you select Cancel, the move will be canceled. Click OK if you want to overwrite the data.

6. After you have moved the row, the original row will still be there, but it will be empty.

Drag a Column to a New Location

Moving a column isn't that different from moving a row. To move an entire column, select the column and place your pointer on the border, where it becomes a four-headed arrow. Then, as you hold the mouse button down, drag the column to a new location.

Move Rows or Columns by Cutting

When you cut a row or column, you have the option of pasting it to a new location, overwriting anything that was already there. Alternatively, you can tell Excel to insert the data. When you choose the insert option, Excel moves the existing data over before pasting the cut selection. The space that was cut will be filled as Excel shifts data up (for cut rows) or to the left (for cut columns).

1. Select the row you want to cut.

2. On the Home tab, select Cut.

3. Select the row where you want the cut row to go. For example, if the cut row needs to be where the data in row 5 is, select row 5.

4. On the Home tab, select Insert Cut Cells from the Insert drop-down. Excel will insert a new row before pasting the data. It will delete the original row, shifting all the data beneath it up.

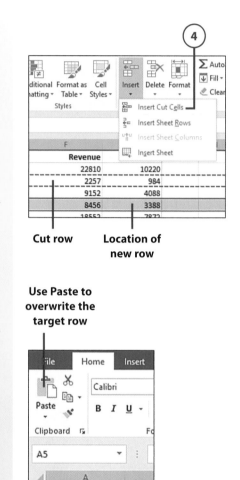

Cut row   **Location of new row**

Use Paste to overwrite the target row

Cut row

Target row

Overwrite Data

If you want to overwrite data in an existing row, instead of Insert Cut Cells, on the Home tab, select the Paste button. Excel will overwrite the data in the selected row. It will not remove the original row—only the data in the cells.

It's Not All Good

Accidental Overwrite

When you cut and paste a selection over existing data, Excel won't give you any warning—it will just do it. To undo the overwrite, click the Undo button in the QAT or press Ctrl+Z.

Cut a Column

Cutting a column isn't that different from cutting a row. Select the column letter and then click the Cut button of the Home tab. Select the column you want
to replace and then select either Paste to overwrite it or Insert Cut Cells to shift
it over.

Copy Rows or Columns

When you copy a row or column, you
have the option of pasting it to a new
location, overwriting anything that was
already there. Alternatively, you can
tell Excel to insert the data. When you
choose the insert option, Excel shifts the
existing data over before pasting the
copied selection.

1. Select the row you want to copy.

2. On the Home tab, select Copy.

3. Select the row where you want
   the copied row to go. For example, if the copied row needs to be
   row 5, select row 5.

4. On the Home tab, select Insert
   Copied Cells from the Insert drop-
   down. Excel will insert the new
   row, shifting the rows below it
   down.

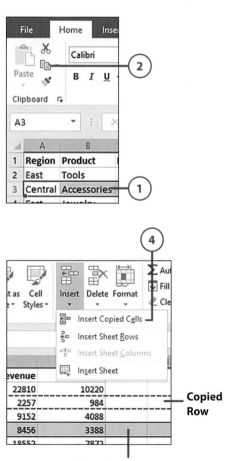

Copied Row

Location of new row

Overwrite Data

If you want to overwrite data, instead of Insert Copied Cells, on the Home tab, select the Paste button. Excel will over-write the data in the selected row.

Do It Quicker

To quickly copy a row, select the row and then hold down the Ctrl key as you click on the border and drag the row to the other location.

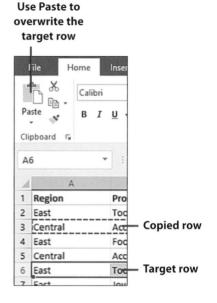

Use Paste to overwrite the target row

— Copied row

— Target row

It's Not All Good

Insert Multiple Copies

Suppose you need to make several copies of a specific row (or column). You select the row, select where you want it to go, choose Insert Copied Cells. You then go to the next row where you need the duplicate data… and the option Insert Copied Cells is no longer available. You look at the original row and see it is still selected. So what's up?

The copied data is still in the clipboard. You can still paste it. However, by design, the insert functionality is removed. To get it back, you'll need to copy the data again.

Copy a Column

Copying a column isn't that different from copying a row. Select the column heading and then click the Copy button of the Home tab. Select the column you want to replace and then select either Paste to overwrite it or Insert Copied Cells to shift it over.

Working with Cells

Just like you can insert, move, and delete entire rows and columns, you can also insert, move, and delete cells. This section shows you how to quickly jump to a cell you can't currently see on your sheet, select noncontiguous ranges, and insert, move, and delete cells.

Select a Cell Using the Name Box

Chapter 1, "Understanding the Microsoft Excel Interface," explains how each cell has an address made up of the column and row it resides in. The basics of navigation were touched upon—you can either click a cell or use the keyboard to select a cell.

You can also jump to a cell by typing the cell address in the Name box, located above the sheet in the left corner. This is a great way of traveling quickly to a specific location on a large sheet.

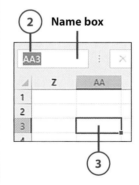

1. Click in the Name box.

2. Type the desired cell address. For example, if you want to jump to cell AA3, type in AA3; typing 3AA won't work.

3. Press Enter and the currently selected cell will be cell AA3.

When Column Headings Are Numbers

If you have R1C1 notation turned on—you'll have numbers instead of letters in the column heading—A1 notation won't work. To turn off R1C1 notation, go to File, Options and select the Formulas menu. Under Working with Formulas, unselect R1C1 Reference Style.

Select Noncontiguous Cells and Ranges

You don't always want to select cells right next to each other. For example, you might want to select only the cells with negative values and make them bold. You can use the Ctrl key to select noncontiguous cells and then apply your desired format (or perform some other action).

1. Select the first cell to include.

2. Hold down the Ctrl key.

3. Select the next cell to include. Repeat this step until all the desired cells are selected.

4. Release the Ctrl key. Do what you need to the selection, such as making the cells bold.

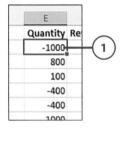

You Can't Deselect

Once a range has been selected using the Ctrl key method, you cannot deselect it without deselecting all other selected cells. If you make a mistake in your cell selection, you have to start over.

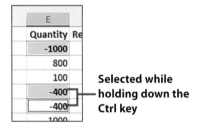

Selected while holding down the Ctrl key

Insert Cells

When you insert or delete rows and columns, Excel shifts all the other data on the sheet. If you only want part of the data shifted, you need to select the specific range where you want empty cells.

1. Select the cells you need to shift.

2. On the Home tab, click the Insert drop-down and select Insert Cells.

3. Choose which direction you want to shift your existing data. If you want the selected cells to shift downward, choose Shift Cells Down. If you want the selected cells to shift to the right, choose Shift Cells Right.

4. Click OK. New cells will be inserted and the selected data shifted.

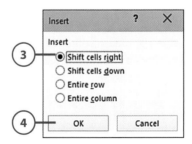

It's Not All Good

Watch Out for Misaligned Data

When you use this method for inserting cells, versus inserting entire rows or columns, Excel inserts only the number of cells that you have selected. This has the potential to mess up your data layout if you don't select the entire range that needs to be affected.

This also applies to deleting cells—Excel will delete only as much data as you have selected, shifting data over to fill in the empty space.

Delete Cells

When you delete a range, you remove the cells from the sheet, thus shifting other data to fill in the empty space. If you aren't cautious, you can ruin the careful layout of your sheet—for example, moving data from the credit column to the debit column.

1. Select the cells you want to delete.

2. On the Home tab, click the Delete drop-down and select Delete Cells.

3. Choose either Shift Cells Left or Shift Cells Up.

4. Click OK. The selected cells will be deleted and the remaining data shifted.

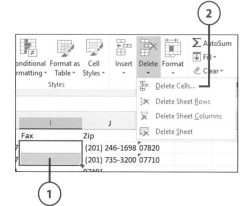

Clear Data But Leave Cells Intact

If what you really want is to remove the data from the cells, leaving the cells intact, Excel calls this "clearing the contents." For specifics on clearing contents, see the section "Clearing the Contents of a Cell," in Chapter 4, "Getting Data onto a Sheet."

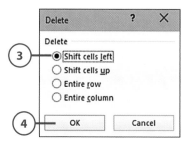

Move Cells

You have to be careful when moving a range—you could end up overwriting other cells.

1. Select the range you want to move.

2. Place your pointer over the selection's border until a four-headed arrow appears.

3. Click the border and hold the mouse button down.

4. Drag the selection to a new location and let go of the mouse button.

5. If there is any data in the new location, Excel asks if you want to overwrite it. If you select Cancel, the move will be canceled. Click OK if you want to overwrite the data.

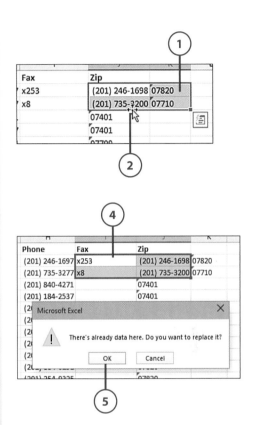

Move Cells by Cutting and Pasting

You can also move cells by cutting and pasting the range. But be warned! Whereas the dragging method prompts to let you know you're overwriting data, Excel won't be so kind if you paste the data. So before you cut and paste, make sure the new location is big enough for your dataset.

2015 Customer Revenue

Customer	Revenue
Amazing Yardstick Partners	$ 22,810.00
Inventive Opener Corporation	$ 2,257.00
Magnificent Tackle Inc.	$ 11,240.00
Leading Yogurt Company	$ 9,204.00
Excellent Doorbell Company	$ 18,552.00
Paramount Doghouse Inc.	$ 9,152.00
Flexible Instrument Partners	$ 8,456.00
Honest Chopstick Company	$ 21,730.00
Wonderful Faucet Corporation	$ 13,806.00
Special Doghouse Inc.	$ 16,416.00
Ideal Vise Corporation	$ 21,015.00
Guaranteed Bicycle Company	$ 21,465.00
Astonishing Thermostat Corporation	$ 21,438.00
Trustworthy Yogurt Inc.	$ 9,144.00
Bright Toothpick Inc.	$ 6,267.00
Remarkable Banister Supply	$ 1,740.00
Safe Shoe Company	$ 2,401.00
Vibrant Vise Company	$ 9,345.00
Forceful Furnace Company	$ 11,628.00
Guarded Zipper Corporation	$ 5,961.00
	$ 244,027.00

Reported created May 8, 2015 with data 1/1/15 - 4/1/15

Printed: 5/8/2015 9:39

Change row height

Currency format

Increase column width

Border

Wrap Text

Date & Time format

Formatting data is important—it makes it easier to interpret the data and pulls the user's eye to important parts. You also need to know how to resize rows and columns so more of your data is visible. This chapter includes the following topics:

6

→ Merging cells

→ Formatting dates

→ Centering data in a cell

→ Quickly copying a format from one range to another

→ Switching between number formats

Formatting Sheets and Cells

Now that you have your data on a sheet, you need to format it so that it's easy to decipher and readers can quickly make sense of it. From formatting the font, wrapping text, and merging cells to changing how a number is displayed in a cell, Excel has the tools you need to make reports visually interesting.

Changing the Font Settings of a Cell

Changing font aspects allows you to add emphasis to an entire cell. Two ways you can access the font-changing tools in Excel are from the ribbon and from the mini toolbar, which is accessed by right-clicking over a range.

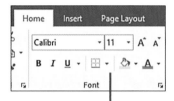

Font controls on mini toolbar

Font controls on ribbon

>>>Go Further

CHANGE MULTIPLE FONT SETTINGS AT A TIME

The following sections will outline how to change one font setting at a time, but on the Font tab of the Format Cells dialog box, you can change multiple settings at one time.

To open the dialog box, select Format Cells from the Format drop-down on the Home tab or right-click over a selected range and choose Format Cells.

Ribbon menu

Right-click menu

Select a New Font Typeface

The default font in Excel is Calibri, but many others are available.

1. Select the range for which you want to change the font.

2. On the Home tab, open the Font drop-down and click the desired font.

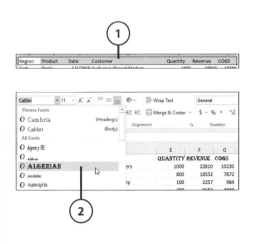

Use the Mini Toolbar

You can also change the font using the mini toolbar. Right-click over the selected range and click a font from the Font drop-down of the mini toolbar.

Preview Your Selection

If the selected range is in view, you can preview the font change as you move your mouse pointer across fonts on the list. When you find the one you want, click it to make the change stick.

Increase and Decrease the Font Size

The default font size in Excel is 11, but you can make it smaller or larger.

1. Select the range for which you want to change the font size.

2. On the Home tab, open the Font Size drop-down and click the desired size.

Other Ways to Change the Font Size

You can change the font using the mini toolbar. Right-click over the selected range and select a size from the Font Size drop-down of the mini toolbar.

Both the ribbon and mini toolbar include buttons to increase and decrease the font size. Click the Increase Font Size button and the font will increase to the next size; click the Decrease Font Size button and the font will decrease to the previous size.

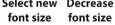

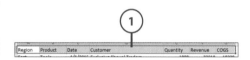

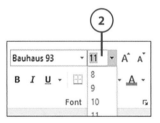

Increase font size

Select new font size   **Decrease font size**

Apply Bold, Italic, and Underline to Text

In addition to changing the font type or size to add emphasis to data, you can bold, italicize, or underline the values.

1. Select the range you want to format.

2. On the Home tab, click the desired font style.

Use the Mini Toolbar

You can bold and italicize the font using the mini toolbar. Right-click over the selected range and select the desired font style on the mini toolbar.

Use Keyboard Shortcuts

The popular keyboard shortcuts for bold (Ctrl+B), italic (Ctrl+I), and underlining (Ctrl+U) also work in Excel.

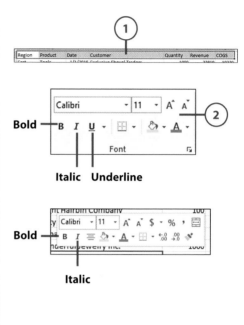

Apply Strikethrough, Superscript, and Subscript

The strikethrough, superscript, and subscript effects are available only through the Format Cells dialog box.

1. Select the range to which you want to apply an effect.

2. Right-click over the selection and select Format Cells.

3. Select the desired effect(s) from the Effects group and click OK.

4. The effect will be applied to the selected range.

Change the Font Color

Emphasis can also be added to a range by using color, or you can use color to just make the data look pretty.

1. Select the range for which you want to change the font color.

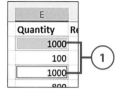

2. On the mini toolbar, open the Font Color drop-down and click on the desired color.

3. The range will update to the selected color.

More Colors

If you don't see the color you want in the drop-down, click More Colors to open the Color dialog box to access all the colors available. The dialog box will also allow you to enter the RGB and HSL values for colors.

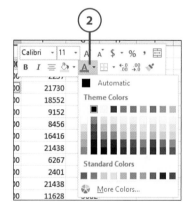

Reapply the Default Color

To quickly return to the default color, usually black, select the Automatic option at the top of the Font Color drop-down.

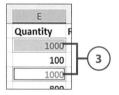

Format a Character or Word in a Cell

You can change the font settings of a single character or word in a cell, not just the entire cell contents.

1. Double-click the cell so that the cursor appears in the cell and you can select the desired character or word.

Select Text in the Formula Bar

You can also select the desired text via the formula bar. Select the cell and then select the character or word in the formula bar.

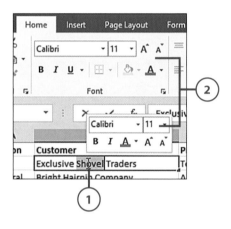

2. A modified mini toolbar will appear when you are done with the selection and when you right-click over the selected text. You can make selections from this smaller toolbar or make your selections from the options on the Home tab.

Format Quickly with the Format Painter

The Format Painter enables you to quickly copy the formatting of one range to another. Copied formatting includes font, color, and number formatting; it does not include row heights or column widths.

1. Select the range with the formatting to duplicate.

2. Click the Format Painter button. The pointer changes to a paint-brush with a plus sign.

3. Click the cell in the upper-left corner of the destination range if the range is the same size. If the destination range is larger, select the entire range.

4. The formatting is applied, and the pointer changes back to normal.

Paint Multiple Ranges

By default, the Format Painter is a one-shot tool. To get it to stay on until you are done pasting the formatting every-where you want to apply it, double-click the Format Painter button. The button will remain on until you press the Esc key or double-click the button to turn it off.

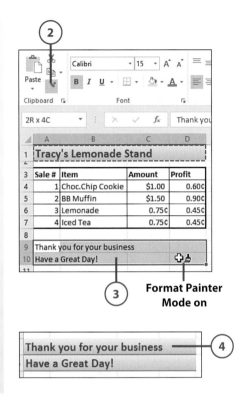

Format Painter Mode on

Adjusting the Row Height

If the text is wrapping to the next line in your cell, you might not be able to see all of it. This is especially true if you have merged cells—Excel won't automatically adjust the row height for merged cells as it will for non-merged cells.

Modify the Row Height by Dragging

You can quickly change the row height by adjusting the line between the row headings.

1. Place your pointer on the line below the row heading of the row to resize. For example, if you want to resize row 3, move your pointer onto the line below row 3.

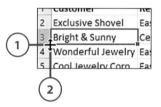

Resize Multiple Rows at a Time

You can resize multiple rows at a time. Select the rows then place the pointer below any row heading in the selection.

2. When the pointer changes to a two-headed arrow, click and hold down the mouse button.

3. As you drag to resize the row to the desired height, a ScreenTip will appear by the pointer, showing the current height. Let go of the mouse button when you've reached the desired height.

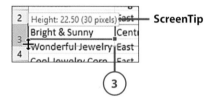

ScreenTip

Set the Maximum Needed Height

If there are no merged cells in the row to resize, you can use the double-click method to have Excel calculate the required maximum height of the row. When you get the two-headed arrow, double-click and Excel will size the row for you.

Modify the Row Height by Entering a Value

Row heights are based on points. If there are no cells with wrap turned on, then the default row height will be slightly larger than the largest font size in the row. You can change this by entering a specific value.

1. Select a cell in the row you want to adjust. Cells in multiple rows can be selected.

2. On the Home tab, select Row Height from the Format drop-down.

3. Enter the new height and click OK.

4. The row height will adjust to the new value.

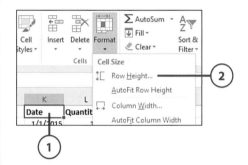

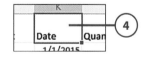

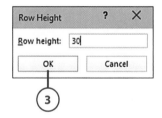

Use Font Size to Automatically Adjust the Row Height

The default row height is based on the largest font size in the row. For example, if cell F2 has a font size of 26, even if there is no other text in the row, the row automatically adjusts to approximately 33 points, providing a little empty space above and below the text. You can take advantage of this to set the height of a row, instead of manually setting the row height. The advantage is that when a user tries autofitting the row height, your setting won't change.

1. Select a blank cell in the row to adjust. You want a cell that won't ever have text in it, or the text will be that font size.

2. On the Home tab, from the Font Size drop-down, select a new font size.

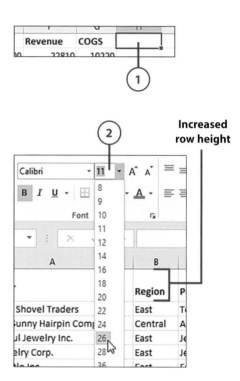

Height Doesn't Adjust Completely

If manual height adjustments have been applied to a row, the font size method will not work right away. If that happens, use the double-click method to reset the automatic adjustment functionality for the row.

Adjusting the Column Width

If you can't see all the data you enter in a cell or the data in a column doesn't use up very much of the column, you can adjust the column width as needed.

Modify the Column Width by Dragging

You can quickly change the column width by adjusting the line between the column headings.

1. Place the pointer on the line to the right of the column heading of the column you want to resize. For example, if you want to resize column D, move your pointer over the line between headings D and E.

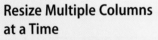

Resize Multiple Columns at a Time

You can resize multiple columns at a time. Select the columns and then place the pointer to the right of any column heading in the selection.

ScreenTip

---

2. When the pointer changes to a two-headed arrow, hold down the mouse button.

3. As you drag to resize the column to the desired width, a ScreenTip will appear by the pointer, showing the current width. Let go of the mouse button when you've reached the desired width.

Set the Maximum Needed Width

If your cells aren't merged or wrapped, you can use the double-click method to have Excel calculate the required maximum width of the column. When you get the two-headed arrow, double-click and Excel will size the column for you based on the cell with the longest entry.

If you have multiple columns selected, each column will adjust to its own required maximum width.

Modify the Column Width by Entering a Value

You can adjust the column width to a specific value. This value represents the number of characters that can be displayed in a cell formatted with the default font style.

1. Select a cell in the column you want to adjust. Cells in multiple columns can be selected.

2. On the Home tab, in the Format drop-down, select Column Width.

3. Enter the new width and click OK.

4. The column width will adjust to the new value.

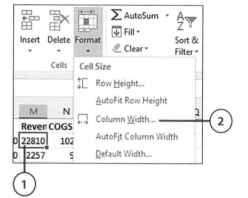

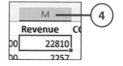

Aligning Text in a Cell

Excel allows you to change the vertical and horizontal alignment of data in a cell. By default, text is left aligned in a cell and numbers are right aligned. Both are bottom aligned.

Change Text Alignment

You can change the horizontal and vertical alignment of text in a cell so that it appears as you need it.

1. Select the range for which you want to change the alignment.

2. On the Home tab, select a vertical and/or horizontal alignment option.

3. The range's alignment will change to match your selection(s).

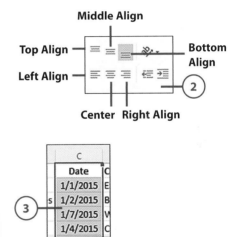

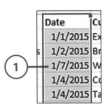

Merging Two or More Cells

The process of merging cells takes two or more adjacent cells and combines them to make one cell. For example, if you are designing a form with many data-entry cells and you need space for a large comment area, resizing the column might not be practical because it will also affect the size of the cells above and below it. Instead, select the range you want the comments to be entered in and merge the cells. Any existing text in cells other than the upper-left cell of the selection is deleted as the newly combined cell takes on the identity of this first cell.

It's Not All Good

Merged Cells Limit Excel

Use caution when merging cells because it can lead to potential issues:

- Users will be unable to sort if there are merged cells within the sort range.
- Users will be unable to cut and paste unless the same cells are merged in the paste location.
- Column and row AutoFit won't work.
- Lookup-type formulas will return a match only for the first matching row or column.

Merge and Center Data

Excel makes it easy to merge cells and center the data by having a single button that does both these actions right on the Home tab.

1. Select the cells to merge.
2. On the Home tab, select Merge & Center.
3. The selected cells will merge, and any data in the leftmost cell will be centered.

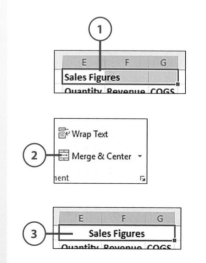

Merge But Don't Center

If you want to merge cells but not center the data, open the Merge & Center drop-down and select Merge Cells. The alignment of the leftmost cell in the selection will be applied to the merged cell.

Merge Across Columns

When you select a range that contains both multiple columns and multiple rows, Excel merges the entire range into a single cell. If you want to merge only the columns, creating a separate merged cell in each row, you can use the Merge Across option. This keeps the rows separate but merges the columns.

1. Select the rows and columns you want to merge. You don't have to select the same number of columns in each row.

2. On the Home tab, from the Merge & Center drop-down, select Merge Across.

3. The selected columns in each row will be merged together.

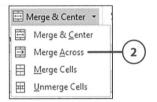

Unmerge Cells

Unmerge cells to revert them to their individual state.

1. Select one or more merged cells.

2. On the Home tab, from the Merge & Center drop-down, select Unmerge Cells.

3. The cells will unmerge with any data appearing in the upper-left cell only.

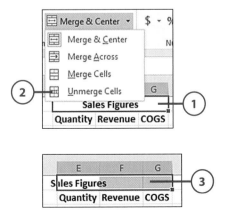

Centering Text Across Multiple Cells

As noted in the earlier section "Merging Two or More Cells," merging cells can cause problems in Excel, limiting what you can do with a dataset. If you need text to span across several columns, instead of merging the cells, you can center the text across the multiple columns.

Center Text Without Merging

Centering text across a selection gives the illusion of merged cells without the complications.

1. Enter your title in the leftmost cell of the dataset.

2. Select the title cell and extend the range to include all cells you want the title centered over.

3. From the Home tab, click on the Alignment group's dialog box launcher.

4. From the Horizontal drop-down, select Center Across Selection.

5. Click OK.

6. The title will be centered above the dataset, but still consists of individual cells.

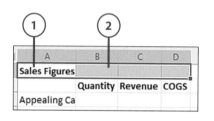

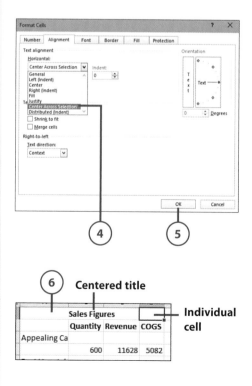

Centered title

Individual cell

Wrapping Text in a Cell to the Next Line

When you type a lot of text in a cell, it continues to extend to the right beyond the right border of the cell if there is nothing in the adjacent cell. You can widen the column to fit the text, but sometimes that may be impractical.

Wrap Text in a Cell

Set a cell to wrap text, moving any text that extends past the edge of the column to a new line in the cell.

1. Select the range you want to set to wrap.

2. On the Home tab, select Wrap Text.

3. The data in the selection will wrap, and the rows will automatically adjust their heights to show the extra lines.

It's Not All Good

AutoFit Row Height Isn't Working Right

Normally, when you wrap a cell, the row height automatically adjusts to fit the text. But if you've manually adjusted the row height any time before pasting or if you have merged cells, Excel will not autofit the row. If there are merged cells, unmerge them. Then, reset the AutoFit setting by manually forcing an autofit (see the "Adjusting the Row Height" section). The row height will begin to automatically adjust again.

Reflowing Text in a Paragraph

If you paste text into a cell, it may continue to the right, beyond what you can see on your screen. You could manually insert line breaks in the text, or you could flow the text to fit in a selected range.

Fit Text to a Specific Range

You can reflow text so that it uses the specified rows and columns. Unlike wrapped text, this doesn't affect the row height.

Select a Big Enough Range

Be careful when selecting the range, because if you don't have enough empty rows available for the text to flow into, Excel will, after warning you, over-write the rows below the selection.

1. Ensure that the text is contained in a single column of cells. The text can overflow into adjacent columns to the right, but the leftmost column must contain the text and the remaining columns must be blank.

2. Select a range as wide as the finished text should be. Ensure that the upper-left cell of the selection is the first line of text.

3. On the Home tab, from the Fill drop-down, select Justify.

4. The text reflows so that each line is within the range selected in step 2.

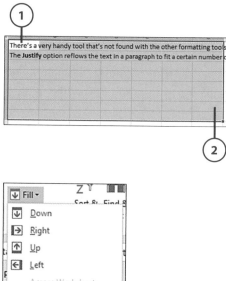

There's a very handy tool that's not found with the other formatting tools. The **Justify** option reflows the text in a paragraph to fit a certain number o

There's a very handy tool that's not found with the other formatting tools. It is hidden in the Editing group on the Home tab. The button is the Fill button (a blue down arrow) and the option within it is Justify. The Justify option reflows the text in a paragraph to fit a certain number of columns. For example, if you paste a paragraph directly into a cell, the height of the cell will increase, but the column width will be unaffected.

Indenting Cell Contents

By default, text entered in a cell is flush with the left side of the cell, whereas numbers are flush to the right. To move a value away from the edge, you might be tempted to add spaces before or after the value. However, if you change your mind about this formatting at a later time, it can be quite tedious to remove the extraneous spaces.

Indent Data

Use the indent tools instead of spaces to change the indention of data in a cell.

1. Select the range for which you want to change the indent.

2. Click the Increase Indent button until the data is increased the desired amount.

3. Click the Decrease Indent button to remove an indent.

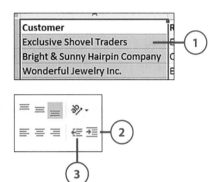

It's Not All Good

Indenting Right-Aligned Numbers

If you use the indent buttons with a right-aligned number, the number will become left aligned and adjust from the left margin.

To get a right-aligned number to indent from the right side of a cell, go to the Alignment tab of the Format Cells dialog box, set the Horizontal alignment to Right, and then set the Indent value.

Set right indent

Set the Indent value

Applying Number Formats

The way you see number data in Excel is controlled by the format applied to the cell. For example, you may see the date as August 12, 2015, but what is actually in the cell is 42106. Or you may see 10.5%, but the actual value in the cell is 0.105. This is important because when you're doing calculations, Excel doesn't care what you see. It deals only with the actual values.

General is the default format used by all cells on a sheet when you first open a workbook. Decimal places and the negative symbol are shown if needed. Thousand separators are not.

Modify the Number Format

By default, the Number format uses two decimal places but does not use the thousands separator. You can change the number of decimals shown or add a thousands separator, formatting the number as needed.

1. Select the range you want to format.

2. Click Comma Style on the Home tab to add a thousands separator.

3. Click Increase Decimal to increase the number of decimals shown. You may also have to resize the column to see all the numbers.

4. Click Decrease Decimal to decrease the number of decimals shown.

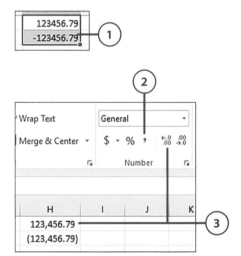

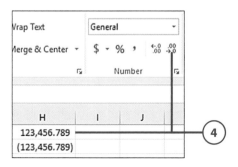

Change the Format of Negative Numbers

Negative numbers can be formatted in a variety of ways: with a leading unary symbol (the dash before a negative number), wrapped in parentheses, or colored red.

1. Select the range you want to format.

2. From the Home tab, select the Number group's dialog box launcher.

3. On the Number tab, select the Number category.

4. From the Negative Numbers list, select the desired negative number format.

5. Click OK.

6. Negative numbers will update with the new formatting.

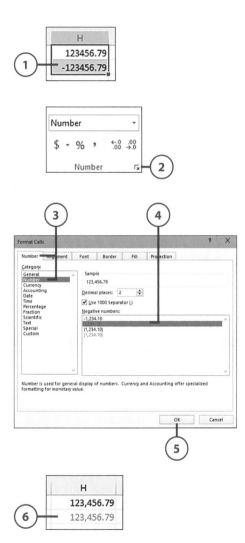

Apply a Currency Symbol

The default currency symbol is based on your Windows settings, but you can use any symbol available.

1. Select the range you want to format.

2. On the Home tab, click Accounting Number Format to apply the symbol shown on the button.

3. To apply a different symbol, open the Accounting Number Format drop-down and choose the desired symbol.

4. The default Accounting number format settings will be applied.

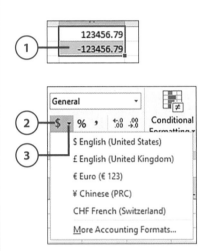

Accounting Format vs. Currency Format

The Accounting and Currency formats are similar in that they both apply a currency symbol, thousands separator, two decimal places, and black negative numbers surrounded by parentheses.

How they differ is in the alignment of the symbol and value. Accounting lines up the currency symbols on the left side of the cell and decimals points to the right side of the cell. Currency places the symbol directly to the left of the value, and the decimal points might not line up.

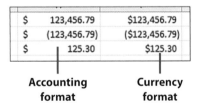

Format Dates and Times

The Number Format drop-down on the Home tab has limited date and time formatting options. More options are available through the Format Cells dialog box, such as showing the date and time together in one cell or showing only the month and year of a date.

1. Select the range you want to format.

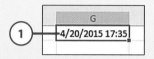

2. On the Home tab, from the Number Format drop-down, select a date or time format. If you don't see one you like, choose More Number Formats.

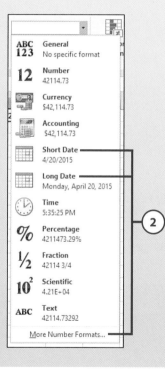

3. Click either the Date or Time category.

4. Scroll through the various types. If you want to see what your data will look like with that format, highlight it and view the sample.

5. Click OK when you've found the desired format.

Times in Excel

Excel sees times on a 24-hour clock. That is, if you enter 1:30, Excel assumes you mean 1:30 a.m. But if you enter 13:30, Excel knows you mean 1:30 p.m.

If you need to display times beyond 24 hours, such as if you're working on a timesheet adding up hours worked, use the time format 37:30:55.

Format as Percentage

When you apply the percentage format, Excel takes the value in the cell, multiplies it by 100, and adds a % symbol at the end. For example, if you have 50 in a cell and apply the percentage format to it, you will see 5000%. If you actually want 50%, you need the decimal value, 0.5, in the cell.

When you use the cell in a calculation, the actual (decimal) value is used. For example, if you have a cell showing 90% and multiply it by 1,000, the result will be (in General format) 900 (0.9*1,000).

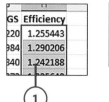

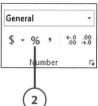

Excel Tries to Help

If you include the % symbol when you type the value in the cell, Excel converts the value to its decimal equivalent and then applies the percentage format to the cell.

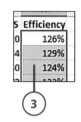

1. Select the range you want to format.

2. On the Home tab, click Percent Style.

3. The values will be multiplied by 100 and a % symbol added.

Format as Text

When you type a number with leading zeros into a cell, such as 06012, Excel drops the zero and only 6012 appears in the cell. That's because real numbers don't start with zeroes. But there are some cases, such as invoices and ZIP codes, where those leading zeroes are needed. In such cases, you should format the range as text before entering the value.

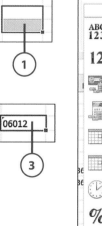

1. Select the range you want to format.

2. On the Home tab, select Text from the Number Format drop-down.

3. Select a cell in the range and type the desired value, such as 06012. The zero won't get dropped.

Use an Apostrophe Instead

You can also tell Excel you want a number treated as text by typing an apostrophe before the number (for example, '06012). One advantage of this method is the cell isn't converted to the Text format, so if you type a number later on, the number formatting applied to the cell will be retained.

It's Not All Good

Formatting Existing Values

Excel gets a little strange when it comes to applying the Text format to a cell with numbers in it. If you apply this format to formatted numbers, Excel strips any number formatting from the cell and aligns the number to the left side of the cell. However, you can still use the cells for calculations. The full conversion to "numbers as text" doesn't happen until you reenter the value in the cell. At this point, you can no longer use the cells for calculations.

Apply the Special Number Format

The Special category provides formats for numbers that are not actually numbers—ZIP codes, phone numbers, and Social Security numbers. Remember, when you change the formatting of a cell, you change only its *appearance*. The value in the cell is not affected.

1. Select the range you want to format.

2. From the Home tab, select the Number group's dialog box launcher.

3. On the Number tab, select the Special category.

4. Select a type. If you want to see what your data will look like with that format, highlight it and view the sample.

5. Click OK when you've found the desired format.

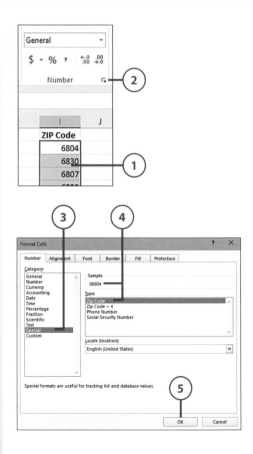

6. The format of your values will update.

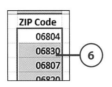

Adding a Border Around a Range

The Borders drop-down on the Home tab includes 13 of the most popular border options. When you're applying a border, Excel sees the entire selection as one object and applies the border you have chosen to the selection, not the individual cells that make it up. For example, if you select a range consisting of five rows and apply the Bottom Border, the border appears only in the last cell, not at the bottom of each cell in the selection.

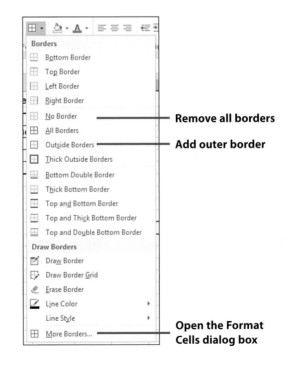

Format a Range with a Thick Outer Border and Thin Inner Lines

You can apply multiple border formats on top of each other by using the Format Cells dialog box.

1. Select the range to be formatted.

2. Select More Borders from the Borders drop-down.

3. Select a thick border style.

4. Select the Outline preset.

5. Select a thin border style.

6. Select the Inside preset.

7. Click OK.

8. The borders will be applied to the selected range.

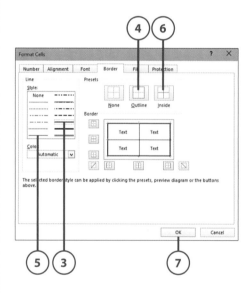

>>>Go Further

APPLY SELECTIVE LINES

The Format Cells dialog box allows you to get very specific in the application of borders to a range. You can mix and match the border styles, such as dotted lines and double lines. You can choose where they're applied within the range, whether it's the outer border, an inner line, or a diagonal line across the entire range.

Use the sample area of the Format Cells dialog box to build your border design. You can click within the box to add the lines or choose from the buttons surrounding the sample area.

Add a Colored Border

An underline applied to a value underlines only the characters. If you want to cover a larger area—such as the title over a table—apply a bottom border to the cell(s).

1. Select all the cells to which you want to apply the border.

2. Right-click over the selection and select More Borders from the Borders drop-down on the mini toolbar.

Tracy's Lemonade Stand ①

Calibri	15	A A $ %
B I	A	H .0 .0

ofit
| 0.60C |
| 0.90C |
| 0.45C |
| 0.45C |

⊞ Bottom Border
⊞ Top Border
⊞ Left Border
⊞ Right Border
⊞ No Border
⊞ All Borders
⊞ Outside Borders
⊞ Thick Outside Borders
⊞ Bottom Double Border
⊞ Thick Bottom Border
⊞ Top and Bottom Border
⊞ Top and Thick Bottom Border
⊞ Top and Double Bottom Border
⊞ More Borders...

②

3. Select a color from the Color drop-down.

4. Select a thick border style.

5. Click the bottom border button.

6. Click OK.

7. The colored border is added to the bottom of the selection.

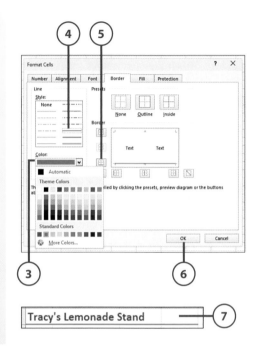

Coloring the Inside of a Cell

Fill color refers to the color applied inside of a cell. You can also apply fill effects, such as patterns, styles, and gradient fills. The pattern color and pattern style work together to fill a cell with a pattern (various dots or lines) in the selected color. This effect is placed on top of the background color.

The Color Palette Has Changed!

You send a workbook to a co-worker and when you get it back, you see a different set of colors in the drop-down. What happened?

In a new, blank workbook, you get the standard color palette. However, Excel allows you to create and share custom color palettes within themes. Themes are good ways to ensure uniformity of color in an organization (see the Chapter 7 section "Using Themes to Ensure Uniformity in Design" for more information).

Apply a Two-Color Gradient to a Cell

A gradient fill is where a color slowly changes from one color to another within a cell. Instead of filling a cell with a single solid color, you can apply a two-color gradient to a range.

1. Select the range you want to format. If you select multiple cells, the gradient will repeat across the range.

2. On the Home tab, select Format Cells from the Format drop-down.

3. Select the Fill tab.

4. Click the Fill Effects button.

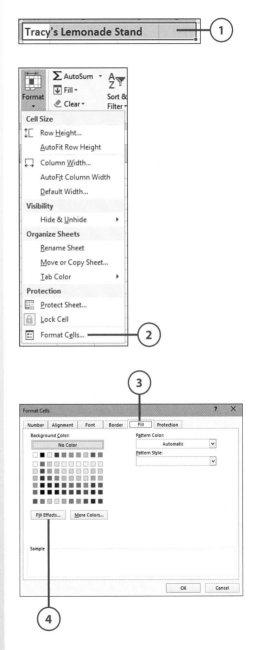

5. Select a color from the Color 1 drop-down.

6. Select a different color from the Color 2 drop-down.

7. Select a shading style from the Shading Styles section.

8. Make a selection from the Variants section. The Sample box updates to reflect your selection.

9. Click OK twice.

10. The fill effect will be applied to the range.

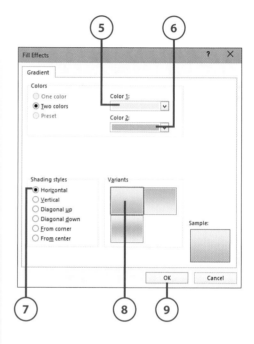

Cell styles —

Add cell icons

Highlight duplicates —

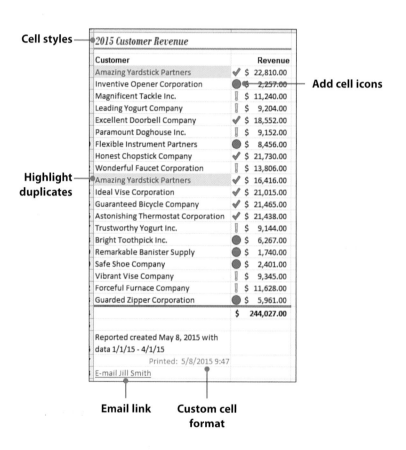

2015 Customer Revenue

Customer	Revenue
Amazing Yardstick Partners	✓ $ 22,810.00
Inventive Opener Corporation	● $ 2,257.00
Magnificent Tackle Inc.	$ 11,240.00
Leading Yogurt Company	$ 9,204.00
Excellent Doorbell Company	✓ $ 18,552.00
Paramount Doghouse Inc.	$ 9,152.00
Flexible Instrument Partners	● $ 8,456.00
Honest Chopstick Company	✓ $ 21,730.00
Wonderful Faucet Corporation	$ 13,806.00
Amazing Yardstick Partners	✓ $ 16,416.00
Ideal Vise Corporation	✓ $ 21,015.00
Guaranteed Bicycle Company	✓ $ 21,465.00
Astonishing Thermostat Corporation	✓ $ 21,438.00
Trustworthy Yogurt Inc.	$ 9,144.00
Bright Toothpick Inc.	● $ 6,267.00
Remarkable Banister Supply	● $ 1,740.00
Safe Shoe Company	● $ 2,401.00
Vibrant Vise Company	$ 9,345.00
Forceful Furnace Company	$ 11,628.00
Guarded Zipper Corporation	● $ 5,961.00
	$ 244,027.00

Reported created May 8, 2015 with
data 1/1/15 - 4/1/15

Printed: 5/8/2015 9:47

E-mail Jill Smith

Email link   **Custom cell format**

In this chapter, you'll find out how to set up formatting that changes as the data changes. You'll see how you can use themes to provide consistency in design between workbooks. Topics in this chapter include the following:

→ Creating custom number formats

→ Emphasizing the top 10

→ Highlighting duplicate values in a list

→ Ensuring consistency with themes and cell styles

→ Creating hyperlinks

Advanced Formatting

Custom formats allow you to create your own number formats, such as including text in a cell but still allowing calculations. With conditional formatting, you can apply a variety of formatting to data that automatically changes as the data updates. You can also design your own styles and themes to keep a consistent look among your workbooks.

Creating Custom Number Formats

Despite all the number formats available, not all the possible situations are covered. For example, you may need to add a *K* to show thousands in a cell. However, you can't actually have the text in the cell because it would interfere with calculations. That's why there's the option of custom formats, allowing you to create a format specific to your situation.

Once you've created a custom number format, you can apply it to any cell in the workbook, just like a built-in number format. Custom number formats are found under the Custom category of the Format Cells dialog box. The newest custom number format is found at the bottom of the Type list.

Custom number formats

Sharing Custom Formats

Custom formats are saved with the workbook they are created in. To share the format, copy a cell with the format and paste it in the other workbook.

The Four Sections of a Custom Number Format

A custom format can contain up to four different sections, each separated by a semicolon: positive; negative; zero; text.

Each section can have its own format rules, and you don't have to include all the sections in your custom format. If you specify only two sections, the first section is used for positive numbers and zeros, and the second section is used for negative numbers. If there is only one section, it's used for all numbers. To skip a section but include one that follows it, you must include the ending semicolon for the section you skipped.

Positive number in millions

Display "No Sales" for zero

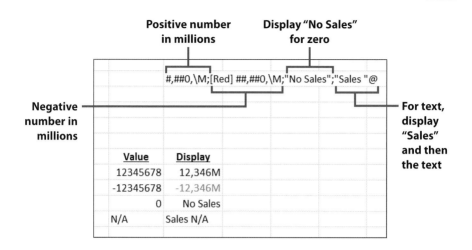

`#,##0,\M;[Red] ##,##0,\M;"No Sales";"Sales "@`

Negative number in millions

For text, display "Sales" and then the text

Value	Display
12345678	12,346M
-12345678	-12,346M
0	No Sales
N/A	Sales N/A

Optional Versus Required Digits

Use the pound (#) sign as a placeholder if you would like to display a certain number of characters that are not necessary. If the numbers are required, use zeros instead.

1. Select the range you want to format.

2. From the Home tab, select the Number group's dialog box launcher.

3. On the Number tab, select the Custom category.

4. In the Type field, replace the existing entry with the following to format the positive section to always show three decimal places and the negative section to show only what's entered:

   0.000;-0.###

5. Click OK.

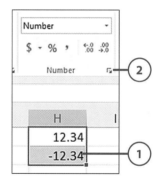

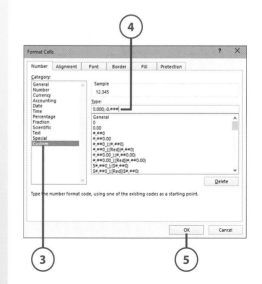

Preserve Leading Zeros

When you enter a number starting with a zero, Excel drops the leading zero. You can format the cell as text, but what if you forget to type the zero? Enter the following to ensure seven values to the left of the decimal:

0000000

Example with custom format designed

12.340 — 0.000;-0.###

-12.34

0001234 — 0000000

Example with leading-zeros custom format applied

Use the Thousands Separator, Color Codes, and Text

When you have large numbers, one way to make them more readable is to include a thousands separator (usually a comma). Another is to scale the number so that thousands, millions, or billions are represented by letters. For example, 2,000,000 could be shown as 2B.

1. Select the range you want to format.

2. From the Home tab, select the Number group's dialog box launcher.

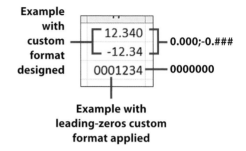

3. On the Number tab, select the Custom category.

4. In the Type box, enter the following:

   #,##0,,,"B";[Red]#,##0,,,"B";"-"

Custom Format Explanation

This custom format will remove the nine rightmost digits from the value and add a *B* at the end, symbolizing billions. In the negative portion of the format, the unary symbol (minus sign) is not used. Instead, the **[Red]** code colors the negative number red. In the zero portion of the format, a dash will be shown instead of a zero. The text portion is not used.

5. Click OK.

6. The custom format is applied to the range, but the original values are retained in the cell.

Requested	Enacted
2B	-
449B	342B
37B	37B
88B	94B
18B	20B
111B	96B
1,534B	1,478B
43B	45B
1,056B	1,065B

449000000000

>>>Go Further

FORMAT OPTIONS IN DETAIL

To include a thousands separator, use a comma in the format, such as **#,###.0**. To scale a number by thousands (for example, to show 22,000 as 22), include a comma at the end of the numeric format for each multiple of 1,000 (**#,##0,**).

You can use eight text color codes in a format: red, blue, green, yellow, cyan, black, white, and magenta. For other colors, you use numbered color codes (color1–color56). You place the color in square brackets, such as **[cyan]** or **[color35]**. The color should be the first element of a numeric formatting section.

To add text to a numeric format, place the characters in quotation marks. The following characters are an exception to this rule and do not require quotation marks:

: $ - + / ( ) : ! ^ & ' ~ { } = < > and the space character

Line Up Decimals

Use an underscore (_) in a format to make a character to the right of the underscore, such a parentheses, invisible in the cell but still take up space. You can use this formatting option to line up a column of positive and negative numbers.

1. Select the range you want to format.

2. From the Home tab, select the Number group's dialog box launcher.

3. On the Number tab, select the Custom category.

4. Enter the following:

   0.00_);(0.00)

5. Click OK.

6. The decimals of the positive and negative values in the column now line up.

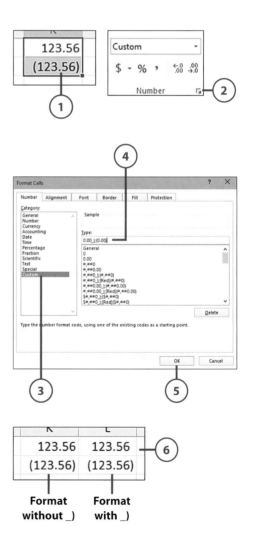

Fill Leading and Trailing Spaces

Instead of you typing in extra characters to fill the blank area in a cell, an asterisk (*) followed by a character will automatically display and adjust extra characters as the column is resized. As a bonus, the extra characters won't interfere with calculations because they aren't really in the cell.

1. Select the range you want to format.

2. From the Home tab, select the Number group's dialog box launcher.

3. On the Number tab, select the Custom category.

4. In the Type box, enter ***-#,###** to fill leading spaces.

   Or

5. Enter **#,###-*** to fill trailing spaces.

6. Click OK.

7. The extra character will fill the cell.

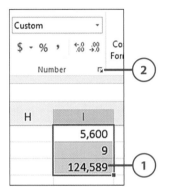

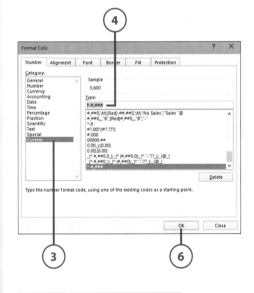

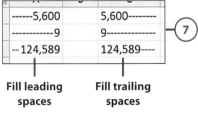

Fill leading spaces   **Fill trailing spaces**

Show More Than 24 Hours in a Time Format

When you have time values greater than 24, Excel doesn't seem to provide the proper answer. For example, you have a timesheet with daily start and end times for hours worked. You've calculated the hours worked each day and now you want to sum the entire month. But when you do, you get a value such as 7:26, which isn't correct. The correct answer is there—it's just a matter of formatting to see it.

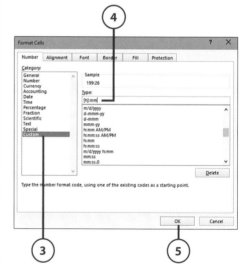

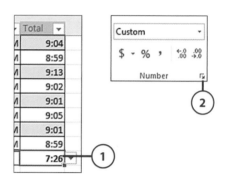

1. Select the range you want to format.

2. From the Home tab, select the Number group's dialog box launcher.

3. On the Number tab, select the Custom category.

4. Enter the following:

   [h]:mm

5. Click OK.

6. The correct total number of hours is shown.

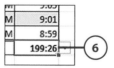

>>>Go Further

DATE AND TIME CODE OPTIONS

Date and time formats have the greatest variety of codes available when it comes to creating number formats. There isn't a real difference between the codes ## and ###; however, the difference between formatting a date cell **mm** or **mmm** is more obvious.

The following table lists the available date and time codes you can use when creating a format.

To Display This:	Use This Code:
Months as 1–12	m
Months as 01–12	mm
Months as Jan–Dec	mmm
Months as January–December	mmmm
Months as the first letter of the month	mmmmm
Days as 1–31	d
Days as 01–31	dd
Days as Sun–Sat	ddd
Days as Sunday–Saturday	dddd
Years as 00–99	yy
Years as 1900–9999	yyyy
Hours as 0–23	H
Hours as 00–23	hh
Minutes as 0–59	m
Minutes as 00–59	mm
Seconds as 0–59	s
Seconds as 00–59	ss
Hours as 4 AM	h AM/PM
Time as 4:36 PM	h:mm AM/PM
Time as 4:36:03 P	h:mm:ss A/P
Elapsed time in hours (for example, 25:02)	[h]:mm
Elapsed time in minutes (for example, 63:46)	[mm]:ss
Elapsed time in seconds	[ss]
Fractions of a second	h:mm:ss.00

Here are a couple things to keep in mind when creating date and time formats:

- If the time format has an AM or PM in it, Excel bases the time on a 12-hour clock. Otherwise, Excel uses a 24-hour clock.

- When you're creating a time format, the minutes code (m or mm) must appear immediately after the hour code (h or hh) or immediately before the seconds code (ss); otherwise, Excel displays months instead of minutes.

Creating Hyperlinks

Hyperlinks allow you to open web pages in your browser, create emails, and jump to a specific cell on a specific sheet in a specific workbook. For web and email addresses, Excel automatically recognizes what you've typed in and applies the format accordingly, turning the cell into a clickable link.

Create a Hyperlink to Another Sheet

Being able to create a hyperlink to a sheet can be useful if you want to create a table of contents for a large workbook or a series of workbooks.

1. Select the cell where you want the link. It can contain the text you want to use as a hyperlink or it can be blank.

2. Click the Hyperlink button on the Insert tab.

   Or

3. Right-click over the selection and select Hyperlink.

4. Click Place in This Document.

5. Select the sheet you want the link to jump to and enter the cell address you want selected.

   Or

6. Select a range name from the Defined Names list.

7. Enter the text to display in the cell.

8. Click OK.

9. The link will appear blue and underlined.

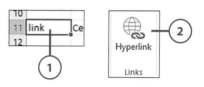

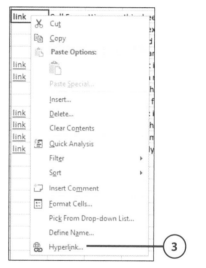

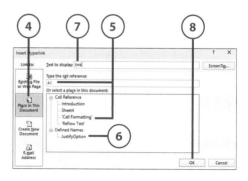

Select a Hyperlink Cell to Edit or Remove

A link is triggered when you click it with the mouse. To select the cell without triggering it, use the keyboard arrow keys to navigate to the cell. You can then edit the cell, such as changing the font color.

To edit or remove a hyperlink, right-click the link and select Edit Hyperlink or Remove Hyperlink. When you remove the hyperlink, the text remains in the cell.

>>>*Go Further*

LINK TO OTHER FILES

Links can be created to other workbooks and other file types, such as Word documents. You can even create a new file from scratch.

Click Existing File or Web Page in the Insert Hyperlink or Edit Hyperlink dialog box to link to another file. You can choose the file from a list or browse to it. When the user clicks the link, the file will open in its parent application. For example, if link is to a Word document, Word will open.

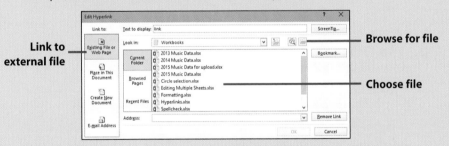

Link to external file

Browse for file

Choose file

Click Create New Document in the Insert Hyperlink or Edit Hyperlink dialog box to create a new file and link to it. You can enter the filename with extension or click Change to open the Create New Document dialog box. This dialog box allows you to choose an extension from the Save As Type drop-down, choose a new file location, and enter the filename.

Create a new document

Enter the filename

Change the extension or location

Link to a Web Page

You can add a link that opens a web page in the user's default web browser.

Create a Simple Link

You can create a simple link by typing the web address directly in a cell, such as www.tsyrstad.wordpress.com. When Excel see's the www, it knows it's a web page, and once you press Enter, it converts the text to a link. But if you want to hide the address and have some other text appear in the cell instead, you must use the Hyperlink dialog box.

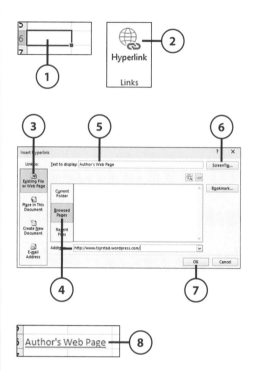

1. Select the cell where you want the link.

2. Click the Hyperlink button on the Insert tab.

3. Click Existing File or Web Page.

4. Click Browsed Pages. Select from the list or enter a new address.

5. Enter the text to display in the cell.

6. If you want, enter a ScreenTip to appear when the pointer is over the link.

7. Click OK.

8. The link will appear blue and underlined.

Dynamic Cell Formatting with Conditional Formatting

Conditional formatting allows you to apply formatting and icons that will automatically update as the data does. You can create your own formatting rule (see "Create a Custom Rule") or use one of the predefined rules found on the Conditional Formatting drop-down.

Use Icons to Mark Data

You can use icons to mark how values compare to each other. For example, use a green check mark for values in the top 67%, a red stoplight for values below 33%, and a yellow exclamation point for everything in between.

1. Select the range of values to which you want to apply the formatting.

2. Select Icon Sets, More Rules from the Conditional Formatting drop-down on the Home tab.

Use Existing Icon Group

You can choose an icon group from the Icon Style drop-down instead of creating one from scratch. If you do use an existing icon group, then continue to step 6.

3. Click the first drop-down under the Icon heading and select the green check mark.

4. Click the second drop-down and select the yellow exclamation point.

5. Click the third drop-down and select the red stoplight.

6. To the right of the first drop-down, select >=, enter 67, and select Percent.

7. To the right of the second drop-down, select >=, enter 33, and select Percent.

8. Click OK.

9. The icons will be added to the range. When a value in the range changes, the icon will update accordingly.

⊿	A	B	C	D
1	Customer	Revenue		
2	Amazing Yardstick Partners	✓ 22810		
3	Inventive Opener Corporation	● 2257		
4	Magnificent Tackle Inc.	▯ 11240		
5	Leading Yogurt Company	▯ 9204		
6	Excellent Doorbell Company	✓ 18552		

9

Edit Default Icon Sets

Excel has several default icon sets you can quickly apply from the Conditional Formatting drop-down, but you may still need to modify the logic used for each icon. If you select an icon set from the Conditional Formatting drop-down and need to edit the logic values, see the section "Edit Conditional Formatting."

Highlight the Top 10

You can format the top 10 values in a dataset so they stand out.

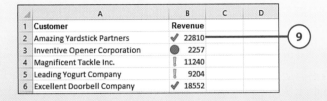

1. Select the range to which you want to apply the formatting. The comparison and formatting will apply to all numerical values selected, even if they are in different columns.

2. Select Top/Bottom Rules, Top 10 Items from the Conditional Formatting drop-down on the Home tab.

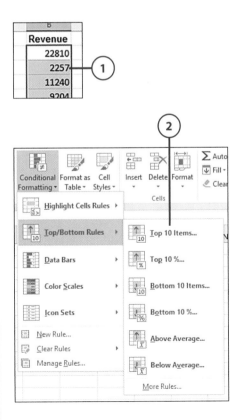

3. Change the value if you want something other than the top 10.

4. Select the desired formatting option. As you choose, your dataset will update so you can see how the formatting looks.

More Formatting Options

If you click Custom Format from the list of formatting options in the dialog box, the Format Cells dialog box will open up and you can use it to create your own format.

5. Click OK.

6. The conditional format will be applied to the dataset. As the values change, the formatting will automatically update.

Highlight Entire Row

If you need to highlight the entire row of the dataset, you'll have to set up a conditional format using a formula rule. See "Create a Custom Rule" for more information.

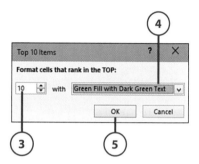

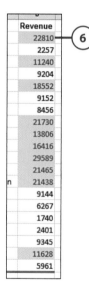

>>>Go Further

MORE PREDEFINED RULES

The Conditional Formatting drop-down contains more predefined rules under Highlight Cells Rules and Top/Bottom Rules:

- Cells containing values greater than, less than, between, or equal to the value you specify

- Cells containing specific text

- Cells containing a date from the last day, two days, and so on

- Cells containing duplicate values

- Cells containing the top or bottom *n* items

- Cells containing the top or bottom *n*%

- Cells containing values above or below the average

You can apply multiple predefined rules to a single selection—for example, highlight the top 10 and those values that fall within a certain range.

Highlight Duplicate or Unique Values

Use the preset conditional formats to highlight duplicate or unique data in a range.

1. Select the range to which you want to apply the formatting.

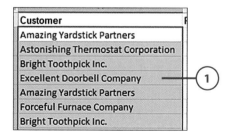

2. Select Highlight Cells Rules, Duplicate Values from the Conditional Formatting drop-down on the Home tab.

3. Select Duplicate to highlight the duplicate data. Select Unique to highlight the unique data.

4. Select the desired formatting option. As you choose, your data-set will update so you can see how the formatting looks.

5. Click OK.

6. The duplicate or unique data will be highlighted.

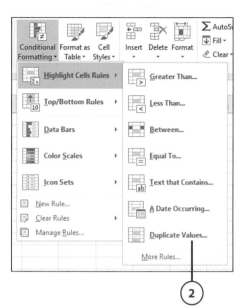

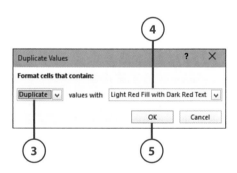

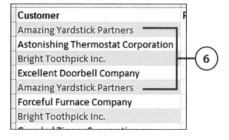

Create a Custom Rule

You can customize any of the prebuilt rules, but if what you need is not listed, such as highlighting a row based on a selection from a drop-down, you'll want to build your own conditional formatting rule based on a formula.

1. Select the range to which you want to apply the formatting, including all the columns you want highlighted.

2. Select New Rule from the Conditional Formatting drop-down on the Home tab.

3. Select the Use a Formula to Determine Which Cells to Format option.

4. Enter a logical formula that will evaluate to True or False. For example:

    =$A$1=$A4

5. Click the Format button to open the Format Cells dialog box.

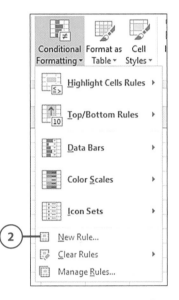

	A	B
1	Amazing Yardstick Partners	
2		
3	Customer	Revenue
4	Amazing Yardstick Partners	22810
5	Inventive Opener Corporation	2257
6	Magnificent Tackle Inc.	11240
7	Leading Yogurt Company	9204

Conditional Formatting · Format as Table · Cell Styles ·

- Highlight Cells Rules ▸
- Top/Bottom Rules ▸
- Data Bars ▸
- Color Scales ▸
- Icon Sets ▸
- New Rule...
- Clear Rules ▸
- Manage Rules...

New Formatting Rule   ?   ✕

Select a Rule Type:

- ► Format all cells based on their values
- ► Format only cells that contain
- ► Format only top or bottom ranked values
- ► Format only values that are above or below average
- ► Format only unique or duplicate values
- ► Use a formula to determine which cells to format

Edit the Rule Description:

Format values where this formula is true:

=$A$1=$A4

Preview: No Format Set   Format...

OK   Cancel

6. Select the desired formatting options (for example, a light blue fill).

7. Click OK when you're done formatting.

8. Click OK to return to the sheet.

9. When a different name is entered in a cell, for example A1, the corresponding record will be highlighted.

Format Cells

Number | Font | Borders | Fill

Background Color:

No Color

Pattern Color:

Automatic

Pattern Style:

Fill Effects...   More Colors...

Sample

Clear

OK   Cancel

New Formatting Rule

Select a Rule Type:

- Format all cells based on their values
- Format only cells that contain
- Format only top or bottom ranked values
- Format only values that are above or below average
- Format only unique or duplicate values
- Use a formula to determine which cells to format

Edit the Rule Description:

Format values where this formula is true:

=$A$1=$A4

Preview: No Format Set   Format...

OK   Cancel

	A	B
1	Magnificent Tackle Inc.	
2		
3	Customer	Revenue
4	Amazing Yardstick Partners	22810
5	Inventive Opener Corporation	2257
6	Magnificent Tackle Inc.	11240
7	Leading Yogurt Company	9204

>>>Go Further

UNDERSTANDING THE FORMULA

Conditional formulas must evaluate to True or False.

In the previous example, $A$1 is the cell with the company name to match. The reference is absolute so that as the value is compared to other cells in the selected range, the address won't change, similar to copying down a formula. If we need to match values in column B, then the address would be $B$1.

$A4 is the first cell in the selected range that has a possible match. Only the column is absolute so that when the comparison is done to values in column B, the column reference doesn't change. However, when the comparison is done to another row, the row number does update. For example, the formula in B4 is (if you could see it) $A$1=$A4; the formula in A5 is $A$1=$A5; the formula in B5 is $A$1=$A5.

For more information on absolute versus relative referencing, see Chapter 8, "Using Formulas."

Clear Conditional Formatting

With a few clicks of the mouse, you can clear all conditional formatting from a selected range.

Delete Specific Rules

If you need to delete specific rules, refer to the section "Edit Conditional Formatting" to learn how to open the dialog box from which you can select and delete rules.

1. Select the range from which you want to clear the conditional formatting.

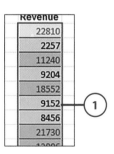

Revenue
22810
2257
11240
9204
18552
9152
8456
21730

2. From the Clear Rules submenu in the Conditional Formatting drop-down on the Home tab, select Clear Rules from Selected Cells.

3. The rules will be cleared from the selection. If there are other ranges with one or more of the same rules, the rules will still apply to those ranges. If there are no other ranges, the rules will be deleted.

Edit Conditional Formatting

You can edit conditional formatting to change the rule itself, the range to which it is applied, or both.

1. Select Manage Rules from the Conditional Formatting drop-down on the Home tab.

2. Choose which rules you want to view. For example, choose This Worksheet to view all the rules on the sheet.

3. Highlight the rule you want to edit.

4. Click Edit Rule.

5. Make the desired changes to the rule.

6. Click Format to change the formatting used.

7. Click OK.

8. To change the range to which the rule is applied, click in the address field and then select a new range on the sheet. You can also type the address directly in the field, but ensure the cell addresses are absolute.

9. Click OK to apply the changes.

⑧

Conditional Formatting Rules Manager				? ✕

Show formatting rules for: This Worksheet ▾

🗋 New Rule...   📝 Edit Rule...   ✕ Delete Rule   ▲ ▼

Rule (applied in order shown)	Format	Applies to		Stop If True
Cell Value = 15664.5	AaBbCcYyZz	=$B$2:$B$21	📷	☑
Cell Value between 0 an...	AaBbCcYyZz	=$B$2:$B$21	📷	☐
Top 10	AaBbCcYyZz	=$B$2:$B$21	📷	☐

OK   Close   Apply

⑨

Using Cell Styles to Apply Cell Formatting

You're probably familiar with using styles in Word but never realized that styles are also available in Excel. Styles provide a great way of quickly applying consistent formatting in your workbooks.

Apply a Style

As you move your pointer over the styles, the selected range will update, providing a preview of the style on the sheet.

1. Select the range to which you want to apply the style.

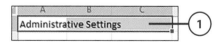
①

2. On the Home tab, click the Cell Styles drop-down to view the styles.

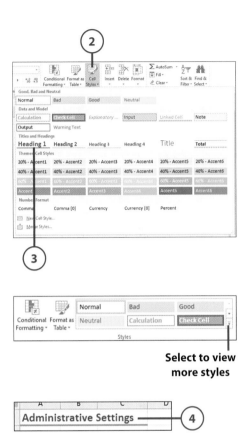

No Cell Styles Button Visible

If your monitor is large enough and resolution set high, you won't see the Cell Styles button—you'll see a selection of styles directly on the ribbon. Click the drop-down in the bottom-right corner to view more styles.

3. Select the desired style, such as Heading 1.

4. The selected range will update to the new style.

Select to view more styles

Style a Table

If your dataset is setup as a table (when you select a cell in the dataset, you see the Table Tools ribbon tab), you have the additional option of using the Table Styles on the Table Tools, Design tab. Note that Cell Styles will overwrite Table Styles.

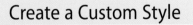

Administrative Settings

Create a Custom Style

You aren't limited to these predefined styles. You can create and save your own style for use throughout the workbook it's saved in.

1. Apply the desired formatting to a cell. You can also start from a pre-existing style and make changes to it. Select the cell.

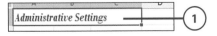

Administrative Settings

2. On the Home tab, select New Cell Style from the Cell Styles drop-down.

3. Enter a new style name.

4. Select the options you want included in the style.

5. Click OK.

6. The custom style will appear at the top of the style drop-down. See the section "Apply a Style" for instruction on how to apply the style.

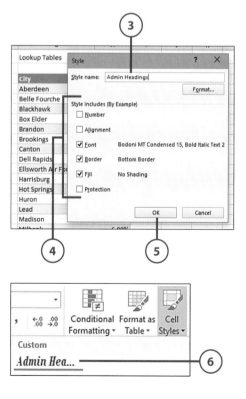

Using Themes to Ensure Uniformity in Design

Themes are collections of fonts, colors, and graphic effects that can be applied to a workbook. This can be useful if you have a series of company reports that need to have the same color and fonts. Only one theme can affect a workbook at a time.

Excel includes several built-in themes, which you can access from the Themes drop-down on the Page Layout tab. You can also create and share themes you design.

A theme has the following elements, which you can apply individually instead of applying an entire theme package:

- **Fonts**—A theme includes a font for headings and a font for body text.

- **Colors**—There are 12 colors in a theme: four for text, six for accents, and two for hyperlinks.

- **Graphic effects**—Graphic effects include lines, fills, bevels, shadows, and so on.

Apply a New Theme

Excel has a variety of themes you can choose from.

1. On the Page Layout tab, open the Themes drop-down.

2. As you move the pointer over a theme, the objects (fonts, charts, and so on) on the active sheet will change to reflect that theme. When you find one you like, click it, and it will be applied to the workbook.

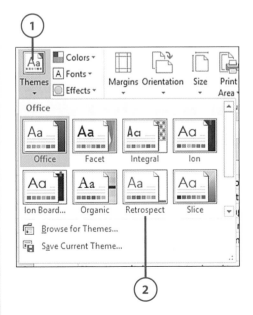

3. If you like some elements of a theme, but not others, open the drop-down corresponding to the element you want to change (Colors, Fonts, or Effects) and select a new palette.

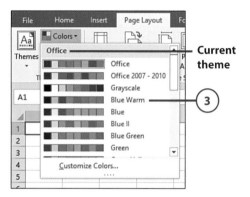

Current theme

Create a New Theme

When you create and save a theme, you can apply it to other workbooks or share it with other people. First change the colors, fonts, and/or effects as desired and then save that combination as a new theme.

1. Select Customize Colors from the Colors drop-down on the Page Layout tab.

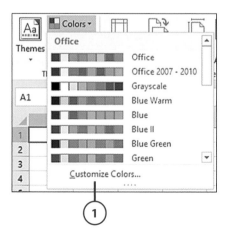

2. To change the color for one of the color placeholders, such as Accent 3, choose its drop-down to open the color palette.

3. When you find the desired color, click it to apply it to your theme.

4. Repeat steps 2 and 3 for each color placeholder you want to change.

5. Type a name for your color theme.

6. Click Save.

7. Select Customize Fonts from the Fonts drop-down on the Page Layout tab.

8. Click the Heading Font drop-down and choose a new font.

9. Click the Body Font drop-down and choose a new font.

10. Type a name for your font theme.

11. Click Save.

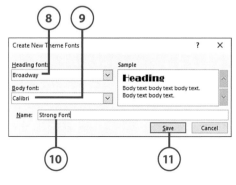

12. Select an effect from the gallery of built-in effects from the Effects drop-down on the Page Layout tab.

13. Select Save Current Theme from the Themes drop-down on the Page Layout tab.

14. Browse to a location to save the theme and enter a name for it. Click Save.

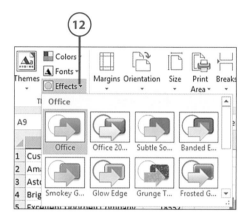

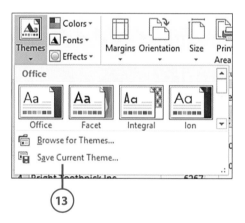

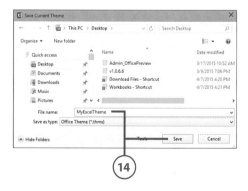

Share a Theme

To share a theme with other people, you must send them the *.thmx file you saved when you created the theme (refer to "Create a New Theme").

When the other people receive the file, they should save it to either their equivalent theme folder or some other location and then use the Browse for Themes option under Themes on the Page Layout tab.

Name box   Named range   Formula bar

	A	B	C	D	E	F	G
					SUM	▾	:	×	✓	fx	=(F4/E4) *(1+TaxRate)	
1	Region	Product	Date	Customer	Quantity	Revenue	Price Per
2	Central	Laser Printe	2/8/2015	Appealing Calculator	0	1817	#DIV/0!
3	Central	Laser Printe	4/6/2015	Alluring Shoe Compa	300	5886	#NAME?
4	Central	Laser Printe	4/13/2015	Appealing Calculator	400	8016	=(F4/E4) *(
5	Central	Laser Printe	6/13/2015	Alluring Shoe Compa	700	12838	19.07
6	Central	Laser Printe	8/5/2015	Bright Eggbeater Cor	800	15288	19.87
7	Central	Laser Printe	8/18/2015	Compelling Raft Com	1000	21120	21.96
8	Central	Laser Printe	8/28/2015	Bright Hairpin Compa	300	6309	21.87
9	Central	Laser Printe	9/22/2015	Appealing Calculator	600	10602	18.38
10	Central	Laser Printe	9/26/2015	Alluring Shoe Compa	900	17712	20.47
11	Central	Laser Printe	10/17/2015	Appealing Calculator	400	7520	19.55
12	Central	Laser Printe	10/19/2015	Appealing Calculator	800	14136	18.38
13	Central	Laser Printe	10/30/2015	Alluring Shoe Compa	500	9475	19.71
14	Central	Laser Printe	11/29/2015	Bright Hairpin Compa	300	5592	19.39
15	Central	Laser Printe	12/26/2015	Alluring Shoe Compa	100	1861	19.35
16							#NAME?

Color-coded formulas   Formula errors

Excel is great for simple data entry, but its real strength is its capability to perform calculations. After you design a sheet to perform calculations, you can easily change the data and watch Excel instantly recalculate. This chapter includes the following topics:

8

→ Entering a formula into a cell

→ Comparing absolute and relative referencing

→ Using array formulas

→ Converting formulas to values

→ Troubleshooting formulas

Using Formulas

This chapter not only shows you how to enter a formula, but also teaches you fundamental basics, such as the difference between absolute and relative referencing, which is important when you want to copy a formula to multiple cells, and how to use a name to refer to a cell instead of having to memorize a cell address. You'll take the formula basics you learn here and apply them later in Chapter 9, "Using Functions," to really crank up the calculating power of your workbook.

Entering a Formula into a Cell

Typing a formula is similar to entering an equation on a calculator, with one exception. If one of the terms in your formula is already stored in a cell, you can point to that cell instead of typing in the number stored in the cell. The advantage of this is that if that other cell's value ever changes, your formula automatically updates.

Enter Formula Mode

When the first thing in a cell is an equal sign (=), Excel expects a formula to be entered. If you don't want to trigger formula mode, type an apostrophe (') first.

Calculate a Formula

Use Excel to calculate the tax on items with a 6% tax rate. The item value is already entered in a cell, but you need to type the tax rate into the formula.

1. Select the cell you want the formula to be in.

2. Type an equal sign (=).

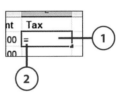

3. Select the cell with the value to include in the formula and then type ***.06**. The asterisk (*) is the multiplication symbol in Excel. Note that the cell address in the formula and the corresponding highlighted cell have the same color.

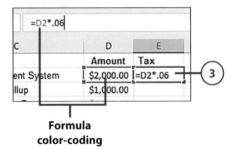

Formula color-coding

Reference Another Sheet

If the range you need to reference is on another sheet in this or another open workbook, simply go to the sheet and select the range. You can continue entering the formula from the other sheet, or return to the original.

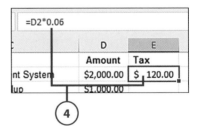

4. Press Enter to complete the formula. Select the cell with the formula to view the formula in the formula bar. It should look like this:

=D2*0.06

>>>Go Further

ORDER OF OPERATIONS

Excel evaluates a formula in a particular order if it contains many calculations. Instead of calculating from left to right like a calculator, Excel performs certain types of calculations, such as multiplication, before other calculations, such as addition.

You can override this default order of operations using parentheses. If you don't, Excel applies the following order of operations:

1. Unary minus (the dash before a negative number)
2. Exponents
3. Multiplication and division, left to right
4. Addition and subtraction, left to right

For example, if you have the formula

=6+3*2

Excel returns 12, because first it does 3*2 and then adds the result (6) to 6. But, if you use parentheses, you can change the order of operations:

=(6+3)*2

This produces 18 because now Excel will do the addition first (6+3) and multiply the result (9) by 2.

View All Formulas on a Sheet

You can toggle between viewing values and formulas on a sheet. To do this, on the Formulas tab, select Show Formulas.

Toggle the visibility of formulas in cells

Select All Formulas

If you just want to see what cells have formulas, but don't need to see the formulas themselves, you can use the Formulas option in the Go to Special dialog box. Press Ctrl+G and click Special to open the dialog box. Select Formulas and click OK, and all formula cells on the sheet will be selected.

Relative Versus Absolute Referencing

When you copy a formula, such as =D2*H1, down a column, the formula automatically changes to =D3*H2, then =D4*H3, and so on. Excel's capability to change cell D2 to D3 to D4 and so on is called *relative referencing*. This is Excel's default behavior when dealing with formulas, but it might not always be what you want to happen.

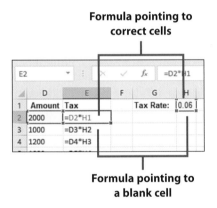

Formula pointing to correct cells

Formula pointing to a blank cell

If the cell address must remain static as the formula is copied, you need to use absolute referencing. This is achieved through the strategic placement of dollar signs ($) before the row or column reference.

Lock the Row When Copying a Formula Down

When you copy a formula down a column, the row number increases by one. You can stop this behavior by making the row reference absolute.

1. Select the formula cell.

2. Type a dollar sign ($) to the left of the row number that needs to remain static.

3. Press Enter to calculate the formula.

4. Copy the formula down (see "Copy by Dragging the Fill Handle," later in this chapter). Notice that the row number with the dollar sign does not change.

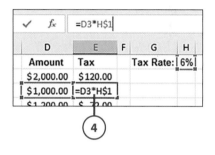

Lock the Column When Copying a Formula Across

To lock the column when copying a cell across a row, place the $ to the left of the column letter, making the column absolute.

>>>Go Further

USING F4 TO CHANGE THE CELL REFERENCING

Instead of typing the $ manually, press the F4 key right after entering the cell address. Each press of the key changes the cell address to another reference variation. For example, if the cell address is A1, the rotation would be A1, $A$1, A$1, $A1, and then back to A1.

If you need to change a reference after you've already entered the formula, you can still place the insertion point in the cell address and use the F4 key to toggle through the references.

Copying Formulas

Once you enter a formula, you may want to copy it: across the row, down the column, or to another workbook. You might just have to copy it to a few cells or into thousands of cells. You might want to copy the formula, but not the formatting. There are many combinations of how you might need to copy the formula, and Excel has methods you can use to cover all of them, without retyping the formula.

Copy and Paste Formulas

When you copy and paste a formula, not only is the formula pasted, but the formatting of the originating cell is too, unless you choose otherwise. Any relative cell addressing updates accordingly.

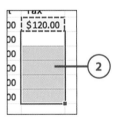

1. Right-click over the cell you want to copy and click Copy.

2. Select the range you want to copy the formula into.

3. Right-click over the selection and click Paste.

4. The formula and formatting is pasted to the new range.

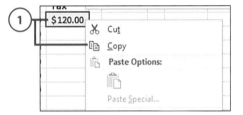

Paste Formulas Without Formatting

If you want to paste the formulas without any of the formatting, use the Formulas option available when you right-click over the selection to paste to. Any relative cell addressing updates accordingly.

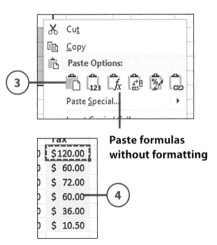

Paste formulas without formatting

Copy by Dragging the Fill Handle

This method is useful if you need to copy your formula across a row or down a column. Any formatting in the originating cell will also be copied.

1. Select the cell with the formula.

2. Place your pointer over the fill handle until a black cross appears.

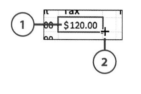

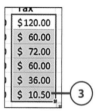

Missing Fill Handle

If you don't get the fill handle, it's possible you have the option turned off. Go to File, Options, Advanced and ensure Enable Fill Handle and Cell Drag-and-Drop is selected.

3. Hold the mouse button down as you drag the fill handle. Release the mouse button when you've copied the formula to all the desired cells.

Copy Without Formatting

If you hold the right mouse button down as you drag, instead of the left, you can choose Fill Without Formatting, which will copy the formula but not the formatting.

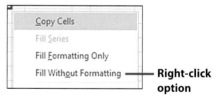

Right-click option

Copy Rapidly Down a Column

If you need to copy a formula into just a few rows, dragging the fill handle is fine. But if you have several hundred rows to update, you could zoom right past the last row. And if you have thousands of rows, using the fill handle can take quite some time.

1. Select the cell with the formula.

2. Place your pointer over the fill handle until a black cross appears.

3. Double-click, and the formula will be copied down the sheet until it reaches the end of the dataset (a fully blank row).

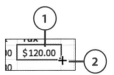

0	$120.00	

	$ 300.00	$ 18.00
ort	$ 335.00	$ 20.10
nparisons	$ 460.00	$ 27.60
nse Form	$ 185.00	$ 11.10
	$ 110.00	$ 6.60

Blank row

It's Not All Good

Formula Doesn't Copy All the Way Down

This double-click method relies on having your data set up so that Excel can properly identify it. If Excel can't figure out the full dataset, then the method won't work properly.

Excel uses fully blank rows and columns to mark the end of a dataset. You can have a blank cell here and there within the dataset. If you want to test if Excel will properly identify the dataset, select a cell within it and press Ctrl+A. If you see any blank columns or rows interfering with the desired selection, add some temporary text and then try the selection again.

Copy Between Workbooks Without Creating a Link

Sometimes when you copy a formula from one workbook to another, a link to the source workbook is created in the target workbook. This is most common when the formula includes names or links to other sheets. You'll have to do things a little differently if you don't want that link.

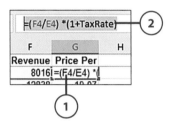

1. Select the cell with the formula.

2. Highlight the formula in the formula bar. This places Excel in Edit mode, so be careful not to make unwanted changes.

Resize the Formula Bar

If you can't see the entire formula, click the down arrow at the right end of the formula bar. This will make the formula bar taller. Click the arrow again to shrink the bar back to normal.

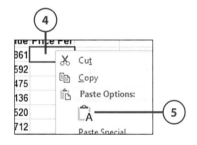

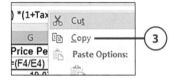

3. Right-click over the formula bar selection and click Copy. Press Esc on the keyboard to exit Edit mode.

4. Select the cell in the target workbook where you want to paste the formula.

5. Right-click over the cell and click Paste.

6. The formula will paste exactly as you copied it. When you copy a formula in this way, it's like copying text, so Excel does not update any relative cell addresses or link to the original file.

Converting Formulas to Values

Formulas take up a lot of memory, and the recalculation time can make working in a large workbook a hassle. At times, you need a formula only temporarily; you just want to calculate the value once and won't ever need to calculate it again. You could manually type the value over the formula cell, but if the result is a long number, or if you have a lot of calculation cells, this isn't convenient.

Paste as Values

Use paste options to get rid of formulas, but retain values and formatting.

1. Select the range of formulas.

2. Right-click over the selection and click Copy.

3. With the range still selected, right-click over it and select Values.

4. The formulas will be replaced with the calculated values.

Keep Numeric Formatting

If you want to keep the numeric format, use the Values & Number Formatting option available in the Paste drop-down on the Home tab.

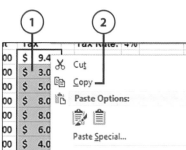

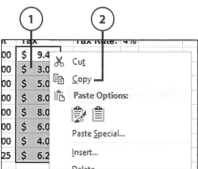

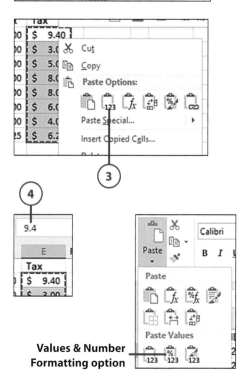

Values & Number
Formatting option

Select and Drag

This method is quite a bit faster than the previous.

1. Select the range of formulas.

2. Place your pointer on the edge of the dark border around the range so that it turns into a four-headed arrow.

3. Hold the right mouse button down and drag the range to the next column and then back to the original column. Release the right mouse button and a special right-click menu will appear.

Location Matters

Be very careful that you place the range exactly where it was originally. Excel allows you to use this method to place the range in a new location.

---

4. Select Copy Here as Values Only.

5. The formulas will be replaced with the calculated values.

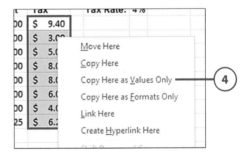

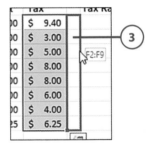

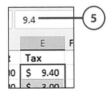

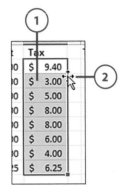

Using Names to Simplify References

It can be difficult to remember what cell you have a specific entry in when you're writing a formula. And if the cell you need to reference is on another sheet, you have to be very careful writing out the reference properly, or you must use the mouse to go to the sheet and select the cell.

Instead of remembering a cell address, use a name, such as TaxRate, in your formula. After a name is applied to a range, any references to the range can be done by using the name instead of the address.

Create a Named Cell

Quickly create a name to make it easier to reference a range.

1. Select the range you want to apply the name to.

2. In the Name Box, type in the name. It cannot contain spaces.

3. Press Enter for Excel to accept the name. Whenever you select the range, you will see the name instead of a cell address in the Name Box.

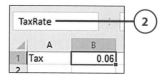

>>>Go Further

RULES FOR CREATING NAMES

You only need to remember a few limitations when creating a name:

- The name must be one word. You can use an underscore (_), backslash (\), or period (.) as a spacer.

- The name cannot be a word that might also be a cell address. This was a real problem when people converted workbooks from legacy Excel to Excel 2007 or newer because some names, such as TAX2009, weren't cell addresses before. Now in Excel 2007 and newer versions, such names cause problems when you open a legacy workbook. So name carefully!

- The name cannot include any disallowed characters, such as a question mark (?), exclamation mark (!), or hyphen (-). The only valid special characters are the underscore (_), backslash (\), and period (.).

- Names are not case sensitive. Excel will see "sales" and "Sales" as the same name.

- You should not use any of the reserved words in Excel, even though Excel will let you. These words are Print_Area, Print_Titles, Criteria, Database, and Extract.

Use a Name in a Formula

Once you create a name, you'll want to use it in new or existing formulas.

1. Select the cell with the formula.

2. In the formula bar, highlight the cell address you want to replace.

3. Type the name and press Enter to update the formula.

AutoComplete Box

As you type the name, an AutoComplete Box appears. When you see the name, you can select it either with the mouse or by highlighting it and pressing Tab.

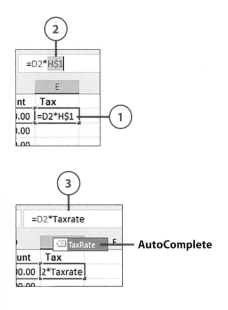

>>>Go Further

GLOBAL VERSUS LOCAL NAMES

Names can be global, which means they are available anywhere in the workbook. Names can also be local, which means they are available only on a specific sheet. With local names, you can have multiple references in the workbook with the same name, but they will only work on the sheet they're scoped to. Global names must be unique to the workbook. If you don't specify a sheet when creating a name, the name will be global.

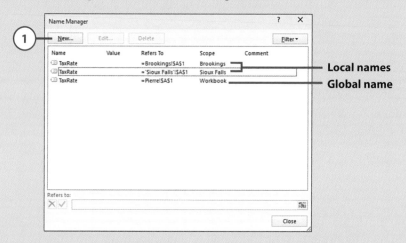

Local names

Global name

The Name Manager dialog box (click Name Manager on the Formulas tab), lists all the names in a workbook, even a name that has been assigned to both the global and local levels. The Scope column lists the scope of the name, whether it is the workbook or a specific sheet such as Brookings.

If you have a name that is scoped both globally and locally, Excel will automatically reference the global name, unless you are referencing the local name on the sheet on which it resides. In that case, Excel will let you choose which scope you want to reference.

You can create a local name from the Name Manager.

1. Click New.

2. Enter the name.

3. Select the sheet to which it should be scoped.

4. Click OK.

New Name   ?   ✕

Name: TaxRate   **2**

Scope: Rapid City   ▾

Comment: **3**

Refers to: ='Rapid City'!$A$1   ▦

4   OK   Cancel

Inserting Formulas into Tables

Names are automatically created when you define a table. A name, or a specifier, for each column and the entire table is created. Just like you can use names to simplify references in your standard formulas, you can use specifiers to simplify references to the data in your table formulas.

Define a Table

See the "Define a Table" section in Chapter 4, "Getting Data onto a Sheet," for information on defining a table.

Write a Formula in a Table

Excel uses the column specifier instead of the cell address when you reference table cells in your formulas.

1. If you don't already have a column ready for the formula, add one by typing a header in a new column adjacent to the table. Excel will automatically extend the table to include the new column.

2. Select the first data cell in the column.

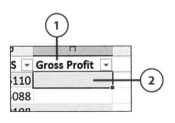

3. Type an equal sign (=) and then select the first cell in the formula. You will notice that column specifiers are used in the formula instead of cell addresses. Enter the rest of the formula.

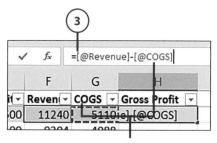

Column specifiers

When You See a Cell Address

If you select a cell in a different row than that of the formula cell, you will see a cell address. Excel expects formulas in a table to reference the same row or an entire column or table.

4. Press Enter, and Excel copies the formula down the column of the table. Notice the formula is the same in every cell.

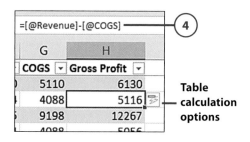

Table calculation options

Table Calculation Options

After you enter the formula, a lightning bolt drop-down appears by the cell. If you don't want the formula copied down the column, select Undo Calculated Column or Stop Automatically Creating Calculated Columns.

If you stop the process, you will have to turn the option back on under the AutoCorrect options. To do this, go to the File tab, select Options, Proofing, AutoCorrect Options, and on the AutoFormat As You Type tab, select Fill Formulas in Tables to Create Calculated Columns.

Write Table Formulas Outside the Table

Writing formulas with specifiers is very handy, and the ability isn't limited to formulas within tables.

1. Select a cell outside the table where you want to place the formula. The cell should not be adjacent to the table; otherwise, Excel will make it part of the table.

2. Begin entering the formula. When you get to the point where you want to refer to a table component, type the name of the table. You can type the entire name or press Tab when you see it highlighted in the AutoComplete Box.

3. Type a left square bracket. A list of specifiers, including the column headers, will appear. Highlight the desired specifier, or type it in, and press Tab.

4. Type the closing bracket, finish entering the formula, and press Enter. The formula will calculate.

Find the Table Name

Select a cell in the table and click the Table Tools, Design tab. The table name appears in the Table Name field. Use this name in formulas to reference the entire table.

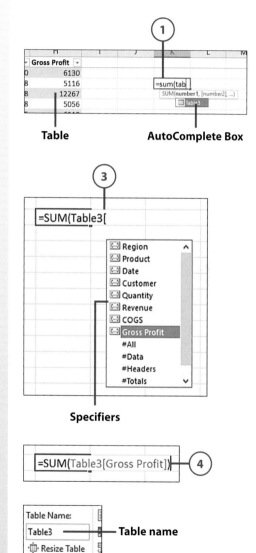

>>>*Go Further*

MORE RULES AND SPECIFIERS

Besides starting the table reference with the table name and enclosing specifiers in square brackets (TableName[Specifier]), you have a few more rules to keep in mind:

- If you're using multiple specifiers, each specifier must be surrounded by square brackets and separated by commas. The entire group of specifiers used must be surrounded by square brackets, like this:

TableName[[Specifier1],[Specifier2]]

- To create an absolute reference to a column, refer to the specifier twice, separated by a colon and surrounded by square brackets, like this:

TableName[[Specifier1]:[Specifier1]]

- If no specifiers are used, the table name refers to the data rows in the table. This does not include the headers or total rows.

In addition to the table and column specifiers, Excel provides five more to make it easier to narrow down a particular part of a Table:

- **#All**—Returns all the contents of the Table or specified column.

- **#Data**—Returns the data cells of the Table or specified column.

- **#Headers**—Returns all the column headers or that of a specified column.

- **#Totals**—Returns the Total Rows or the total of a specified column. If the Total Row option is not on for the table, a #REF error is returned.

- **@ – This Row**—Returns the current row in which the formula is being typed.

You can combine these specifiers with the column specifiers. For example, to return the total of a column, if Total Rows is on, you could do this:

=TableName[[#Totals][Column Specifier]]

Using Array Formulas

An array holds multiple values individually in a single cell. An array formula allows you to do calculations with those individual values.

You can tell if a formula is an array formula because it's surrounded by curly braces ({}). These braces are not typed in. They appear after you press Ctrl+Shift+Enter (CSE). If you edit the formula, the braces will go away and you'll have to press the CSE combination to get them to come back, or press Esc to exit the cell and undo any changes.

Enter an Array Formula

1. If you're typing the formula, select a cell and enter the formula. Do not press Enter or Tab. Do not type the curly braces ({ }).

   Or

2. If you've copied the formula from another source, double-click the cell so the insertion point is in the cell and then paste the formula. Do not press Enter or Tab. Also, make sure you didn't include the curly braces ({}) when you copied the formula.

3. Press Ctrl+Shift+Enter (CSE). Excel will place the curly braces around the entire formula and calculate it. Any time you edit the formula, remember to press the CSE combination instead of Enter or Tab when you are done.

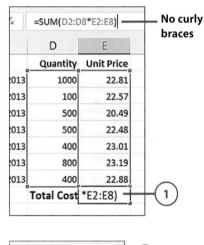

No curly braces

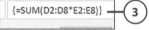

Multicell Array Formulas

If you need to return multiple values from the array formula, select the range the formula needs to be in before entering the formula. Once you press the CSE combination, the formula will be copied into the entire range. In some ways, the range will be treated like a single cell. A change in the formula in one cell will affect all the other cells in the range. You won't be able to insert rows or columns within the range, nor will you be able to move just a part of it.

Delete a Multicell Array Formula

A normal array formula can be cleared like any other formula, but you cannot delete just one cell of a multicell array formula. The message "You can't change part of an array" will appear if you try to delete just a portion of the range containing the formula. The entire range containing the array formula must be selected before you can delete it.

1. Select a cell in the multicell array range.

2. Press Ctrl+G to bring up the Go To dialog box.

3. Click the Special button.

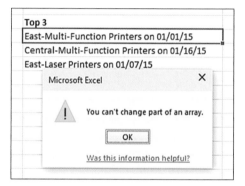

4. Select Current Array.

5. Click OK.

6. The entire array formula range is selected. Press Delete to delete it.

Resize a Multicell Array

If you need to resize a multicell array, you have to delete its entire range, select the new range, and re-enter the formula. You can extend the formula to more cells, but the new cells won't be part of the original range. If you make a change to the formula in the original range, the change won't extend to the new cells.

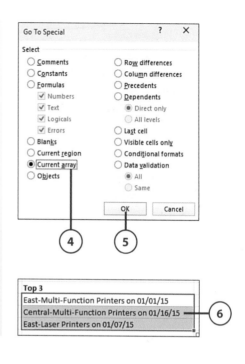

Working with Links

A link is created when a formula in a cell references a range in another workbook or when a chart is copied between workbooks. A link can sometimes be created when you copy a formula from one workbook to another. The workbook that receives information from other sources is the one that is considered linked and will generate prompts to update the data when it is opened.

Invisible Links

If the link is in a formula in a name, instead of a formula in a cell, Excel will not prompt to update the link. The Edit Links option will not be available, either. However, if that name is then used in a cell formula, the prompt and Edit Links option will become available.

Control the Prompt

You can control whether the prompt appears and whether the link is updated when the workbook is opened.

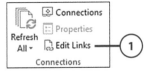

1. On the Data tab, select Edit Links.

2. Select Startup Prompt.

3. Select the desired option.

4. Click OK.

5. Click Close.

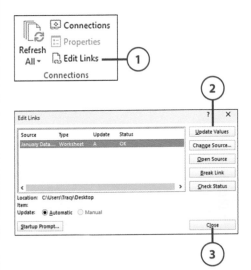

Refresh Data

If you didn't update the link when the workbook first opened but now want to, or you need to force a refresh, you can choose to update the values.

1. On the Data tab, select Edit Links.

2. Click Update Values.

3. Click Close.

Recalculate a Single Cell

To update a single cell, force it to recalculate by double-clicking the cell and then pressing Enter or Tab.

Change the Source Workbook

You don't have to recreate your linked formulas if the referenced cells are in another workbook. As long as location of the cell is the same, you can just point Excel to the new file.

1. On the Data tab, select Edit Links.

2. Highlight the source you want to change and select Change Source.

3. Select another workbook and click OK.

4. If a source sheet isn't found, Excel will give you the chance to select a new one. Select it and click OK.

5. Click Close.

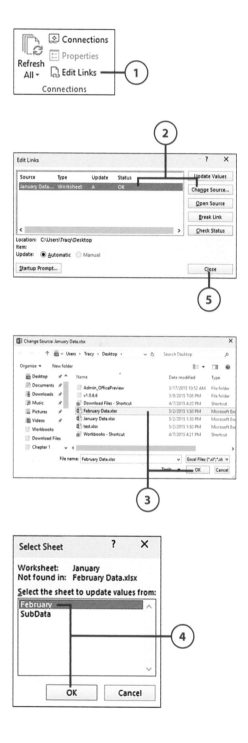

Break the Link

You can break the formula links, replacing the formulas with the calculated values.

1. On the Data tab, select Edit Links.

2. Select Break Link.

3. Excel warns you that the formulas will be lost and that this action cannot be undone. Click Break Links to continue.

4. Any cell formulas with links to external workbooks will be replaced with just the values. This will not affect named ranges with formulas.

Keep the Formulas

If you want to break the link to the source workbook but keep the formulas intact, you can point the links to the linked workbook itself. Use the Change Source option and select the active workbook. Keep in mind that the active workbook must contain any sheets and named ranges that the source had, else, the action will generate errors.

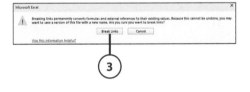

Troubleshooting Formulas

It can be frustrating to enter a formula and have it return either an incorrect value or an error. An important part of solving the problem is to understand what the error is trying to tell you. After you have an idea of the problem you're looking for, you can use several tools to look deeper into the error.

Fix ###### in a Cell

This isn't usually an error but a matter of the column being too narrow.

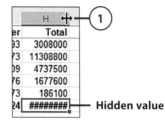

Hidden value

1. If your formula isn't dealing with dates, increase the column width by placing your pointer between column headings and clicking and dragging the column wider.

2. When the column is wide enough, the data will be displayed.

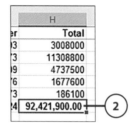

Understand a Formula Error

Excel returns different errors depending on what's causing the issue.

Function Errors

If your formula contains a function, look up the function in the Help to get specific details on what the error means.

Divisor is 0

1. Select the cell with the error.

2. If the error is #DIV/0!, a value in the cell is being divided by a 0. If the divisor is a cell, look at that cell and check that it is correct and not zero or blank.

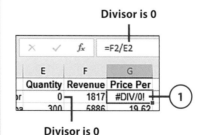

Divisor is 0

3. If the error is #NAME?, Excel is unable to resolve a reference in the formula (for example, a mistyped name or nonexistent cell address).

4. If the error is #VALUE!, the formula is trying to do math with nonnumeric data.

5. If the error is #REF!, a cell reference isn't valid. The cell has likely has been deleted. There's no direct way to trace back to the original reference.

6. If you're unable to see the issue from looking at the formula, click the exclamation icon next to the formula.

7. Select Help on This Error to open the Excel Help dialog box for more information on the error.

8. Select Trace Error to have Excel highlight the cells used in the formula. See the "Trace Precedents and Dependents" section for more information on using this tool.

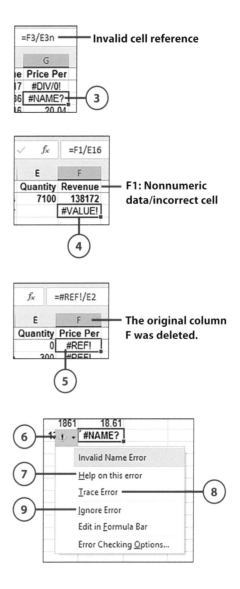

Show Calculation Steps Instead of Trace Error

Select Show Calculation Steps to open the Evaluate Formula dialog box. See the "Use the Evaluate Formula Dialog Box" section for information on using this dialog box.

9. Select Ignore Error to hide the error icon. It will reappear if the formula is edited.

10. Select Edit in Formula Bar, and the insertion point will be placed in the formula bar, highlighting any cells in the formula that are on the active sheet.

11. Select Error Checking Options to open the Options dialog box to the Formulas section, where you can modify how Excel interacts with you when it comes to errors.

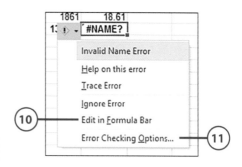

Missing Error Icon

If the error icon is not appearing by cells with errors, it's possible that error checking in Excel has been turned off. To check, and turn it back on, go to File, Options, Formulas and select Enable Background Error Checking. If the option is checked, it's possible that all errors have been ignored. In that case, click the Reset Ignored Errors button.

Use Trace Precedents and Dependents

Use Trace Precedents to locate cells used by the selected formula. Use Trace Dependents to find out if the selected cell is used in a formula in another cell. When you click one of the trace buttons, arrows appear, linking the cell to other cells.

1. Select the cell you want to trace.

2. To see what cells the selected formula references, click Trace Precedents on the Formulas tab.

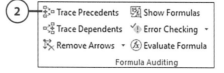

3. Arrows will appear, pointing from the cells used in the formula to the formula cell.

4. Click the button again to see if there are precedents to these cells.

5. To see what formulas the selected cell is used in, click Trace Dependents on the Formulas tab. Arrows appear, pointing from the selected cell to the formulas using it.

	G
e	Price Per
7	19.26
6	20.80
6	21.24
8	19.44
8	20.26
0	22.39
9	22.29
2	18.73
2	20.86
0	19.93
6	18.73
5	20.09
2	19.76
1	19.73
	283.50

③

	Quantity	Revenue	Price Per
r	1	1817	19.26
a	3	5006	20.80
r	4	8016	21.24
a	7	12030	19.44
r	6	15200	20.26
m	10	21120	22.39
a	3	6309	22.29
r	6	10602	18.73
a	9	17712	20.86
r	4	7520	19.93
r	6	14136	18.73
a	5	9475	20.09
a	300	5592	19.76
a	100	1861	19.73
			283.50

④

	Quantity	Revenue	Price Per
r	100	1817	19.26
a	300	5886	20.80

⑤

6. Click the button again to see if there are dependents to these cells.

7. If one of the arrows has a dashed line with a sheet icon, the referenced cell is on another sheet. Double-click the dashed line to follow the trace.

8. Select a reference to inspect and then click OK. Excel will activate the sheet the reference is on and select the cell.

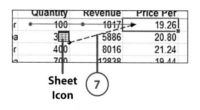

Clear Arrows

To clear all the arrows, select Remove Arrows. To remove precedent arrows, click the Remove Arrows drop-down and select Remove Precedent Arrows. To remove dependent arrows, select Remove Dependent Arrows.

Sheet Icon ⑦

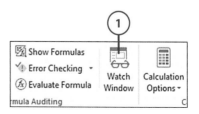

Track Formulas on Other Sheets with Watch Window

The Watch Window allows you to watch a cell update as you make changes to other cells that will affect it.

1. On the Formulas tab, click Watch Window.

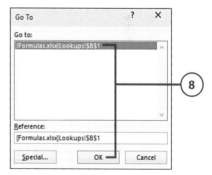

2. Click Add Watch.

3. Select the cell you want to watch update and click Add.

4. Leave the Watch Window open (you can drag it out of the way) and make changes to cells that will affect the watched cells. The Watch Window will update as Excel recalculates.

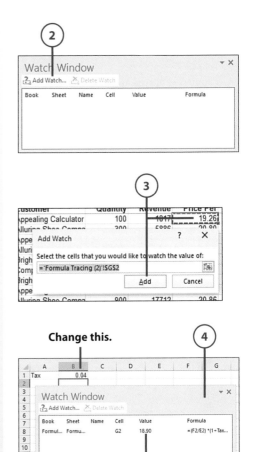

Change this.

This updates.

Use the Evaluate Formula Dialog Box

Use Evaluate Formula to watch how Excel calculates each part of a formula.

1. Select the formula cell.

2. On the Formulas tab, select Evaluate Formula.

3. Click Step in to have the under-lined portion evaluated.

4. The value appears in the second window.

5. Click Step Out.

6. The calculated value replaces its reference.

7. You can continue to step in and out, or jump ahead by clicking Evaluate to calculate the underlined portion.

8. If there are additional portions to calculate, repeat the previous steps until the entire formula is evaluated.

9. Click Restart to go through the steps again, or click Close to return to Excel.

Evaluate with F9

Use F9 to instantly evaluate the highlighted portion of a formula.

1. Select the formula cell.

2. In the formula bar, highlight the part you want to evaluate, including any relevant parentheses. Excel will be in Edit mode.

3. Press F9. The highlighted portion will calculate.

4. To exit Edit mode, press Esc. If you don't, Excel replaces your formula with the value you just evaluated to.

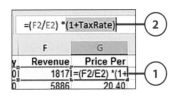

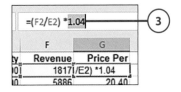

Adjusting Calculation Settings

By default, Excel recalculates whenever you open or save a workbook, or make a change to a cell used in a formula. At times, this isn't convenient— such as when you're working with a very large workbook with a long recal- culation time. In times like this, you will want to control when calculations occur. The setting is saved with each workbook.

Set Calculations to Manual

When you set calculations to manual, formulas will only calculate when you first insert them or edit them.

1. On the Formulas tab, click the Calculation Options drop-down.

2. Select Manual.

3. To turn calculations back to auto- matic, return to the drop-down and select Automatic.

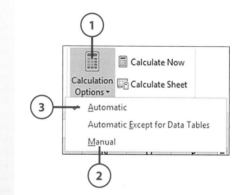

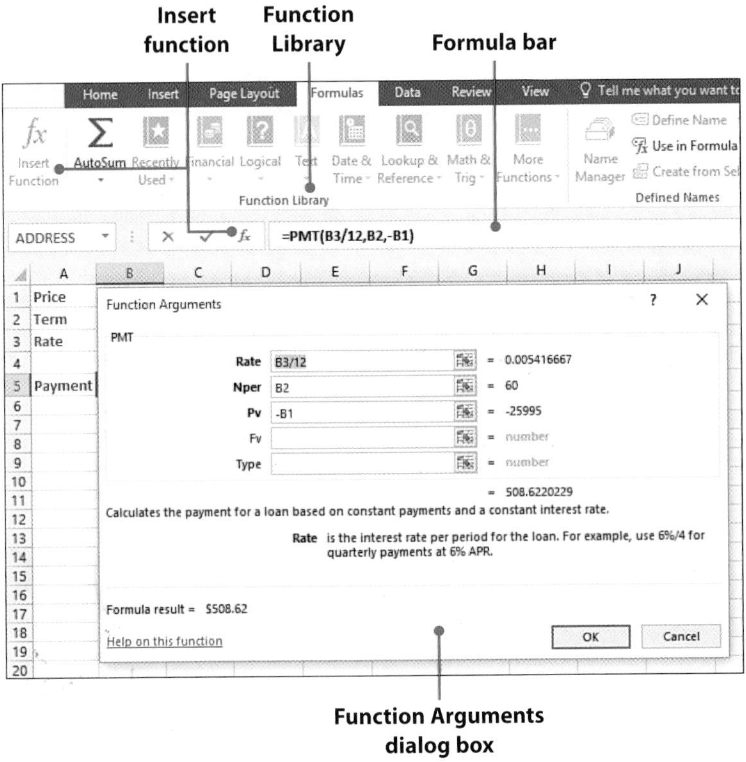

Insert function · Function Library · Formula bar

Function Arguments dialog box

Formula bar contents: `=PMT(B3/12,B2,-B1)`

Function Arguments

PMT

Rate	B3/12		= 0.005416667
Nper	B2		= 60
Pv	-B1		= -25995
Fv			= number
Type			= number

= 508.6220229

Calculates the payment for a loan based on constant payments and a constant interest rate.

Rate is the interest rate per period for the loan. For example, use 6%/4 for quarterly payments at 6% APR.

Formula result = $508.62

Help on this function   OK   Cancel

Spreadsheet cells:
1 Price
2 Term
3 Rate
5 Payment

This chapter shows you how to look up functions available in Excel and reviews some functions helpful for everyday use. Goal Seek is also introduced. Other tasks in this chapter include the following:

9

→ Using the Function Arguments dialog box

→ Using multiple criteria to look up values

→ Calculating the number of workdays between two dates

→ Creating formulas using multiple functions

→ Troubleshooting formulas

Using Functions

A function is like a shortcut for using a long or complex formula. If you've ever summed cells using

=A1+A2+A3+A4+A5

you could have instead used the SUM function, like this:

=SUM(A1:A5).

Understanding Functions

Excel offers more than 400 functions. These include logical functions, lookup functions, statistical functions, financial functions, and more.

More Functions

Only a handful of Excel's functions are reviewed here. For a more in-depth review of functions and possible scenarios you'd use them in, see *Excel 2016 In Depth*, by Bill Jelen (ISBN 978-0-7897-5584-1).

Look Up Functions

You can always search Excel's Help to find a function, but you may get more than just the function information you're looking for. Instead, narrow down the results by using tools provided to specifically search for functions.

1. Select the cell in which you want the function to appear.

2. On the Formulas tab, select Insert Function.

The Other fx Button

To the left of the formula bar is the symbol fx. This symbol is actually a button that opens the Insert Function dialog box.

---

3. Enter a search term in the Search for a Function field or select a category from the drop-down.

4. Select a function from the list box and review the description.

5. Click OK.

6. The function will appear in the active cell, and the Function Arguments dialog box will appear to help you fill in the rest of the arguments.

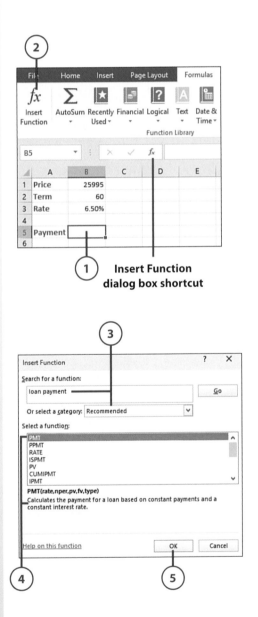

Insert Function dialog box shortcut

Use the Function Arguments Dialog Box

The Function Arguments dialog box assists in entering the arguments for a selected function. A field exists for each argument. If the function has a variable number of arguments, like the SUM function, a new field will be automatically added when needed.

Function name   **Argument name**   **Argument values**   **Resolved value of the argument**   **Argument type**

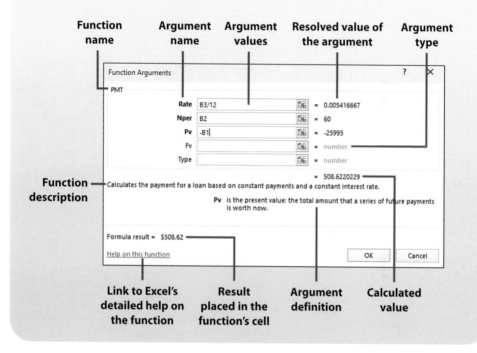

Function description

Link to Excel's detailed help on the function   **Result placed in the function's cell**   **Argument definition**   **Calculated value**

1. Select the cell that will hold the formula.

2. Click the Insert Function (fx) button by the formula bar.

3. If you know the name of the function, such as FIND, type it in. If not, refer to the section "Look Up Functions." Select Go.

4. Select the desired function from the list and click OK.

5. Select a field to enter an argument. Bold arguments are required; non-bold arguments are not. The argument type and description provide more information about the selected argument.

6. To select a range on a sheet, click in the field in the dialog box first; then select the range on the sheet.

7. To enter a value in the field, type it in. If the value is a word, wrap it in quotation marks; if the value is a number, don't use quotation marks, or else the number will be treated as a word.

8. After you have filled in the required arguments, click OK to have the cell accept the function.

Enter Functions Using Formula Tips

If you are already familiar with the function you need, you can type it in the cell or formula bar directly.

1. Select the cell that will hold the formula.

2. Type an equal sign (=), the function name, then a left parenthesis. The formula tip appears. The current argument is bold. Optional arguments appear in square brackets.

3. Use a comma to separate the arguments.

4. When you're finished entering all the arguments, type the right parenthesis.

5. Press Enter or Tab to have the cell accept the formula.

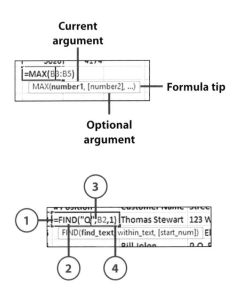

Current argument

Formula tip

Optional argument

Move the Formula Tip

If the formula tip is in the way, place your pointer on the tip where you can get a four-headed arrow then click and drag it out of your way.

Using the AutoSum Button

Excel provides one-click access to the SUM function through the AutoSum button. With two clicks, you can access a few more functions. In both cases, Excel will guess which cells you are trying to calculate and select them for you.

The functions available from the AutoSum button are as follows:

- **Sum**—Adds the values in the selected range by default
- **Average**—Averages the values in the selected range
- **Count Numbers**—Returns the number of cells containing numbers
- **Max**—Returns the largest value in the selected range
- **Min**—Returns the smallest value in the selected range

Calculate a Single Range

Use the AutoSum button to quickly calculate a range.

1. Select the range to sum, including the cell in which the formula will be placed.

Skip the Range

You don't have to pre-select the range you want to calculate. Instead, select only the cell where you want to place the formula. Excel will then try to figure out the range for you. You can accept it or select the one you want.

2. On the Home tab, click the AutoSum button.

Apply Other Auto Functions

From the AutoSum drop-down, you can select another function, such as Average, to apply to the range.

3. The formula is placed in the blank cell that is the far-right or bottom cell of the selection, and the value is calculated.

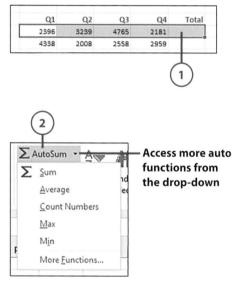

Access more auto functions from the drop-down

It's Not All Good

Excel Misassumptions

You should keep an eye out for a couple of things when using the AutoSum function:

- Be careful of numeric headers (such as years) when letting Excel select the range for you. Excel cannot tell that the header isn't part of the calculation range, and you will need to correct the selection before accepting the formula.

- Excel will look for a column to sum before summing a row. The default selection by Excel is the range of numbers above the selected cell, instead of the adjacent row of numbers.

Sum Rows and Columns at the Same Time

You can sum multiple, nonadjacent ranges at the same time.

1. Select the range to sum, including an extra row and column for the formulas.

2. While holding down the Ctrl key, select the other range with additional cells for the formulas.

3. Click the AutoSum button, or select an option from its drop-down.

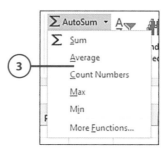

	Q1	Q2	Q3	Q4	Total
East	2396	3239	4765	2181	
Central	4338	2008	2558	2959	
West	3026	4174	4956	1613	
Total					

	2005	2006	2007	2008	Total
East	2396	3239	4765	2181	
Central	4338	2008	2558	2959	
West	3026	4174	4956	1613	
Total					

Σ AutoSum ▾ A▾

Σ Sum

    Average

    Count Numbers

    Max

    Min

    More Functions...

4. Excel will enter the formulas in the extra cells.

④

	Q1	Q2	Q3	Q4	Total
East	2396	3239	4765	2181	12581
Central	4338	2008	2558	2959	11863
West	3026	4174	4956	1613	13769
Total	9760	9421	12279	6753	38213

	2005	2006	2007	2008	Total
East	2396	3239	4765	2181	12581
Central	4338	2008	2558	2959	11863
West	3026	4174	4956	1613	13769
Total	9760	9421	12279	6753	38213

Quick Calculations

You can use the status bar or the Quick Analysis icon to perform quick calculations with functions.

Calculate Results Quickly

If you just need to see the results of a calculation and not include the information on a sheet, Excel offers six quick calculations you can preview in the status bar.

Changing the Status Bar
Changes to the status bar affect the application, not just the active workbook or sheet.

---

1. Select the range to calculate.

2005	2006	2007	2008
2396	3239	4765	2181
4338	2008	2558	2959
3026	4174	4956	1613

①

2. Right-click the status bar.

3. Select the functions you want to view or remove in the status bar.

4. Click away from the menu to return to Excel.

5. The selected results will appear in the status bar.

Customize Status Bar	
✓ Cell Mode	Ready
✓ Flash Fill Blank Cells	
✓ Flash Fill Changed Cells	
✓ Signatures	Off
✓ Information Management Policy	Off
✓ Permissions	Off
Caps Lock	Off
Num Lock	On
✓ Scroll Lock	Off
✓ Fixed Decimal	Off
Overtype Mode	
✓ End Mode	
✓ Macro Recording	Not Recording
✓ Selection Mode	
✓ Page Number	
✓ Average	3184.416667
✓ Count	12
Numerical Count	
Minimum	
Maximum	
✓ Sum	38213
✓ Upload Status	
✓ View Shortcuts	
✓ Zoom Slider	
✓ Zoom	100%

Average: 3184.416667 | Count: 12 | Sum: 38213

Using Quick Analysis Functions

When you select multiple adjacent cells, the Quick Analysis icon appears in the bottom-right corner of the selection. Click the icon, select TOTALS, and various quick calculations will appear.

1. Select the range to calculate.

2. Click the Quick Analysis Icon.

3. Select Totals.

4. Choose the desired function. Use the arrows on the left and right sides of the icons to scroll through the list.

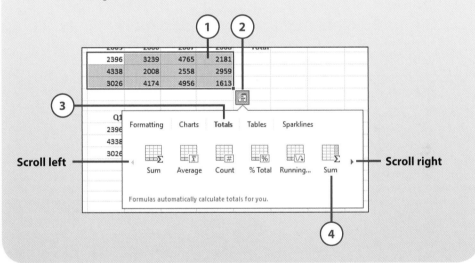

Using Lookup Functions

This section reviews some of the lookup functions. There are functions that can return a value dependent on its position in a list or return a value in the same row as a match. You can even combine multiple functions to return a value by looking up and matching multiple variables.

Use CHOOSE to Return the nth Value from a List

The CHOOSE function returns a value from the list based on an index number. The syntax of the CHOOSE function is as follows:

CHOOSE(index_num, value1, [value2],…)

In the following example, the numeric grade is used as the index number, and a letter grade is supplied based on its position in the list. For example, if the numeric grade is "1," the letter in the first position, "F," is returned.

1. Select the cell for the formula.

2. Type the following:

   =CHOOSE(

3. Select the cell with the index number and then type a comma.

4. Select the cell with the first value argument, or type it in. If it's an alphabetic character, wrap it in quotation marks.

5. Type a comma then enter the next value. Repeat until all the values are entered.

6. Type the closing parentheses and press Enter or Tab.

7. Based on the index number, Excel will return the corresponding value.

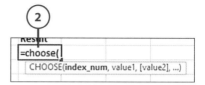

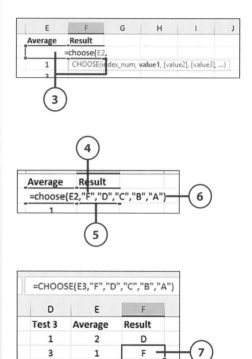

Function Rules

Here are a few rules to keep in mind when using CHOOSE:

- If the index_num is a decimal, it will be rounded to the next lowest integer. For example, if it is 4.8, the formula will use 4.

- If the index_num is less than 1 or greater than the number of available values, the function will return a #VALUE! error.

- You can enter 1 to 254 argument values.

- Arguments can be numbers, cell references, names, formulas, functions, or text.

Use VLOOKUP to Return a Value from a Table

The VLOOKUP function matches your lookup value to a value in a data-set and returns data from a specified column in the matching row. For example, based on a customer's name, you can use VLOOKUP to fill in the street address and phone number. The syntax of the VLOOKUP function is as follows:

VLOOKUP(lookup_value, table_array, col_index_num, [range_lookup])

1. Select the cell for the formula.

2. Type **=VLOOKUP(** and then press the fx button by the formula bar.

3. Select the cell with the value to look up. Press F4 to change the cell address from relative to abso-lute. That way, when you copy the formula, the Lookup_value address won't change.

4. Click in the Table_array field and then select the lookup range, ensuring that the lookup value is in the leftmost column of the selection. Press F4 to change the cell address from relative to absolute.

5. Enter the index number of the column to return in the Col_index_num field. This is based on the lookup range and may not be equivalent to the column heading. For example, if the selected range begins in column C and the col_index_num is 2, a value from column D will be returned.

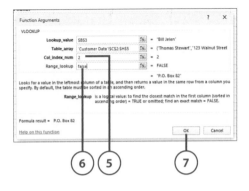

6. Enter **False** if you want to return an exact match to the lookup value.

7. Click OK to complete the function.

>>>Go Further
TROUBLESHOOT VLOOKUP ERRORS

If VLOOKUP returns an error or incorrect value but you can manually verify that the lookup value is present in the table, the issue may be one of the following:

- If you're using FALSE for the range_lookup, the entire cell contents must match 100%. If you're looking up "Bracelet" and the term in the table is "Bracelets," Excel will not return a match.

- Be careful of extra spaces before and after a word. "Bracelet " and "Bracelet" are not matches—the first occurrence has a space at the end.

- If you're matching numbers, make sure both the lookup value and the matching value are formatted the same type—for example, both as General or one as General and the other as Currency. This allows Excel to still see them as numbers. Sometimes when you're importing data, numbers get formatted as Text. If you have a lookup value formatted as General and the matching value is formatted as Text, Excel will not see this as a match. Refer to the section "Fixing Numbers Stored as Text" in Chapter 4, "Getting Data onto a Sheet," for instructions on how to force the numbers stored as text to become true numbers.

- Make sure the table_array encompasses the entire dataset.

Use INDEX and MATCH to Return a Value from the Left

VLOOKUP works only when returning data from columns to the right of the lookup column. If your data is also to the left of the lookup column, use MATCH and INDEX together. The INDEX function returns a value based on a row and column number. The MATCH function looks up a value and returns its position (row or column) in a dataset.

The syntax of the INDEX function is as follows:

INDEX(array, row_num, [column_num])

Two Ways to Use INDEX

The INDEX function has two syntaxes—array and reference—but this section will only use the array version.

And here is the syntax of the MATCH function:

MATCH(lookup_value, lookup_array, [match_type])

1. Select the cell for the formula.

2. Type the following:

    =INDEX(

3. Select the range you want to return data from, press F4 to make the address absolute, and then type a comma.

4. The next argument for the INDEX function is the row_num. Because this is our dynamic value, use the MATCH function to do the lookup and return the row number. Type the following:

    MATCH(

Switching Sheets When Writing Formulas

Sometimes when writing formulas, you have to switch to another sheet to select a range. When you switch back to the sheet you are entering the formula on, Excel includes the sheet name in the formula. It's up to you whether or not you want to keep this unneeded reference.

5. Select the lookup value and then type a comma.

6. Select the lookup range and then type a comma.

7. Enter the match type. The MATCH function is now complete, so type the following:

),

- If the match type is 1, the function returns the largest value that is less than or equal to the lookup_value. The lookup_array must be sorted in ascending order.

- If 0, the function returns the first value that is an exact match to the lookup_value.

- If -1, the function returns the smallest value that is greater than or equal to the lookup_value. The lookup_array must be sorted in descending order.

8. Enter the index number of the column to return. This is based on the lookup range and may not be equivalent to the column heading. For example, if the table begins in column B and the col_index_num is 2, a value from column C will be returned.

9. Enter the closing parenthesis and press Enter or Tab to calculate the formula.

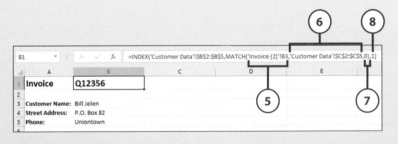

Nested Functions

It's not always easy to type in a formula that uses multiple functions. You may find it easier to place each function in a different cell, referencing the results of a previous function as needed. When you've verified that each piece works, cut the function (without the equal sign) out of its cell and paste it over the cell address in the parent function.

Using SUMIFS to Sum Based on Multiple Criteria

The SUMIFS function sums a single column based on multiple criteria. For example, you can sum revenue between two dates or sum the quantity of a specific product in a specific region.

Here is the syntax of the function (optional arguments are in square brackets):

SUMIFS(sum_range, criteria_range1, criteria1, [criteria_range2, criteria2],...)

SUMIFS Rules

You need to keep a few rules in mind when using this function:

- Each range consists of a single column.

- Each range has the same number of rows.

- Words as well as equality and inequality symbols must be wrapped in quotation marks.

- If you are using equality and inequality symbols with a cell reference, the cell reference should be outside the quotation marks around the symbol. Also, join the symbols and cell reference with an ampersand (&).

Sum a Column Based on Two Criteria

The following example sums the revenue of records within a specific date range with a maximum quantity.

1. Select the cell for the formula.

2. Type the following:

   =SUMIFS(

3. Click the fx button by the formula bar.

	C	D	F	G	H	I
	Date	Quant	Reven		Start Date	1/3/2015
	01/01/15	1000	22810		End Date	1/5/2015
	01/02/15	200	4514		Max Quantity	600
	01/02/15	500	10245		Total Revenue	=SUMIFS(

4. Select the range to sum (in this case, Revenue).

5. Click in the Criteria_range1 field and select the first criteria range, Date. Notice that when you click in the field, more fields are added to the dialog box.

6. The first criteria is dates greater than the start date. Click in the Criteria1 field and type the following:

   ">"&

   Then select the cell with the start date.

7. Click in the Criteria_range2 field and select the second criteria range, which again is the Date column.

8. The second criteria is dates less than or equal to the end date. Click in the Criteria2 field and type the following:

   "<="&

   Then select the cell with the end date.

View More Fields

As fields are filled in, more are added, but the dialog box doesn't get bigger. Use the scroll bar on the right side of the dialog box to scroll down to the next field as needed.

9. Click the in the Criteria_range3 field and select the third criteria range, the Quantity column.

10. The third criteria is quantities less than a set maximum. Click in the Criteria3 field and type the following:

"<"&

Then select the cell with the max quantity.

11. Click OK to have Excel accept the formula and calculate it.

12. Change the dates and max quantity and watch the total revenue update.

Using IF Statements

The IF function lets you build a statement where you perform a logical test, such as comparing two values, and then do one thing if the test evaluates to TRUE and another if it's FALSE. The function syntax is as follows:

IF(logical_test, [value_if_true], [value_if_false])

Compare Two Values

The following example compares the quarter sales for each salesperson. If sales have gone up, "Gain" is entered in the cell; otherwise, "Loss" is entered.

1. Select the cell where the formula will go.

2. Select IF from the Logical drop-down on the Formulas tab.

3. The Logical_test field is where we enter our values to compare. Select the cell containing the first value to compare, enter the comparison symbol < (less than), and then select the cell containing the second value to compare.

4. In the Value_if_True field, type "Gain".

5. In the Value_if_False field, type "Loss".

6. Click OK. Excel will calculate the formula result.

7. Copy the formula to other cells in the dataset.

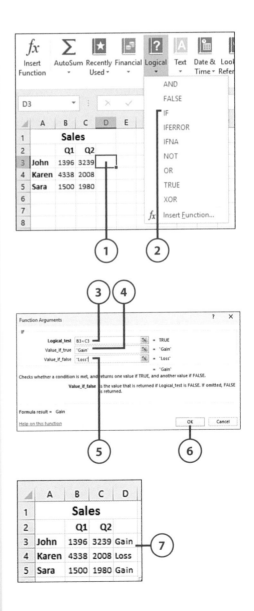

>>>Go Further

COMBINE IF WITH OTHER LOGICAL FUNCTIONS

You can combine the IF statement with AND, OR, and NOT to expand the logical test.

- **AND**—Returns TRUE if all its arguments are TRUE. Returns FALSE if any of the arguments evaluate to FALSE. The function syntax is

  AND(logical1, [logical2], …)

- **OR**—Returns TRUE if any of its arguments are TRUE. Returns FALSE if all the arguments evaluate to FALSE. The function syntax is

  OR(logical1, [logical2, …])

- **NOT**—Reverses the logic of its arguments. The function syntax is

  NOT(logical)

For example, to check if a value in cell B3 is between 2000 and 6000, use AND like this:

=IF(AND(B3>2000,B3<6000),"Between", "Not Between")

To check that the value is not between those numbers, you could do this:

=IF(NOT(AND(B3>2000,B3<6000)),"Not Between", "Between")

Hiding Errors with IFERROR

The IFERROR function returns the value specified if a formula evaluates to an error; otherwise, it returns the result of the formula. The function syntax is as follows:

IFERROR(value, value_if_error)

Hide a #DIV/0! Error

If there's an error in a column being summed, the sum will also be an error. Wrap the calculation that produces the first error in an IFERROR so the sum formula will calculate properly.

1. Select the cell with the formula producing the #DIV/0! error.

2. Place your cursor after the equal sign (=) in the formula bar.

3. Type **IFERROR(** and then place your cursor at the end of the formula.

4. Type a comma and then **"No Sales")** (or some other value).

5. Press Enter or Tab to have Excel accept and calculate the formula.

6. Copy the formula to the rest of the range.

7. The sum formula no longer calculates to an error.

	A	B	C	D	E	F
1	Region	Product	Date	Quantity	Revenue	Unit Price
2	East	Multi-Func	1/1/2015	1000	22810	22.81
3	Central	Laser Print	1/2/2015	200	2257	11.285
4	East	Basic Color	1/2/2015	500	10245	20.49
5	Central	Multi-Func	1/3/2015	0	0	#DIV/0!
6	Central	Multi-Func	1/4/2015	400	9204	23.01
7	East	Laser Print	1/4/2015	800	18552	23.19
8	East	Multi-Func	1/4/2015	400	11240	28.1
9					Total	#DIV/0!

This error is causing the error in the Total below.

②

f_x		=E5/D5	
	D	E	F
	Quantity	Revenue	Unit Price
015	1000	22810	22.81
015	200	2257	11.285
015	500	10245	20.49
015	0	0	=E5/D5
015	400	9204	23.01

①

③

f_x	=IFERROR(E5/D5,"No Sales")		
	D	E	F	G
	Quantity	Revenue	Unit Price	
15	1000	22810	22.81	
15	200	2257	11.285	
15	500	10245	20.49	
15	0	0	o Sales")	
15	400	9204	23.01	

④

⑤

	A	B	C	D	E	F
1	Region	Product	Date	Quantity	Revenue	Unit Price
2	East	Multi-Func	1/1/2015	1000	22810	22.81
3	Central	Laser Print	1/2/2015	200	2257	11.285
4	East	Basic Color	1/2/2015	500	10245	20.49
5	Central	Multi-Func	1/3/2015	0	0	No Sales
6	Central	Multi-Func	1/4/2015	400	9204	23.01
7	East	Laser Print	1/4/2015	800	18552	23.19
8	East	Multi-Func	1/4/2015	400	11240	28.1
9					Total	128.885

⑦

Understanding Dates and Times

Understanding how Excel stores dates and times is important so that you can successfully use formulas and functions when calculating with dates and times.

Dates and times in Excel are not stored the same way we see them. For example, you may type 9/8/15 into a cell, but Excel actually sees 42255. That number, 42255, is called a date serial number. The formatted value, 9/8/15, is called a date value. Storing dates and times as serial numbers allows Excel to do date and time calculations.

Time serial numbers are stored as decimals, starting at 0.0 for 12:00 a.m. and ending at 0.9999884259 for 11:59:59 p.m. The rest of the day's decimal values are equivalent to their calculated percentage, based on the number of hours in a day, 24. For example, 1:00 a.m. is 1/24 or .04166, and 6:00 p.m. would be the 18th hour of the day, 18/24 = 0.75.

Return a New Date *X* Workdays from Date

Excel has a function called WORKDAY that returns a date before or after a specified number of workdays. You also have the option of specifying holidays to skip when calculating the new date.

1. If you want to use the holidays argument, create a list of dates you want the calculation to skip when counting days.

2. Enter the starting date in a cell.

3. Enter the number of days out you want to count.

4. Select the cell for the formula.

5. Select WORKDAY from the Date & Time drop-down on the Formulas tab.

6. Select the cell with the start date.

7. Click in the Days field and then select the cell with the days to count.

8. Click in the Holidays field then select the range of holidays.

9. Click OK. Excel will calculate a new date.

10. Apply a date format to the cell if needed.

Calculate the Number of Days Between Dates

There's a hidden function that can be used to calculate the days, months, or years between two dates. The function doesn't appear when you look at a list of available date functions; Excel includes it for Lotus compatibility, but it can still be used, if you know how to get at it.

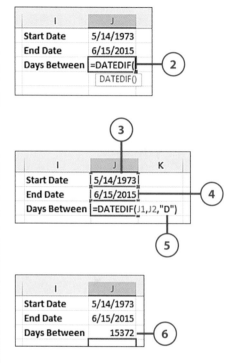

1. Select the cell for the formula.

2. Type the following:

   =DATEDIF(

3. Select the cell with the oldest date and type a comma.

4. Select the cell with the newer date and type a comma.

5. Type the following:

   "D")

6. Press Enter or Tab to calculate the result.

>>>Go Further
MORE THIRD ARGUMENT OPTIONS

Six different options are available for the third argument, providing different ways of counting the time between the dates:

- **"D"**—The number of days between the dates
- **"M"**—The number of months between the dates
- **"Y"**—The number of years between the dates
- **"YM"**—The number of months between the dates, ignoring the days and years in the dates
- **"YD"**—The number of days between the dates, ignoring the years in the dates
- **"MD"**—The number of days between the dates, ignoring the months and years in the dates

Using Goal Seek

Goal Seek adjusts the value of a cell to get a specific result from another cell. For example, if you have the price, term, and rate of a loan, you can use the PMT function to calculate the payment. But what if the calculated payment wasn't satisfactory and you wanted to recalculate with additional prices? You could take the time to enter a variety of prices, recalculating the payment. Alternatively, you could use Goal Seek to tell Excel what you want the payment to be and let it calculate the price for you.

Calculate the Best Payment

Here are a couple things to keep in mind when using Goal Seek:

- You must have the formula in the Set cell. Goal Seek works by plugging values in to your existing formula.

- A clear mathematical relationship between the starting and ending cells must exist.

1. Select the cell whose value you want to be a specific value.

2. Select Goal Seek from the What-If Analysis drop-down on the Data tab.

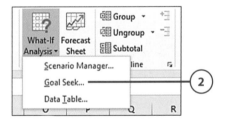

3. In the Set Cell field should be the address of the cell selected in step 1. If not, select the cell for which you are seeking a value.

4. In the To Value field, enter the value you want the Set cell to be, such as 630.

5. In the By Changing Cell field, select the cell whose value you want Excel to change so the Set Cell field calculates to the desired value.

6. Click OK.

7. Excel will attempt to return a solution as close to the desired value as possible. If it succeeds, a message box will appear showing the target value and the actual value it attained.

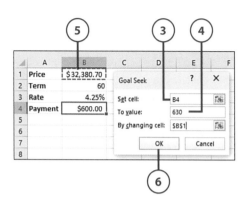

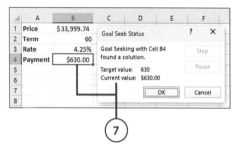

Using the Function Arguments Dialog Box to Troubleshoot Formulas

If you have one function using other functions as arguments and the formula returns an error, you can use the Function Arguments dialog to track down which function is generating the error.

Narrow Down a Formula Error

The Function Arguments dialog box makes it easier to figure out which function in a multifunction formula is causing the problem.

1. Select the cell with the formula to troubleshoot.

2. In the formula bar, place your cursor in the formula's first function.

3. Click the fx button next to the formula bar.

4. If you see the error in the selected function, you can fix it and click OK to recalculate the formula. Otherwise, continue to the next step.

5. If you see the error in a field using another function, place your cursor in that function's name in the formula bar.

Employee	Sales $	Commission
Scott	00	#N/A
Jason	12000	1.0%
Karen	32000	1.3%
Wilma	15000	1.2%

_fx_   =OFFSET($D$1,MATCH(E8,$D$3:$D$5,1),2)

OFFSET(reference, rows, cols, [height], [width])

D		
Min	**Max**	**Rate**
0	9999	1.0%
10000	14999	1.2%
15000	24999	1.3%
25000		1.5%

Employee	Sales $	Commission
Scott	5000	=OFFSET(D
Jason	12000	1.0%
Karen	32000	1.3%
Wilma	15000	1.2%

Function Arguments   ?   ✕

OFFSET

Reference	$D$1	= "Min"
Rows	MATCH(E8,$D$3:$D$5,1)	= #N/A
Cols	2	= 2
Height		= number
Width		= number

= Volatile

Returns a reference to a range that is given number of rows and columns from a given reference.

Reference is the reference from which you want to base the offset, a reference to a cell or range of adjacent cells.

Formula result = Volatile

Help on this function   OK   Cancel

6. The selected function is loaded into the Function Arguments dialog box. Repeat this as needed to find which function is causing the error and fix it. Click OK when you are done.

This range should be $D$2:$D$5.

Quick Sort buttons   **Open Sort dialog box**

	A	B	C	D	E	F	G	H
	Region	Product	Date	Customer	Quantity	Revenue	COGS	Profit
	Central	Laser	1/2/2015	Alluring Shoe Company	500	11240	5110	6130
	Central	Laser	1/3/2015	Alluring Shoe Company	400	9204	4088	5116
	Central	Multi-Function	1/26/2015	Alluring Shoe Company	500	10445	4235	6210
	Central	Basic ColorJet	2/5/2015	Alluring Shoe Company	200	4280	1968	2312
	Central	Basic ColorJet	2/19/2015	Alluring Shoe Company	800	18504	7872	10632
	Central	Basic ColorJet	3/24/2015	Alluring Shoe Company	200	4472	1968	2504
	Central	Multi-Function	4/6/2015	Alluring Shoe Company	300	5886	2541	3345
	Central	Laser	5/17/2015	Alluring Shoe Company	500	10385	5110	5275
	Central	Laser	5/30/2015	Alluring Shoe Company	900	18918	9198	9720
	Central	Multi-Function	6/13/2015	Alluring Shoe Company	700	12838	5929	6909
	Central	Laser	7/1/2015	Alluring Shoe Company	900	21960	9198	12762
	Central	Laser	8/6/2015	Alluring Shoe Company	100	2320	1022	1298
	Central	Multi-Function	8/21/2015	Alluring Shoe Company	800	15544	6776	8768

Sort alphabetically   **Sort numerically**   **Sort by color**

In this chapter, you'll learn the various ways of sorting data, allowing you to view data from least to greatest, greatest to least, and even by color. You'll also learn how to do the following:

→ Sorting data with one click

→ Sorting using a custom, non-alphabetical order

→ Sorting by color or icon

→ Rearranging columns with a few clicks of the mouse and keyboard

Sorting Data

You'll often need to sort your data, whether it be numerically, alphabetically, by color, or by icon. You aren't limited to sorting the rows—columns can also be sorted.

Sorting data allows you to change how you view it. For example, if your dataset has a date column, you can view the oldest data at the top, or you can view the newest data at the top. You can also sort the data so like values, such as product names, are grouped together. You can even combine sorts so that you not only view the products grouped together, but in date order from oldest to newest.

Using the Sort Dialog Box

The Sort dialog box provides the most versatile way of sorting your data because it allows you to specify how you want the data sorted. When you use the dialog box, Excel applies each sort in the order it appears in the list.

Sort by Values

The Sort dialog box makes it easy to sort by multiple columns. A different sort method can be applied for each level. The sorts are done in the order they appear in the list.

1. Select a cell in the dataset. Excel will use this cell to determine the location and size of the dataset.

2. On the Data tab, select Sort.

3. If the data has a header row, but Excel doesn't recognize it, select the My Data Has Headers check box.

4. From the Sort By drop-down, select the first column header by which to sort.

5. From the Sort On drop-down, select Values.

6. From the Order drop-down, select the order by which the column's data should be sorted. Choose A to Z to sort in alphabetical order; choose Z to A to sort in the opposite order. If the data is numerical, the drop-down options will change to Smallest to Largest and Largest to Smallest.

7. Select Add Level to add another sort rule.

8. From the Then By drop-down, select the second column header by which to sort.

9. From the Sort On drop-down, select Values.

10. From the Order drop-down, select the order by which the column's data should be sorted.

11. If you realize a field is in the wrong position, use the up or down arrow at the top of the dialog box to move the field to the correct location.

12. Click OK to sort the data.

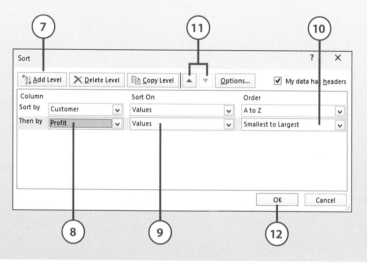

It's Not All Good

Excel Didn't Select the Dataset Correctly

When you sort, Excel will try to help by selecting your dataset for you. You can help Excel do this correctly by not having any blank rows or columns in your dataset. Also, ensure that your header, if you have one, consists of only one row. Only a single header row is allowed—any rows after it are treated as data.

If Excel incorrectly selects your data, exit from the Sort dialog box, delete the blank columns and rows, and start the dialog box over.

If for some reason you can't delete the blank columns or rows, you can pre-select the entire table before starting the Sort dialog box.

Sort by Color or Icon

Excel can also sort data by fill color, font color, or an icon set from conditional formatting.

1. Select a cell in the dataset. Excel will use this cell to determine the location and size of the dataset.

2. On the Data tab, select Sort.

3. If the data has a header row, but Excel doesn't recognize it, select the My Data Has Headers check box.

4. From the Sort By drop-down, select the column header by which to sort.

5. From the Sort On drop-down, select Cell Color to sort by the cell's fill color. You can also choose Font Color to sort by the value's color or Cell Icon to sort by conditional formatting icons.

6. From the first Order drop-down, select the color by which the column's data should be sorted. If sorting by icon, you'll have a choice of icons.

7. From the second Order drop-down, select whether the color should be sorted to the top or bottom of the data. If you select multiple colors to sort at the top of the data, the colors will still appear in the order chosen.

8. Click OK to sort the data.

Color Sorting a Table

If your data is in a table, you don't have to go through the Sort dialog box. Instead, click the arrow in the header, select Sort by Color, and select the color you want sorted to the top of the table.

>>>Go Further
SORTING SHORTCUT

In addition to sorting colors and icons through the Sort dialog box, the following options are also available when you right-click a cell and select Sort from the context menu.

If you use one of the preceding options to sort more than one color or icon, the latest selection will be placed above the previous selection. So, if yellow rows should be placed before the red rows, sort the red rows first, and then the yellow rows.

Color and icon shortcuts

Doing Quick Sorts

The Quick Sort buttons offer one-click access to sorting cell values.

Quick Sort a Single Column

There are several quick methods you can choose from to apply simple sorts to your data.

1. Select one cell in the column to sort by. If you select multiple cells, Excel will sort only the data in the selected range.

2. On the Data tab, select AZ to sort lowest to highest or ZA to sort highest to lowest.

>>>Go Further

OTHER QUICK SORT OPTIONS

There are other ways you can access the quick sort options:

Right-click the cell and select Sort, Sort A to Z or Sort Z to A if your data is text; select Sort Smallest to Largest or Sort Largest to Smallest if the data is numerical.

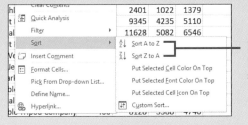

Right-click menu quick sort options

From a filter drop-down, select Sort A to Z or Sort Z to A if your data is text;
select Sort Smallest to Largest or Sort Largest to Smallest if the data is numerical.

Filter
drop-down
quick sort
options

Customer		Quantity	Revenue	
Remarkable	A↓	Sort Smallest to Largest		
Matchless V	Z↓	Sort Largest to Smallest		
Alluring Sho		Sort by Color	▶	
Matchless V	✕	Clear Filter From "Revenue"		
Appealing Ca		Filter by Color	▶	
Reliable Trip		Number Filters	▶	
Unsurpassed				
Exclusive Sh		Search	🔍	

Settings Carry Between Sorts

Sort options are retained for the sheet during an Excel session. So if you set
up a custom sort with Case Sensitive turned on, then later do a quick sort, the
quick sort will be case sensitive.

Quick Sort Multiple Columns

If you keep in mind that Excel keeps previously sorted columns sorted as new
columns are sorted, you can use the Quick Sort feature to sort multiple columns. For example, if the Profit column is organized, Excel doesn't randomize
the data in that column when the Customer column is sorted. Instead, Profit
retains its order to the degree it falls within the Customer sort. The trick is to
apply the sorts in reverse to how they would be set up in the Sort dialog box.

In the following example, we want to
sort by Customer and Profit, both least
to greatest.

1. Select a cell in the column that
   should be sorted last in the Sort
   dialog box (in this case, the Profit
   column).

2. On the Data tab, click the A to Z
   button.

Data	Review	View	♀ Tell me what you want t
ons	A↓ Z A / A Z	Filter	✕ Clear / ↻ Reapply / ▼ Advanced
	Z↓ Sort		Text to Columns

Sort & Filter

	E	F	G	H
	Quantity	**Revenue**	**COGS**	**Profit**
oe Co.	400	9144	4088	5056
oe Co.	400	9204	4088	5116

3. Select a cell in the next column to be sorted (in this case, the Customer column).

4. On the Data tab, click the A to Z button.

5. The table is now sorted by Customer and then Profit within each customer's records.

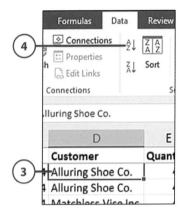

Formulas	Data	Review

Connections · Properties · Edit Links

Connections

Alluring Shoe Co.

D	E
Customer	Quant
Alluring Shoe Co.	
Alluring Shoe Co.	
Matchless Vice Inc.	

Profit is sorted smallest to largest within each customer's record

Customer	Quantity	Revenue	COGS	Profit
Alluring Shoe Co.	400	9144	4088	5056
Alluring Shoe Co.	400	9204	4088	5116
Alluring Shoe Co.	500	11240	5110	6130
Alluring Shoe Co.	500	10445	4235	6210
Alluring Shoe Co.	900	21465	9198	12267
Appealing Calculato	900	17505	7623	9882
Appealing Calculato	1000	19250	8470	10780

Performing Custom Sorts

You aren't limited to sorting data alphabetically and numerically. With a little extra setup work, you can randomize the order or sort by a custom sequence.

Perform a Random Sort

Excel doesn't have a built-in tool to do a random sort, but by using the RAND function in a column to the right of the data and then sorting, you can create your own randomizer.

f_x	=RAND()

C	D
Student Name	Random
Amy Mcmaster	0.3859519
Andrew O'Rasi	
Anja Kennedy	
Bill Jolon	

1. Add a new column to the right of the data and give the column a label in the first cell, such as Random.

2. In the second cell of the new column, type **=RAND()** and press Ctrl+Enter (this will keep the formula cell as the active cell). The formula will calculate a value between 0 and 1.

3. Copy the formula to the rest of the rows in the column.

4. Select one cell in the new column.

5. On the Data tab, click the AZ button.

6. The list will be sorted in a random sequence. Delete the temporary column added in step 1.

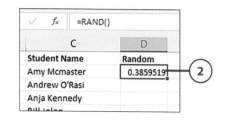
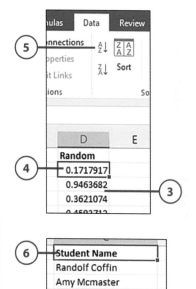

The Numbers Keep Changing

Right after Excel performs the sort, it recalculates the formula in the temporary column, so it may appear that the numbers are out of sequence.

Sort with a Custom Sequence

At times, data may need to be sorted in a custom sequence that is neither alphabetical nor numerical. For example, you might want to sort by month, by weekday, or by some custom sequence of your own. You can do this by sorting by a custom list.

How to Create a Custom List

You'll need to create a custom list before continuing with the following steps. Refer to "Create Your Own List" in Chapter 4, "Getting Data onto a Sheet," for steps on creating one.

1. Select a cell in the dataset.

2. On the Data tab, click Sort.

3. From the Sort By drop-down, select the column header by which to sort.

4. From the Sort On drop-down, select Values.

5. From the Order drop-down, select Custom List.

6. Select the desired list.

7. Click OK.

8. Click OK.

9. The data is sorted by the custom list.

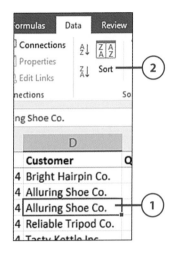

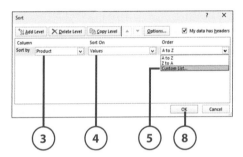

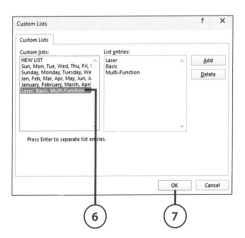

Rearranging Columns

By default, data is sorted by rows, but you can choose to sort columns instead. And with the following trick, you aren't limited to sorting them alphabetically.

Sort Columns with the Sort Dialog Box

Hidden in the Sort dialog box is an option to sort your data left to right, instead of the default top to bottom.

1. Insert a new blank row above the headers by right-clicking the row 1 heading and then selecting Insert.

2. In the new row, type numbers corresponding to the new sequence of the columns, with 1 being the leftmost column, then 2, 3, and so on, until each column has a number denoting its new location.

3. Select a cell in the dataset.

4. Press Ctrl+A to select the current region, including the two header rows.

5. On the Data tab, select Sort.

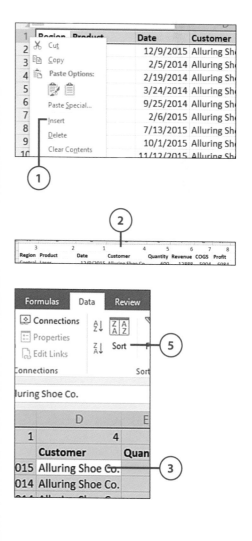

6. Click the Options button.

7. Select the Sort Left to Right option.

8. Click OK to return to the Sort dialog box.

9. In the Sort By drop-down, select Row 1.

10. In the Sort On drop-down, select Values.

11. In the Order drop-down, select Smallest to Largest.

12. Click OK.

13. Excel will rearrange the columns.

14. Delete the temporary row added in step 1.

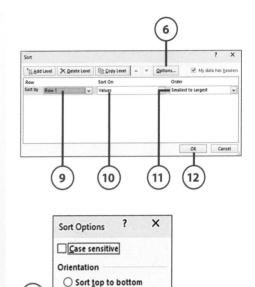

Fixing Sort Problems

If it looks like the data did not sort properly, refer to the following list of possible solutions:

- Make sure no hidden rows or columns exist.

- Use a single row for headers. If you need a multiline header, either wrap the text in the cell or use Alt+Enter to force line breaks in the cell.

- If the headers were sorted into the data, there was probably at least one column without a header.

- Column data should be of the same type. This may not be obvious in a column of ZIP codes where some (such as 57057) are numbers, but others that start with zero are actually text. To solve this problem, convert the entire column to text.

- If you're sorting by a column containing a formula, Excel will recalculate the column after the sort. If the values change after the recalculation, such as with RAND, it may appear that the sort did not work properly, but it did.

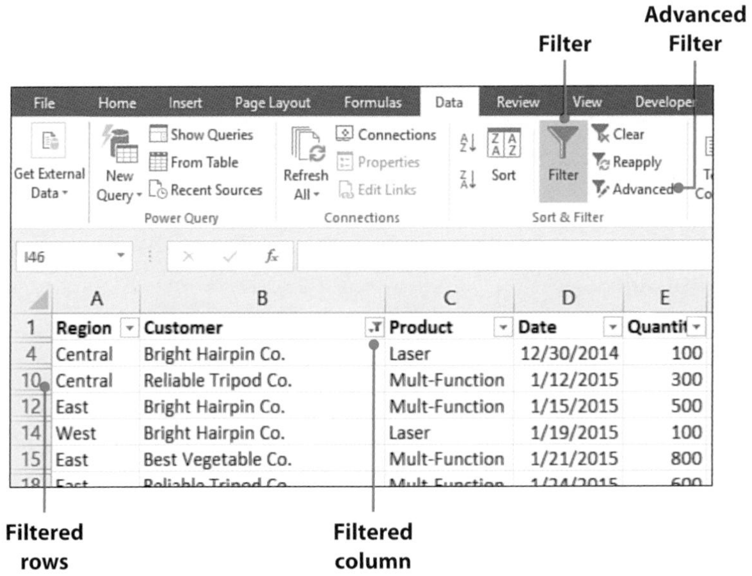
Advanced Filter
Filter
File
Home
Insert
Page Layout
Formulas
Data
Review
View
Get External Data
New Query
Show Queries
From Table
Recent Sources
Power Query
Refresh All
Connections
Properties
Edit Links
Connections
Sort
Filter
Clear
Reapply
Advanced
Sort & Filter
I46
Region
Customer
Product
Date
Central
Bright Hairpin Co.
Laser
12/30/2014
100
Central
Reliable Tripod Co.
Mult-Function
1/12/2015
300
East
Bright Hairpin Co.
Mult-Function
1/15/2015
500
West
Bright Hairpin Co.
Laser
1/19/2015
100
East
Best Vegetable Co.
Mult-Function
1/21/2015
800
Filtered rows
Filtered column

This chapter shows you how to use Excel's filtering functionality to look at just the desired records. It also shows you how to filter by text, values, and dates. Topics in this chapter include the following:

→ Removing duplicate rows

→ Creating a unique list of items

→ Filtering for specific records

→ Consolidating information from multiple workbooks

→ Filtering a protected sheet

→ Focusing on specific data by filtering by color or icon

Filtering and Consolidating Data

Filtering and consolidating data are important tasks in Excel, especially when you are dealing with large amounts of data. The filtering tools can quickly reduce the data to the specific records you need to concentrate on. The consolidation tool can bring together information spread between multiple sheets or workbooks.

Using the Filter Tool

Filtering allows you to view only the data you want to see by hiding the other data. You can apply a filter to multiple columns, thus narrowing down the data. As you filter the data and rows are hidden, the row headings (1, 2, 3, and so on) become blue.

What's AutoFilter?

Occasionally, you may see the term *AutoFilter* used when describing the Filter tool. In older versions of Excel, Excel combined multiple filter tools under the Filter menu, and the AutoFilter was one of them. Now that the tools each have their own button, the old AutoFilter has been simply renamed Filter. But the term still pops up, even in current Excel options.

Apply a Filter

Before you can filter a dataset, you need to turn on the Filter option on the Data tab.

1. Select a cell in the dataset. Excel will use this cell to determine the location and size of the dataset. If you select more than one cell, filtering will be on just for that selection.

2. On the Data tab, select Filter.

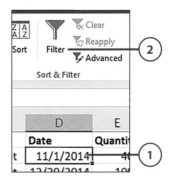

Filter Already On for Tables

When a dataset is converted to a table, the headers automatically become filter headers.

3. Click the drop-down arrow of the column you want to filter.

4. The selected items are the ones that will appear when the column is filtered. Unselect the items you want hidden.

5. Click OK.

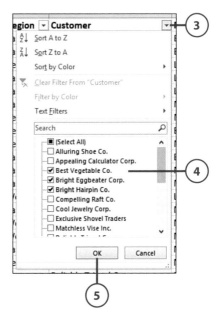

6. The dataset will update, hiding the rows of the items you unselected. Any time you see blue row headings, you know the dataset has been filtered. An icon that looks like a funnel will replace the arrow on the column headers that have a filter applied.

7. Open the drop-down of another column to filter.

8. Unselect the items you want hidden.

9. Click OK.

10. Filters are additive, which means that each time a filter selection is made, it works with the previous selection to further filter the data. The dataset now reflects only the records that were selected for both filters.

Turn Filter Off

The Filter button is a toggle button. Click it once to turn filtering on and click it again to turn filtering off.

Filtered rows

Filtered column

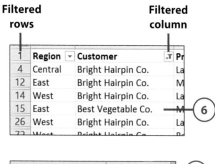

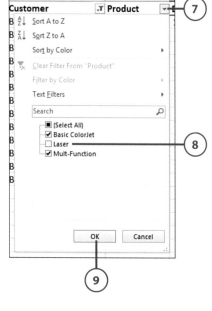

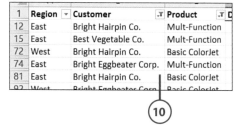

It's Not All Good

Excel Didn't Select the Dataset Correctly

When you apply a filter, Excel will try to help by selecting your dataset for you. You can help Excel do this correctly by not having any blank rows or columns in your dataset. Also, ensure that your header consists of only one row. Only a single header row is allowed—any rows after it are treated as data.

If Excel incorrectly selects your data, turn off the filter, delete the blank columns and rows, and start the previous steps over.

If for some reason you can't delete the blank columns or rows, you can pre-select the entire table before turning on the Filter functionality.

Clear a Filter

A filter can be cleared from a specific column or for the entire dataset.

1. On the Data tab, select Clear to clear all filters of the active dataset.

   Or

2. To clear a specific column, click the column's drop-down and select Clear Filter from "*Column Header*".

   Or

3. To clear a specific column, right-click over the column and from the Filter menu option, select Clear Filter from "*Column Header*".

Reapply a Filter

If data is added to a filtered range, Excel does not automatically update the view to hide any new rows that don't fit the filter settings. You can reapply the filter to work on the extended dataset.

1. On the Data tab, select Reapply.

   Or

2. Right-click a cell in the filtered dataset and select the Filter, Reapply menu option.

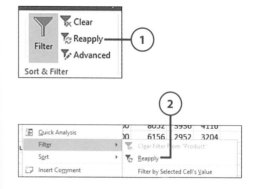

Turn the Filter On for One Column

Filtering can be turned on for a single column or for two or more adjacent columns. Even though you can only select filter items in the columns where the filter drop-downs appear, the filter is applied to the entire dataset.

1. Select the column to turn on the filter for.

2. On the Data tab, select Filter.

3. The filter drop-down will only be available for the selected column, but will apply the filter to the entire dataset.

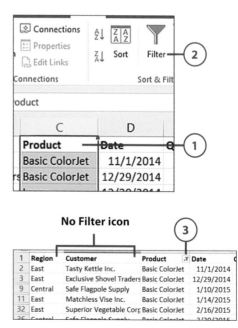

Filtering Grouped Dates

By default, dates in the filter list are grouped by month and year. If you click the + icon by a year, it opens up, showing the months. Click the + icon by a month, and it opens up to show the days of the month. An entire year or month can be selected or unselected by clicking the desired year or month.

Turn On Grouped Dates

The date grouping is controlled by a setting in the Options menu.

1. Select File.

2. Select Options.

3. Select the Advanced menu.

4. Under the Display Options for This Workbook heading, select the Group Dates in the AutoFilter Menu option.

5. Click OK.

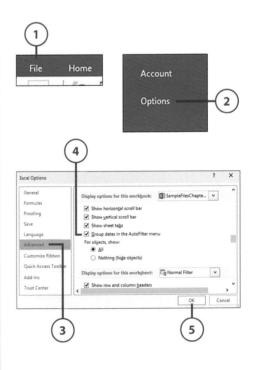

It's Not All Good

Grouped Dates Still Not On

If the group option is selected and the dates still aren't grouped (or if you have some dates grouped, but not others), it could be that the dates are formatted as text, not as true dates. See the section "Fixing Numbers Stored as Text" in Chapter 4, "Getting Data onto a Sheet," for steps to force the dates to be treated as dates.

Date stored as text ⎯⎯⎯⎯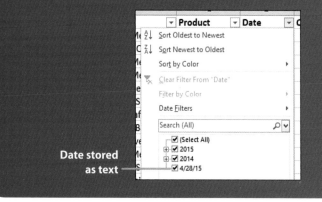

Filter by Date

Once the dates are grouped, you can filter for the desired dates.

1. Select a single cell in the dataset to apply filtering to.

2. On the Data tab, select Filter.

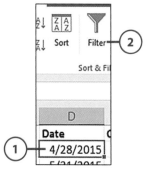

3. Open the drop-down of the date column to filter.

4. Click the + icon to open a group.

5. Click the – icon to close a group.

6. Selecting or unselecting a group parent, such as a month, will affect all the individual items within the group (in this case, the days) the same way.

7. Once the desired filters are in place, click OK. The sheet filters to show only the specified dates.

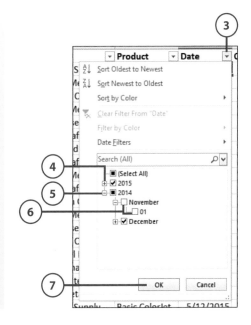

Using Special Filters

There are other ways to filter the data than by selecting from the list of items. You can filter by color, icon, or selection. Additional filter options are available in the filter drop-down depending on which data type (text, numbers, or dates) appears most often in a column.

Filter for Items that Include a Specific Term

Use the special text filters to select only records that include a desired term.

1. Open the filter drop-down.

2. From the Text Filters menu, select Contains.

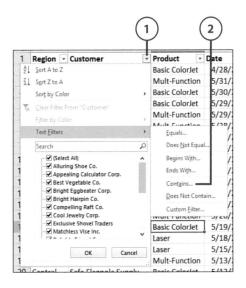

3. Enter the term the cell values should include. Use an asterisk (*) to replace multiple characters or a question mark (?) to replace a single character. For example, to return Supply or Supplies, search for Suppl*.

4. Click OK. The dataset will filter to show the desired records.

Use Conditions in the Custom Filter

The Custom AutoFilter dialog box allows you to combine search criteria. Select the And option if the result must meet both criteria. Select the Or option if the result can meet either or both criteria.

Filter for Values Within a Range

You can filter a numerical column for values that fall within or outside of a specific range.

1. Open the filter drop-down.

2. From the Number Filters menu, select Between.

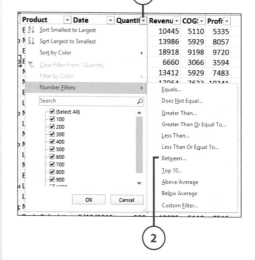

3. Select the desired comparison for the first value.

4. Enter the value.

5. Select And.

6. Select the desired comparison for the second value.

7. Enter the value.

8. Click OK. The dataset will filter to show only those values within the specified range.

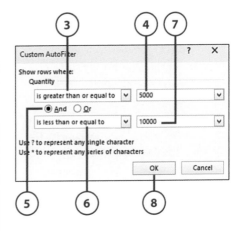

Filter for the Top 25 Items

You can filter to show specific records compared to the whole.

1. Open the filter drop-down.

2. From the Number Filters menu, select Top 10.

3. Select the desired comparison.

4. Enter the number of top values to include.

5. Choose the comparison type.

6. Click OK. The dataset will filter to show only those values that meet the criteria, in this case, the top 25 items.

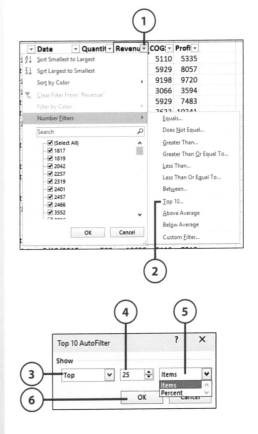

Filter Dates by Quarter

The options dealing with quarters refer to the traditional quarters of a year, with January through March being the first quarter, April through June being the second quarter, and so on.

1. Open the filter drop-down of the Date column.

2. Select a quarter, such as Last Quarter, from the Date Filters menu. The dataset will filter for last quarter's records.

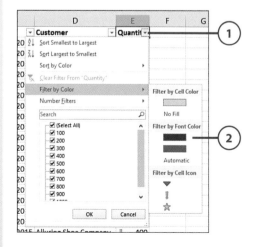

Filtering by Color or Icon

You can filter data by font color, cell color, or icon via the Filter by Color option in the filter listing.

1. Open the filter drop-down of a column with color or icons applied.

2. From the Filter by Color menu, select the desired filter option.

Filtering by Selection

You can filter a dataset without the filter on by right-clicking a cell and choosing to filter by the cell's value, color, font color, or icon. Doing so will turn on the Filter feature and configure the filter for the selected cell's property.

Filters are additive, so you can apply more than one using this method, including mixing and matching text and color.

1. Right-click the cell to filter by.

2. From the Filter menu, select Filter by Selected Cell's Value.

3. Right-click a cell in another column to filter by.

4. From the Filter menu, select the Filter by Selected Cell's Font Color.

5. The dataset is filtered by the two selections.

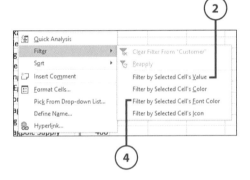

Allowing Users to Filter a Protected Sheet

Normally, if you set up filters on a sheet, protect the sheet, and then send it out to other users, the recipients won't be able to filter the data. But if you set up the protection properly, users won't be able to modify the data you've protected, but they'll be able to use Excel's various Filter tools.

Refer to "Protecting the Data on a Sheet" in Chapter 12, "Distributing and Printing a Workbook," for more information on sheet protection.

Filter a Protected Sheet

Turning on the correct option allows
users to filter a protected sheet.

1. Select a single cell in the dataset
    to apply filtering to.

2. On the Data tab, select Filter.

3. From the Review tab, select
    Protect Sheet.

4. Select Use AutoFilter.

5. Enter a password if desired.

6. Click OK.

7. If you entered a password in
    step 5, Excel will prompt you to
    reenter the password. Do so and
    then click OK.

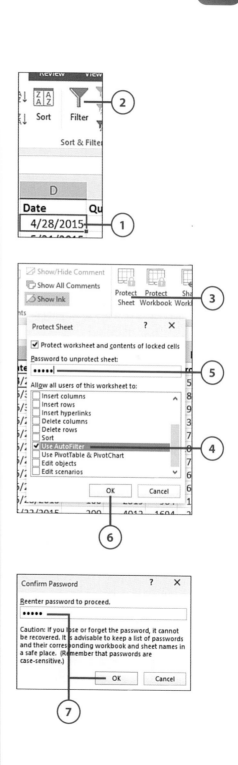

Using the Advanced Filter

Despite the visual simplicity of the Advanced Filter dialog box, it can perform a variety of functions, depending on the options selected and the setup on the sheet.

Reorganize Columns

The Advanced Filter can be used to reorganize columns with a few clicks of the mouse. And if this is something you do often, you can set up a template for reuse.

1. Copy the headers from the data-set to a new sheet (the report).

2. Reorganize the copied headers into the desired order. If the data-set has more columns than you need, delete the ones you won't be needing.

3. Select a cell to the right of the reorganized headers.

4. On the Data tab, select Advanced.

5. Select the Copy to Another Location option.

6. Select the List Range field's range selector button.

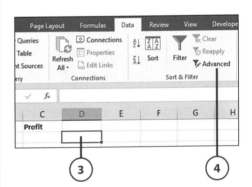

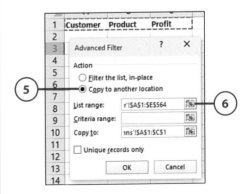

7. Select the entire dataset. Select the range selector button to return to the dialog box.

Keyboard Shortcut to Select Dataset

If you're used to keyboard shortcuts, you may be frustrated that Ctrl+A won't work in this situation. Instead, select the top-left cell of the dataset, press Ctrl+Shift+Right Arrow, and then press Ctrl+Shift+Down Arrow to select the dataset.

8. Select the Copy To range selector button.

9. Select the headers on the report sheet.

10. Select the range selector button to return to the dialog box.

11. Click OK.

12. The data will be copied to the report sheet. Only the columns with headers will be copied, and in the order you set them up.

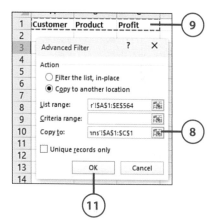

Create a List of Unique Items

When the Unique Records Only option is selected, the Advanced filter can be used to remove duplicates. Unlike with the Remove Duplicates command on the Data tab, the original dataset will remain intact if you choose to copy the results to a new location.

1. On the Data tab, select Advanced.

2. For the List Range field, select the column to create the unique listing from.

Filter the List, In-Place

Select Filter the List, In-Place to only hide the duplicate rows. You can use the Clear button on the Data tab to unhide the rows later.

3. Select Copy to Another Location to place the results in a new location, leaving the original dataset unchanged.

4. Place your cursor in the Copy To field. Select a cell on the sheet for the list to be placed. You cannot place the list on another sheet.

5. Select Unique Records Only.

6. Click OK. The unique list will be created in the selected location.

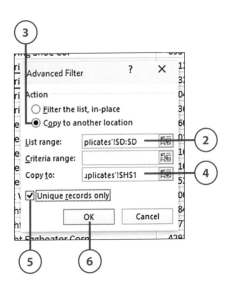

>>>*Go Further*

CREATE A UNIQUE LIST BASED ON MULTIPLE COLUMNS

You can create a list based on multiple columns if the columns are side by side. The List Range field works only with a single range, but if multiple columns are selected together, they are considered a single range.

The steps are the same as for a single column, but when you're filling in the List Range field, select all the desired columns.

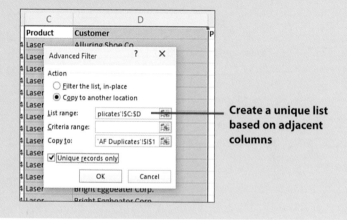

Create a unique list based on adjacent columns

Filter Records Using Criteria

Criteria are the rules by which you want to execute an Advanced Filter. It's an optional field in the Advanced Filter dialog box. Criteria can consist of exact values, values with operators, wildcards, or formulas.

In the following example, we want to create a new report with the following two sets of criteria: Region = West, Product = Laser, Profit > 4000; Region = West, Product = Basic ColorJet, Profit between 5000 and 10000.

1. In row 1 of the dataset sheet, but at least one column away from the dataset, enter the column headers you want to filter on. The text must match exactly, so you may want to copy/paste it. Because the criteria includes a profit range, enter **Profit** twice.

2. Starting in row 2, enter the criteria. For the first criterion, enter **West** under Region, **Laser** under Product, and **>4000** under the first Profit column.

3. Enter the second criterion in row 3. Enter **West** under Region, **Basic ColorJet** under Product, **>=5000** under the first Profit column, and **<=10000** under the second Profit column.

4. Copy the headers from the dataset to a new sheet (the report). You can reorganize or choose the columns filtered over. See "Reorganize Columns" for more information.

5. Select a cell to the right of the headers on the report sheet.

6. On the Data tab, select Advanced.

7. Select Copy to Another Location.

8. Select the List Range field's range selector button.

9. Select the entire dataset. Select the range selector button to return to the dialog box.

10. Select the Criteria Range field's range selector button.

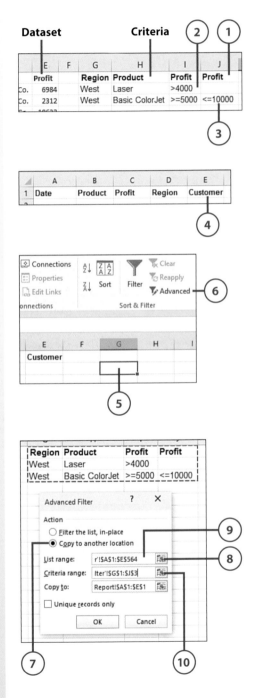

11. Select the criteria, including headers, on the dataset sheet. Select the range selector button to return to the dialog box.

12. Select the Copy To range selector button.

13. Select the headers on the report sheet. Select the range selector button to return to the dialog box.

14. Click OK. The data that fits the two criteria will be copied to the report sheet.

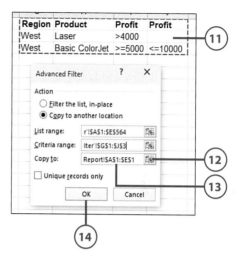

Region	Product	Profit	Profit
West	Laser	>4000	
West	Basic ColorJet	>=5000	<=10000

Advanced Filter

Action
○ Filter the list, in-place
● Copy to another location

List range: r'!$A$1:$E$564
Criteria range: Iter'!$G$1:$J$3
Copy to: Report!$A$1:$E$1

☐ Unique records only

OK   Cancel

>>>Go Further
TAKE CRITERIA TO THE NEXT LEVEL

Here are few rules to keep in mind when setting up criteria:

- Criteria entered on the same row are read as joined by AND.

- Criteria entered on different rows are read as joined by OR.

- If a cell in the criteria range is blank and has a column header, this is read as returning all records that match the column header.

- You can have the same header in the criteria twice (for example, if you're configuring a range).

- If the criteria is for blank cells, enter just an equal sign (=).

- Operators (<, >, <=, >=, <>) can be combined with numeric values for a more general filter.

- Wildcards can be used with text values. An asterisk (*) replaces any number of characters. A question mark (?) replaces a single character. The tilde (~) allows the use of wildcard characters in case the text being filtered uses such a character as part of its value.

Use Formulas as Criteria

You can combine basic criteria with formulas to create your report. If the criterion is a formula, do not use a column header because the formula is applied to the entire dataset. The formula should be one that returns a TRUE or FALSE value.

For example, you need to create a report of customers in the West region from whom you generated more than $4,000 in profit by selling laser print-ers. Your data spans a couple of years, so you want to narrow those results down to February and March of the current year. You also want to return any non-West region profits from January of the current year.

1. Set up the basic criteria and report sheet headers as outlined in the section "Filter Records Using Criteria."

2. In the same row as the criterion for the West region Laser product, enter the formula for the dates. The formula should use relative referencing and refer to the first row of data.

   =AND(YEAR(C2)=YEAR
   (TODAY()),OR(MONTH(C2)=2,
   MONTH(C2)=3))

3. Enter the second formula in the next row. It also refers to the first row of data.

   =AND(A2<>"West",YEAR(C2)=
   YEAR(TODAY()),MONTH(C2)=1)

4. Continue with the steps outlined in "Filter Records Using Criteria" to generate the report, making sure to include the formulas when selecting the criteria.

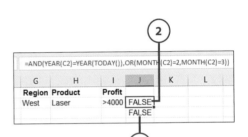

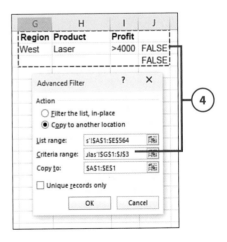

No Basic Criteria, No Problem

If the criteria consists only of formulas and there are no basic criteria with headers, start the formulas in row 2. Also, when selecting the criteria range, include the blank cell in row 1.

Removing Duplicates

The Remove Duplicates tool permanently deletes records from a dataset, unlike other filters, which just hide the rows. The Remove Duplicates dialog box allows you to select the columns to use for finding duplicates.

Delete Duplicate Rows

Because the Remove Duplicates tool permanently removes records from the dataset, you may want to make a backup copy of it.

1. Select a cell in the dataset.

2. On the Data tab, select Remove Duplicates.

3. Excel will highlight the dataset. If columns are missing in the selection, go back and make sure there are no blanks separating columns.

4. If the data has a header row, ensure My Data Has Headers is selected.

5. By default, all the columns are selected. A selected column means the tool will use the column when looking for duplicates. Duplicates in an unselected column will be ignored. In the Columns list box, select the columns to use in the search for duplicates.

6. Click OK.

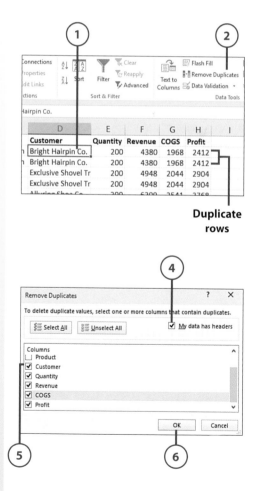

7. The dataset will update, deleting any duplicate rows. A message box will appear informing you of the number of rows deleted and the number remaining in the dataset.

Unique row

	Customer	Quantity	Revenue	COGS	Profit
nction	Bright Hairpin Co.	200	4380	1968	2412
lorJet	Exclusive Shovel Tr	200	4948	2044	2904
lorlet	Alluring Shoe Co	300	6309	2541	3768

Microsoft Excel   ✕

ⓘ   577 duplicate values found and removed; 549 unique values remain.

OK

Was this information helpful?

| nction | Remarkable Motor | 200 | 5508 | 541 | 2067 |

⑦

Consolidating Data

The Consolidate tool creates a report of unique records with combined data from different sheets and workbooks.

Merge Values from Two Datasets

You can merge values found on different sheets or in different workbooks based on their relative positions in the selected datasets. For example, if you're summing the ranges A1:A10 and C220:C230, the calculated results will be A1+C220, A2+C221, A3+C222, and so on.

1. Select the top leftmost cell where the consolidated report should be placed, such as cell A1. If there is other data in the sheet, make sure there is enough room for the new data.

Flash Fill   Consolidate — ②
Remove Duplicates   Relationships
Data Validation ▾   Manage Data Model
Data Tools

2. On the Data tab, select Consolidate.

3. Select the desired function.

4. Select the Reference field's range selector button.

5. Select the first dataset. Don't select any headers because they won't be included in the results. Select the range selector button to return to the dialog box.

6. Click the Add button.

7. Select the Reference field's range selector button.

8. Select the second dataset. Select the range selector button to return to the dialog box.

9. Click the Add button.

10. Click OK.

11. The selected calculation will be applied to the corresponding values in each dataset and placed on the report sheet.

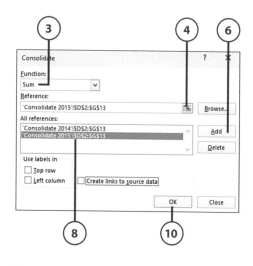

Consolidate with a Closed Workbook

If the dataset is in a closed workbook, you can reference it only by using a range name. Click the Browse button to find and select the workbook. After the exclamation point (!) at the end of the path in the Reference field, enter the range name assigned to the dataset.

Merge Data Based on Matching Labels

You can merge values found on different sheets or in different workbooks based on matching row and column labels. If you're matching row labels, they must be in the leftmost column of the ranges.

1. Select the top leftmost cell where the consolidated report should be placed, such as cell A1. If there is other data in the sheet, make sure there is enough room for the new data.

2. On the Data tab, select Consolidate.

3. Select the desired function.

4. Select the Reference field's range selector button.

5. Select the first dataset. Include the labels that should be used for the matching. Select the range selector button to return to the dialog box.

6. Click the Add button.

7. Select the Reference field's range selector button.

8. Select the second dataset, including the labels. Select the range selector button to return to the dialog box.

9. Click the Add button.

10. Mark the Top Row and/or Left Column checkbox(es) to indicate where the labels are in relation to the data.

11. Click OK.

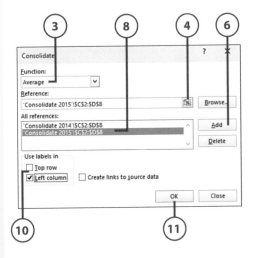

Row labels

12. Excel will match the labels and
apply the selected calculation to
the dataset and place the results
on the report sheet.

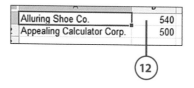

| Alluring Shoe Co. | 540 |
| Appealing Calculator Corp. | 500 |

(12)

>>>Go Further
LINK TO SOURCE DATA

If Create Links to Source Data is selected, the consolidated data will update
automatically when the source is changed. Also, the consolidated data will
be grouped. Click the + icon to the left of the data to open the group and see
the data used in the summary. If row labels were used to consolidate data, the
second column of the report will show the name of the workbook in the first
instance of its data.

Grouping buttons

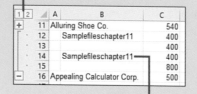

	A	B	C
11	Alluring Shoe Co.		540
12		Samplefileschapter11	400
13			400
14		Samplefileschapter11	400
15			800
16	Appealing Calculator Corp.		500

Originating file

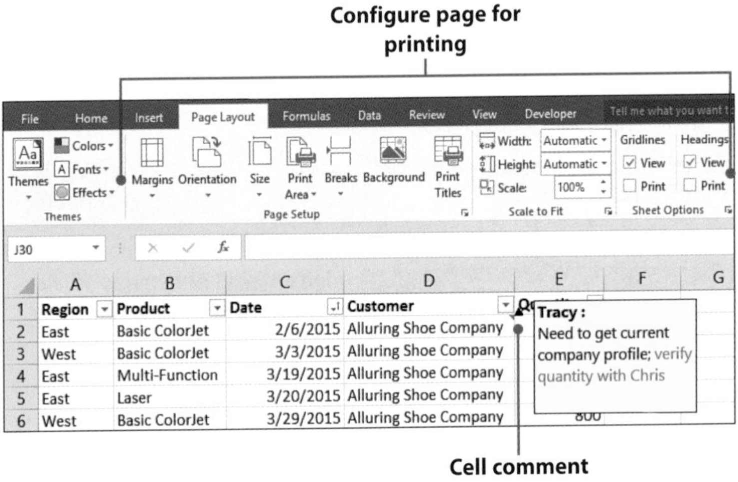

Configure page for printing
File
Home
Insert
Page Layout
Formulas
Data
Review
View
Developer
Themes
Colors
Fonts
Effects
Margins
Orientation
Size
Print Area
Breaks
Background
Print Titles
Page Setup
Width: Automatic
Height: Automatic
Scale: 100%
Scale to Fit
Gridlines
View
Print
Headings
View
Print
Sheet Options
J30
Region
Product
Date
Customer
East Basic ColorJet 2/6/2015 Alluring Shoe Company
West Basic ColorJet 3/3/2015 Alluring Shoe Company
East Multi-Function 3/19/2015 Alluring Shoe Company
East Laser 3/20/2015 Alluring Shoe Company
West Basic ColorJet 3/29/2015 Alluring Shoe Company
Tracy :
Need to get current company profile; verify quantity with Chris
Cell comment

In this chapter, you'll see how easy it is to leave notes in cells for users, freeze rows and columns so they don't move as you scroll, and set up a sheet for printing. Topics also include the following:

→ Allowing multiple users access to your workbook

→ Hiding sheets from other users

→ Customizing your page header or footer by adding a logo

→ Printing one sheet or the entire workbook

→ Protecting formulas or text from accidental overwrite

→ Verifying your workbook will work with different versions of Excel

→ Recovering lost data by retrieving a backup file

Distributing and Printing a Workbook

Once you're done designing your workbook, you probably want to share it with others. But first, you may want to do a little cleanup, such as adding comments so users can understand what goes in specific fields, hiding sheets you don't want users to see, or protecting certain cells so users cannot accidently erase your formulas. You can also protect the file so the wrong eyes can't pry into it.

Once all that's done, you have to decide how you want to share it. For example, will you print it out, put it on the network and allow multiple users access to it at the same time, or email it? And if you have users with a different version of Excel, such as Excel 2007, you need to ensure those users can access all areas of the workbook without a problem. This chapter shows you how to do this and more.

Using Cell Comments to Add Notes to Cells

Cell comments are comments or images you can attach to a cell that appear when the pointer is placed over the cell. By default, the cell comment looks like a yellow sticky note. You can tell if a cell has a comment by the red triangle in the upper-right corner of the cell.

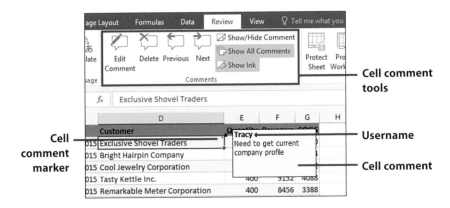

Insert a New Cell Comment

Cell comments are a great way to leave a note for other users. For example, you can explain where the value in a specific cell came from or provide instruction on the type of entry expected in a cell.

1. Select a cell to which to add the comment.

2. On the Review tab, select New Comment.

Another Way to Insert a Comment

You can also insert a comment by right-clicking over the cell, and selecting Insert Comment.

3. Type the desired text. The user-name is automatically entered by Excel.

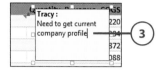

4. Click any cell on the sheet to exit from the comment.

Change the Username

The name shown at the top of the com-ment is controlled by the username in Excel. This can be changed in the Excel Options dialog box's General section.

Edit a Cell Comment

Any text in the comment can be edited, including the username.

1. Select the cell with the comment to edit.

2. On the Review tab, select Edit Comment.

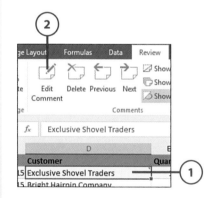

Another Way to Select Edit Comment

Right-click over the cell and select Edit Comment.

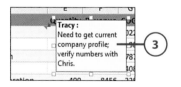

3. Make the desired change to the comment.

4. Click any cell on the sheet to exit from the comment.

Comment Already Visible

If the comment is already visible, just click in the comment box to make changes to the text.

Format a Cell Comment

Once you've inserted a cell comment, you can format it.

1. Select the cell with the comment to edit.

2. On the Review tab, select Edit Comment.

3. Place the pointer on the edge of the comment box so it turns into a four-headed arrow.

4. Right-click and select Format Comment.

5. Select the desired font styling on the Font tab. Font changes affect all the text in the comment.

6. Change the alignment of the selected text on the Alignment tab.

7. Change the color of the comment box and the frame around it on the Colors and Lines tab.

8. Set the size of the comment box on the Size tab.

9. Protect the comment box from accidental changes by selecting the check boxes on the Protection tab and protecting the sheet. When selected, the Locked option prevents the comment box from being moved or resized; the Lock Text option prevents the text from being changed.

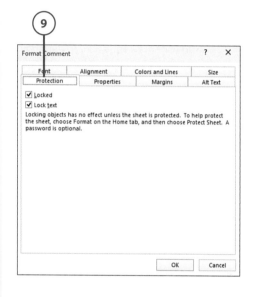

10. Control what happens to the comment box as other cells are sized and moved by choosing the desired option on the Properties tab.

11. On the Margins tab, set the inner margins of the comment box.

12. If you're going to save the file as an HTML type file, you can enter alternative text for the web browser to display by entering it on the Alt Text tab.

13. Click OK.

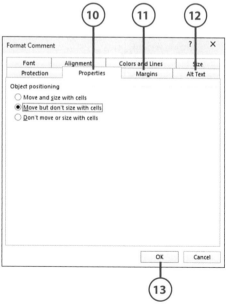

Insert an Image into a Cell Comment

You can insert an image into a cell comment as a background fill. The image will take up the entire box and resize as you resize the box. You can still type text in the comment, and it will appear on top of the image.

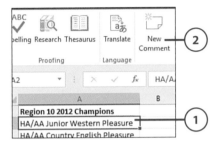

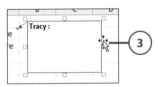

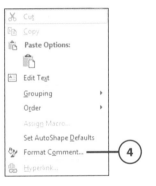

1. Select a cell to which to add the comment.

2. On the Review tab, select New Comment.

3. Place the pointer along the edge of the comment until it turns into a four-headed arrow.

4. Right-click and select Format Comment.

No Colors and Lines Tab

If the Format Comment dialog box that opens only has one tab (Font), close the dialog box and try again. The dialog box that appears should have multiple tabs.

5. On the Colors and Lines tab, select Fill Effects from the Color drop-down.

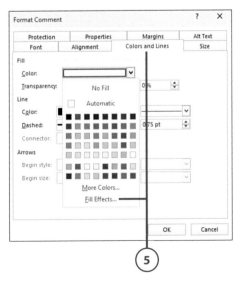

6. On the Picture tab, click Select Picture.

7. Select From a File to browse for the image stored locally, on a network or online drive.

8. Search the Internet for images with a Bing Image Search. Enter keywords in the Search Bing field and press Enter.

Creative Commons

Results returned by Bing may be licensed under Creative Commons. There are different types of CC licenses and you should verify that your usage of the image—for example, if you will be distributing the workbook—falls within the terms of distribution.

More Image Location Options

You might have more image location options listed if you have connected your account to other services, such as OneDrive and Facebook.

9. Select the desired image and click Insert.

10. Select Lock Picture Aspect Ratio to lock the image ratio.

11. Click OK twice to return to Excel.

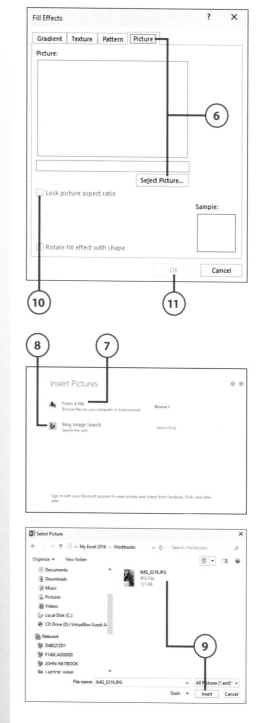

12. Use the sizing handles to resize the comment box.

13. When you click in the comment box, the image is hidden so you can see the text. Highlight the text in the comment box.

14. Right-click within the comment box and select Format Comment.

15. From the Color drop-down of the Font tab, select a new color for the font.

16. Click OK.

17. Click any cell on the sheet to exit from the comment. Place your pointer over the cell comment to view the image.

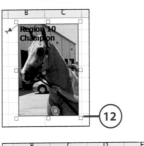

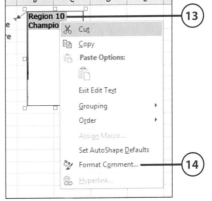

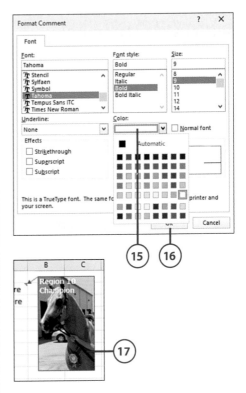

Resize a Cell Comment

Resize a comment so all the text or the entire image can be seen.

1. Select the cell with the comment to edit.

2. On the Review tab, click Edit Comment.

3. Click and drag any of the sizing handles (small white squares) around the comment. When the comment is the size you want, release the mouse button.

4. Click any cell on the sheet to exit from the comment.

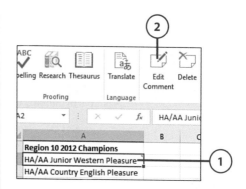

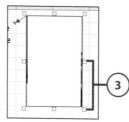

Show and Hide Cell Comments

A cell comment becomes visible when the pointer passes over the cell and then hides again once the pointer moves away from the cell. You can keep all or some cell comments visible at all times.

1. On the Review tab, select Show All Comments to make all comments in the workbook visible.

2. If Show All Comments is active, select it again to hide all comments.

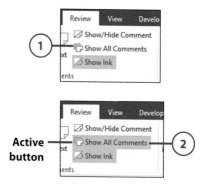

Active button

Show All Comments Not Active

If comments have been individually set to be visible, Show All Comments won't appear active. However, you can still use it to hide all comments by clicking it twice—the first click makes them all visible, the second click hides them.

>>>Go Further
SHOW/HIDE COMMENTS FOR A SINGLE CELL

You can show/hide the comment of a single cell by selecting the cell with the comment and then using one of these methods:

- On the Review tab, select Show/Hide Comment to toggle the comment's visibility.

- Right-click over the cell and select Show/Hide Comments to make the comment visible.

- Right-click over a cell and select Hide Comment to hide that cell's comment.

Review	View	Develop
Show/Hide Comment		
Show All Comments		
Show Ink		

Edit Comment
Delete Comment
Show/Hide Comments

Edit Comment
Delete Comment
Hide Comment

Toggle comment visibility of the selected cell

Show the selected cell's comment

Hide the selected cell's comment

Delete a Cell Comment

Delete a comment to remove it entirely from the cell, including the indicator. If you want to remove the text, refer to the section "Edit a Cell Comment."

1. Select the cell with the comment to delete.

2. On the Review tab, click Delete.

Another Way to Delete a Comment

Right-click over the cell and select Delete Comment.

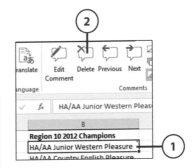

Allowing Multiple Users to Edit a Workbook at the Same Time

Excel workbooks are not designed to be accessed by multiple users at the same time. But Microsoft understands that sometimes there is a need for more than one person to edit a workbook at the same time and has provided a limited option.

It's Not All Good

A Double-Edged Sword

Although Excel allows for multiple user access, what users can do with a shared workbook is severely limited. A shared workbook cannot have tables. Although existing conditional formatting, validation, charts, hyperlinks, subtotals, or scenarios are allowed, new ones cannot be added. Cells cannot be merged and pivot tables cannot be changed. Nor can users write macros or edit array formulas. Basically, only the simplest workbook, such as for data entry, is shareable.

If you need to share a workbook with more advanced options available, such as pivot tables, consider uploading the workbook to your OneDrive. Although not as powerful as the desktop version of Excel, the Excel Web App offers a lot of options. See "Sharing a File Online" later in this chapter for more information.

Share a Workbook

You can turn on workbook sharing and save the file to a network location, allowing multiple users to access it.

1.   On the Review tab, click Share Workbook.

Protect   Protect   Share
Sheet   Workbook Workbook

①

2. Select Allow Changes by More Than One User at the Same Time.

3. Click the Advanced tab.

4. Configure how long the change history should be kept.

5. Choose how copies are updated: when the file is saved or automatically every few minutes.

6. Choose how conflicts should be handled.

7. Select Print Settings if you want users to use their own printings.

8. Select Filter Settings if you want users to use their own filter settings.

9. Click OK.

10. Excel prompts you to save the workbook. Click OK to share the workbook.

Unshare a Workbook

To unshare a workbook, deselect Allow Changes by More Than One User at the Same Time. When you click OK, Excel warns you that the workbook will no longer be shareable, the change history will be removed, and if anyone is currently editing the workbook, changes won't be saved. If you click Yes, Excel will unshare the workbook and save it.

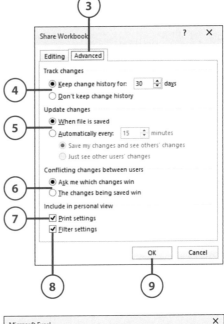

Hiding and Unhiding Sheets

The option of hiding sheets allows you present a cleaner looking workbook to users—there's no need for them to see your raw data or calculation sheets.

Hide a Sheet

You can hide sheets you don't want others to see, just make sure one sheet is left visible.

1. Right-click the sheet's tab and select Hide.

Another Way to Hide a Sheet

With the sheet you want to hide active, on the Home tab, click the Format drop-down. From the Hide & Unhide menu, select Hide Sheet.

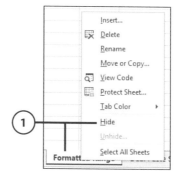

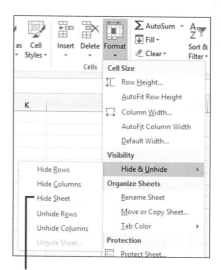

Hide the active sheet

Unhide a Sheet

Unhide sheets when you need to work on them.

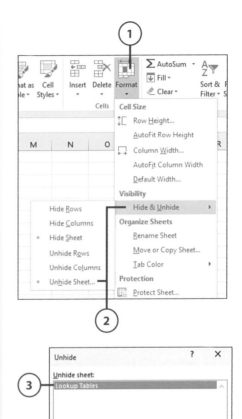

1. On the Home tab, click the Format drop-down.

2. From the Hide & Unhide menu, select Unhide Sheet.

3. Select the sheet to unhide.

4. Click OK.

Can't Hide or Unhide Sheets

If the workbook is protected (Review tab, Protect Workbook), sheets cannot be hidden or unhidden. See "Set Workbook-Level Protection" later in this chapter for more information.

Using Freeze Panes

With the Freeze Panes options, you can force the top rows, leftmost columns, or both to remain visible as you scroll around the sheet.

The Table Exception

If you have your data in a table, you don't need to freeze the top row to keep it visible. Instead, when you scroll the display so that the header row is no longer visible, Excel places the table headers in the headings area for you, replacing the column letters.

Table headers replacing
the column headings

Normal column
heading

If the headers do not appear in the column headings when scrolling, ensure that you don't have the Freeze Panes option turned on and that you do have a cell in the table selected.

Lock the Top Row

You can lock the first row on a sheet so that, as you scroll down the sheet, you can still see the top row.

1. From the Freeze Panes drop-down on the View tab, select Freeze Top Row.

2. To unfreeze the top row, from the Freeze Panes drop-down on the View tab, select Unfreeze Panes.

Lock the First Column

You can lock the leftmost column on a sheet so that, as you scroll across the sheet, you can still see the left column. To do this, select Freeze First Column from the Freeze Panes drop-down on the View tab.

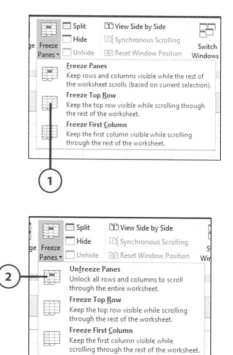

Lock Multiple Rows and Columns

When you use the Freeze Top Row or Freeze First Column option, the selection of one automatically undoes the selection of the other. So, if you want to freeze both the top row and first column, or multiple rows and/or columns, you must use the Freeze Panes option.

These columns will be frozen.

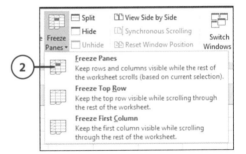

This row will be frozen.

1. Select a cell in the row directly below the row and directly to the right of the column you want to freeze.

Freeze Rows or Columns, Not Both

If you only want to freeze rows, select a cell in column A; if you only want to freeze columns, select a cell in row 1.

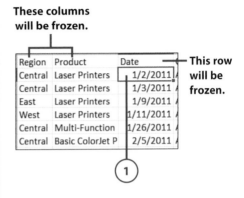

2. From the Freeze Panes drop-down on the View tab, select Freeze Panes.

3. To unfreeze the rows and/or columns, select Unfreeze Panes from the Freeze Panes drop-down on the View tab.

It's Not All Good

You Can't Choose What You Unfreeze

If you have rows and columns frozen, you can't choose to unfreeze one or the other. You must unfreeze them all and then refreeze the part you want to keep frozen.

Configuring the Page Setup

Page setup refers to settings that control how a sheet will look when it is printing. These settings not only include standard print settings, such as the page orientation (portrait or landscape), paper size, and page margins, but they also include settings for repeating rows and columns, printing gridlines, headings, and comments, and more.

Set Paper Size, Margins, and Orientation

You can print your sheet using basic print settings.

1. Click the Page Layout tab.

2. From the Orientation drop-down, select the page orientation.

3. From the Size drop-down, select a paper size.

4. From the Margins drop-down, select a margin configuration.

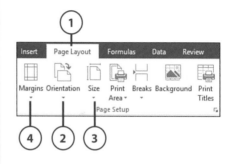

>>>Go Further

CUSTOM MARGINS

If the margins you need aren't found in the drop-down, you can set them up. Select Custom Margins from the Margins drop-down to open the Page Setup dialog box, where you can adjust the margins as needed.

Custom margins set up

Set the Print Area

The *print area* is the portion of the sheet that you want to print. By default, it begins in cell A1 and extends down and to the right to capture any cell that has been used, but this can be changed.

1. Select the range you want to set as the print area.

2. On the Page Layout tab, click Print Area and then select Set Print Area.

3. Print_Area will appear in the Name Box. You can select the name from the drop-down at any time to select (and verify) the print area.

Clear the Print Area

You can reset the print area back to Excel's suggestion by selecting Clear Print Area from the Print Area drop-down on the Page Layout tab.

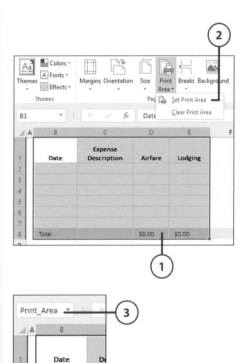

Set Page Breaks

In Page Break Preview, you can see and change breaks. A dashed blue line signifies an automatic page break. A solid blue line signifies a manually set page break.

1. On the View tab, click Page Break Preview.

2. To set a horizontal page break, select the row directly beneath the row where you want the page break. For example, if you want the page break after row 15, select row 16.

3. To set a vertical page break, select the column directly to the right of the column where you want the page break. For example, if you want the page break after column E, select column F.

4. On the Page Layout tab, click Breaks and then click Insert Page Break.

5. A solid blue line will appear to show the manually set page break.

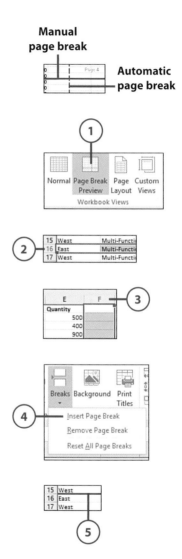

Move Existing Page Breaks

Place the pointer over an existing page break. When it turns into a two-headed arrow, click and drag it to a new location.

>>>Go Further

DELETE PAGE BREAKS

You can delete all the page breaks by selecting the Reset All Page Breaks from the Breaks drop-down on the Page Layout tab. You can also remove a specific page break.

1. To remove a vertical page break, select a cell directly to the right of the page break.

2. To remove a horizontal page break, select a cell directly below the page break.

3. On the Page Layout tab, click Breaks and then select Remove Page Break.

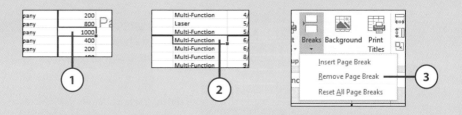

Another Way to Remove a Page Break

Place the pointer over an existing page break. When it turns into a two-headed arrow, click and drag it away from the print area, into the gray area. Note that if you pass over other page breaks, they will also be removed.

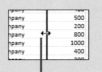

**Drag a page break
away to remove it**

Scale the Data to Fit a Printed Page

There are two ways get your data to fit on a page. You can customize the width and height of the data, and you can adjust the scale.

1. Click the Page Layout tab.

2. From the Width drop-down, select the number of desired pages to force a wide table (many columns) to print to fewer pages.

3. From the Height drop-down, select the number of desired pages to force a long table (many rows) to print to fewer pages.

Automatic Width and Height

When the width or height is set to Automatic, Excel sets the page breaks based on the scale, which means your dataset may print out on more than one page.

4. To print the sheet at its actual size, keep the percentage in the Scale field at 100%. The Scale field is used to adjust the scale of the entire sheet. Values less than 100% will reduce the size of the dataset; values greater than 100% will increase it.

Scale Not Available

To adjust the scale, both Height and Width must first be set to Automatic.

Repeat Specific Rows on Each Printed Page

When you have a report that spans several pages, you can repeat the top rows and leftmost columns on all the printed pages.

1. On the Page Layout tab, click Print Titles.

2. Click the range selector.

3. Select the rows to repeat. You can only select the entire row, not just a few columns of it.

4. Click the range selector again to return to the dialog box.

5. Click OK.

Repeat Specific Columns

To repeat specific columns, use the range selector for the Columns to Repeat at Left field to set up the columns. You can only select the entire column, not just a few rows of it.

Creating a Custom Header or Footer

The header and footer are unique to each sheet. Each header and footer is broken into sections: left section, center section, and right section. You can customize each of these three sections in the following ways:

- Add page numbering
- Add the current date and time
- Add the file path of the workbook
- Add the workbook name

- Add the sheet name

- Insert text

- Format any text, including the preceding options

- Insert and format an image

| Left section | Center section | Right section |

Region	Product	Date	Customer	Quantity
Central	Laser		1/2/2014 Alluring Shoe Company	500
Central	Laser		1/3/2014 Alluring Shoe Company	400
East	Laser		1/9/2014 Alluring Shoe Company	900
West	Laser		1/11/2014 Alluring Shoe Company	400

Add an Image to the Header or Footer

You can insert one image per section of a header or footer.

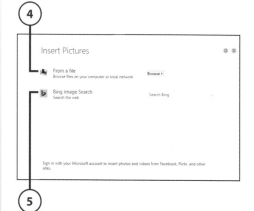

1. On the View tab, select Page Layout.

2. Click the section in which you want to place the image, such as the left section of the header.

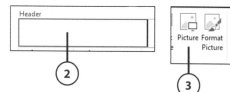

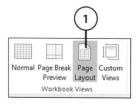

3. On the Header & Footer Tools Design tab, select Picture.

4. Select From a File to browse for the image stored locally, on a network or online drive.

5. Search the Internet for images with a Bing Image Search. Enter keywords in the Search Bing field and press Enter. Note that results returned by Bing may be licensed under Creative Commons.

6. Select the desired image.

7. Click Insert.

Not Seeing the Picture

Any time you're in Edit mode—your pointer is in a section—you will see the code for the picture (that is, &[Picture]). Once you are no longer editing the header or footer, the image will appear.

8. On the Design tab, select Format Picture.

9. Adjust the size of the picture on the Size tab.

10. Click OK.

Lock Aspect Ratio

If you know the needed height for the image to fit in the header but not the width, make sure Lock Aspect Ratio is selected before you adjust the height. The width will automatically adjust, preserving the ratio of the image.

11. Click anywhere outside the header or footer, and the image appears. If you need to modify the image even more, click in the section to re-enter Edit mode.

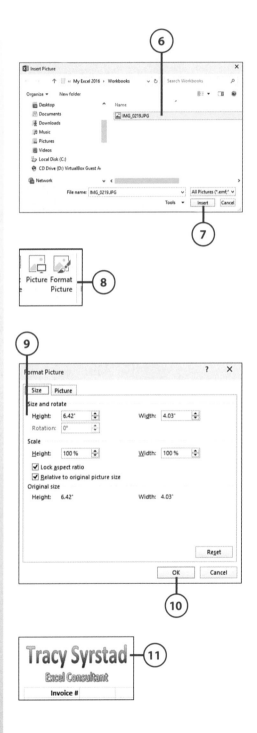

Add Page Numbering to the Header and Footer

You can show just the page number (1, 2, 3, and so on) or you can show the page number out of the total number of pages (1 of 5). If you select multiple sheets when printing, the page numbering will be consecutive for the selected sheets in the order they appear in the workbook.

1. On the View tab, select Page Layout.

2. Click the section you want to place the page numbering in.

3. On the Header & Footer Tools Design tab, select Page Number to place the page number code (&[Page]) in the section.

4. To include the total number of pages, type **of** (with a space on either side of it). Then, on the Design tab, click Number of Pages.

5. Click anywhere outside the footer, and you will see the current page number and the total number of pages.

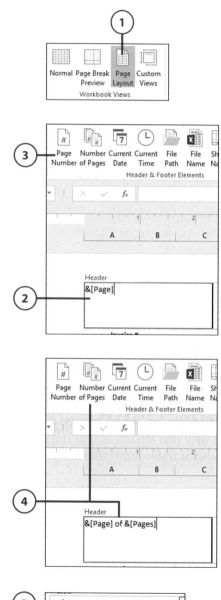

>>>*Go Further*
NONCONSECUTIVE PAGE NUMBERING

If you don't want consecutive page numbering across sheets, you need to force the first page number of each sheet.

To do this, go to Page Layout and click the Page Setup group's dialog box launcher. Near the bottom of the Page tab of the dialog box is a field labeled First Page Number. By default, it is set to Auto, but if you want each page numbering to start at 1 (or another number), you can set the page number here. If you do want the page numbering to be consecutive but it is not, make sure the First Page Number field is set to Auto.

Printing Sheets

Once you've configured a sheet for how you want it to print, printing it is easy.

Configure Print Options

Access to various print settings, such as the number of copies and the printer to print to, is available while previewing your sheet. If there's something you see in the preview that needs adjusting, you can make many adjustments here.

1. Click File to open Backstage view.

2. Select Print, and you'll enter Print Preview.

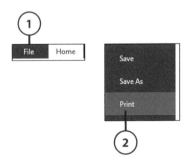

3. To print all visible sheets in the workbook, select Print Entire Workbook from the Print Active Sheets drop-down.

4. To print the selected range of the active sheet, select Print Selection from the Print Active Sheets drop-down.

5. On the right side of the screen is a print preview of the sheet. Move through the pages using the scroll wheel of the mouse, the Page Up and Page Down keys on the keyboard, or the arrows at the lower left of the Print Preview window.

6. Zoom in on the print preview by clicking the Zoom to Page button in the lower-right corner of the Print View window.

7. Click Show Margins to view the margins. You can move a margin by placing the pointer over one and clicking and dragging it to a new location.

8. When the sheet's page settings are properly configured, click Print to print it.

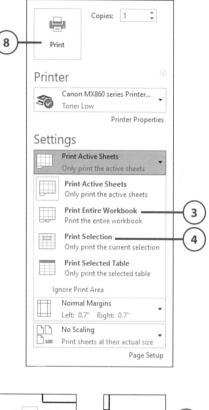

>>>*Go Further*

PRINT SPECIFIC SHEETS

To print specific sheets, you can hide the sheets you don't want to print and then use the Print Entire Workbook option. Alternatively, you can use the Ctrl key to select the tabs of the sheets to print. This second method doesn't require you to select a different print option or hide the sheets, yet it also updates the page numbering.

Protecting a Workbook from Unwanted Changes

After spending time setting up a workbook exactly right, you don't want another user to mess up your hard work. Or, perhaps your workbook contains sensitive data that should only be seen by certain people. Either way, Excel offers various methods of protection you may find useful.

Set File-Level Protection

Set a password at the file level to pre-vent an unauthorized user from opening a workbook. You can also allow a user to open the workbook but not save any changes, except as a new file.

1. In the Save As dialog box, from the Tools drop-down, select General Options.

2. Enter a password in the Password to Open field to prevent an unau-thorized user from opening the workbook.

3. Enter a password in the Password to Modify field to prevent the user from overwriting the workbook, though it can be saved with a new name or to a new location.

4. If you want to suggest to the user that the file be opened in read-only mode, check the Read-Only Recommended box. Note that this does not force the file to be opened read-only—it is provided as an option.

5. Click OK.

6. If you entered a password for opening the file, enter it again. Click OK.

7. If you entered a password for protecting the file from changes, enter it again. Click OK.

8. Click Save.

Remove File Protection

To remove the file protection, return to the General Options dialog box through the Save As option and remove the password. If the file is not read-only, you can overwrite the original file with the new protection settings.

Confirm Password ? ✕

Reenter password to proceed.

•••••

Caution: If you lose or forget the password, it cannot be recovered. It is advisable to keep a list of passwords and their corresponding workbook and sheet names in a safe place. (Remember that passwords are case-sensitive.)

OK   Cancel

6

Confirm Password ? ✕

Reenter password to modify.

••••••••••••••

Caution: Password to modify is not a security feature. This document is protected from unintentional editing. However, the document is not encrypted. Malicious users can edit the file and remove the password.

OK   Cancel

7

Set Workbook-Level Protection

Protection at the workbook level prevents a user from adding, deleting, or moving sheets.

1. On the Review tab, select Protect Workbook.

2. If you want, enter a password.

3. Click OK.

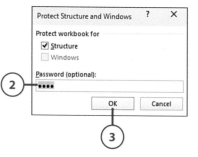

1

Protect Sheet   Protect Workbook   Share Workbook

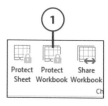

Protect Structure and Windows ? ✕

Protect workbook for

☑ Structure

☐ Windows

Password (optional):

••••

2

OK   Cancel

3

4. If you entered a password, confirm it and click OK.

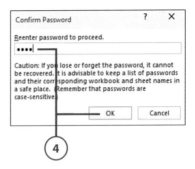

The Windows Option Is Greyed Out

It's not a mistake—the Windows option is greyed out and not usable. At the time of writing, it's no longer an option.

Protecting the Data on a Sheet

Protecting a sheet prevents users from changing the content of locked cells. By default, all cells have the locked option selected, and you purposefully unlock them (see the upcoming section "Unlock Cells").

Protect a Sheet

Sheet protection must be applied to each sheet individually.

1. On the Review tab, select Protect Sheet.

2. Select what actions a user can take on the sheet. If nothing is selected, the user can only scroll around the sheet. As options in the list are selected, the user can do more, such as enter data in unlocked cells or use the filter drop-downs.

3. Enter a password.

4. Click OK.

5. If you entered a password, confirm it and click OK.

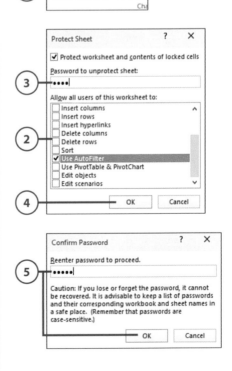

Unlock Cells

While a sheet is still unprotected, you can unlock specific cells so that when the sheet is protected, users can enter information in those cells. By default, all cells are locked.

1. Select the cells you want to unlock.

2. Right-click one of the cells and select Format Cells.

3. Uncheck the Locked option on the Protection tab.

4. Click OK.

5. Protect the sheet to protect the other cells.

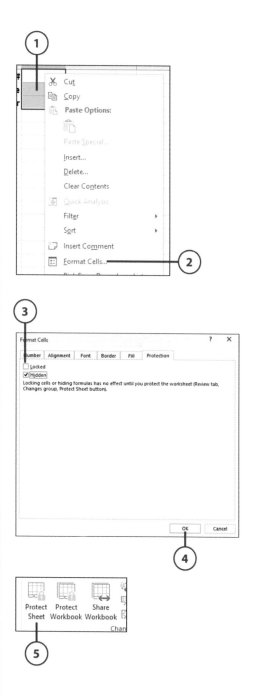

Allow Users to Edit Specific Ranges

Unlocking cells and protecting the sheet is an all-or-none solution. That is, none of your users will be able to modify the protected cells unless they can unprotect the sheet first. The Allow Users to Edit Ranges option lets you assign a password to specific ranges, allowing authorized users to edit those ranges while still protecting the rest of the sheet.

1. Select the cells you want config- ured for authorized users.

2. On the Review tab, select Allow Users to Edit Ranges.

3. Click New.

4. Enter a title for the selected range.

5. Refers to Cells should already reflect the cells you want to con- figure. If not, place your cursor in the field and select the cells on the sheet.

6. Enter the password for editing the range.

7. Click OK.

8. Reenter the password to confirm it and then click OK.

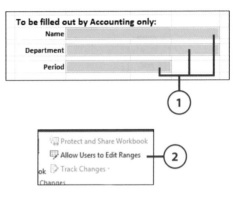

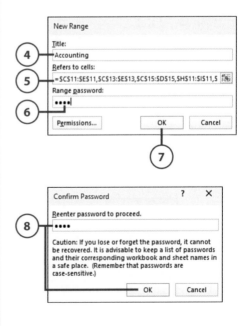

9. Click Protect Sheet.

10. Select the option Select Unlocked Cells; otherwise, users won't be able to select the configured range.

11. Select any other protection options and click OK.

12. The first time a user tries to enter data in the protected range, a password prompt will appear. If the user enters the correct password, the prompt won't appear again until the workbook is closed and then reopened.

Using the Permissions Option

Clicking Permissions allows you to add users or groups that won't have to enter a password to edit the protected range. Your network administrator can help you add the correct names.

Edit Allowed Ranges

To edit the allowed ranges, you must unprotect the sheet first.

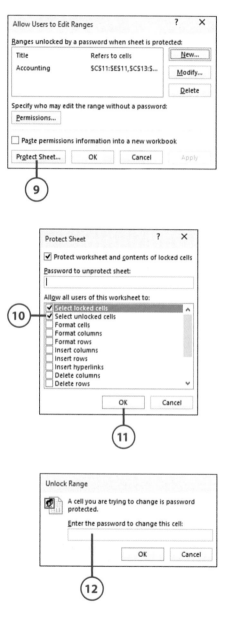

Preventing Changes by Marking a File as Final

You can inform users a workbook is final and shouldn't be edited, though the option to edit it is still available.

Mark a Workbook as Final

When you mark as final, the file becomes read-only.

1. Click File to open Backstage view.

2. On the Info page, select Mark as Final from the Protect Workbook drop-down.

3. Click OK to mark the workbook and save it.

4. Another message box will appear with more information about the final status. Click OK.

5. The workbook is now marked as final, but a button to edit it is available. If you click the button and save the file, repeat the steps to set the status to final again.

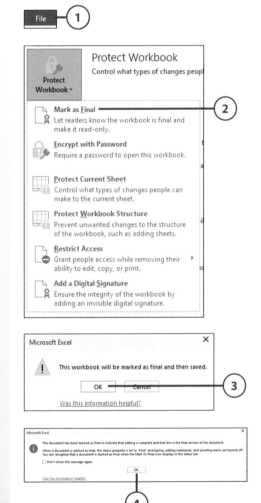

Sharing Files Between Excel Versions

Excel has made many changes over the years. If you plan to send your workbook to users with a version other than Excel 2016, you should ensure that the workbook is compatible with their version(s) of Excel.

Check Version Compatibility

When you check for version compatibility, Excel provides a list of significant and minor issues.

1. Click File to open Backstage view.

2. On the Info page, select Check Compatibility from the Check for Issues drop-down.

3. Select the version(s) to test for. By default, all versions since Excel 97 are selected.

4. Any compatibility issues are listed with a brief explanation, the versions affected, and whether the issue is significant or minor.

5. If it's an issue that must be resolved, such as a function not available in previous versions of Excel, click OK, fix the issue, and run the check again.

6. If a Find link appears next to the issue, Excel takes you directly to the issue when you click the link.

7. Select the check box if you want a compatibility check to automatically run whenever the workbook is saved.

8. Click Copy to New Sheet to copy the list of issues to a new sheet in the workbook.

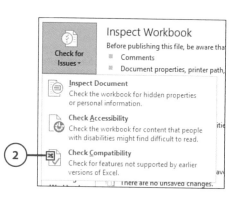

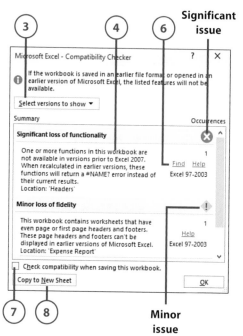

Recovering Lost Changes

Excel automatically creates backups of your workbook as you work on it. Depending on its configuration, it also saves a copy of your workbook if you close it without saving.

Excel won't keep the auto-recovered files forever. The backed-up copies of the workbook will be deleted under the following circumstances:

- When the file is manually saved
- When the file is saved with a new filename
- If you turn off AutoRecover for the workbook
- If you deselect Save AutoRecover in Excel Options
- When you close the file
- When you quit Excel

Configure Backups

Configure Excel to save backups of your open workbooks. Keep in mind that backing up large files often can slow down Excel.

1. Click File to open Backstage view.

2. Select Options.

3. Select Save.

4. Select the Save AutoRecover Information Every x Minutes option.

5. Set the number of minutes to a time frame that will work best for all of your workbooks.

6. Select Keep the Last Autosaved Version If I Close Without Saving and Excel saves the last backup copy it made if you close the workbook without saving.

7. Click OK.

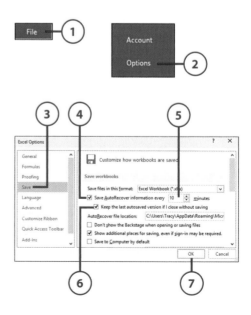

Turn Off AutoRecover on Specific Workbook

Turn off AutoRecover for a specific workbook by going to File, Options, Save. Then, under AutoRecover Exceptions For: Current Workbook, select Disable AutoRecover for This Workbook Only.

Recover a Backup

If Excel crashes, you might be able to recover backups of the workbooks that were open at the time.

1. If Document Recovery didn't open automatically when you started Excel, open the original workbook of which you want to retrieve a backup. Document Recovery lists the available backups for the workbook and any other backups it may have.

2. To open a backup, select Open from the drop-down of the desired workbook. If the currently opened workbook has the same name as the backup, it will be closed.

3. To save a unopened backup, select Save As from the drop-down of the desired workbook. The backup will be opened and the Save As dialog box will open. Save the workbook.

4. Click Close to close the Document Recovery window. Any backups that haven't been opened or saved will be deleted.

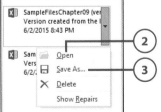

Recover Unsaved Files

If you have a new workbook open long enough for a backup to be created and Excel crashes before you can save it, or you close without saving, there's a chance you can recover the unsaved file.

1. Click File to open Backstage view.

2. On the Info page, select Recover Unsaved Workbooks from the Manage Workbook drop-down.

3. Select a workbook and click Open. The workbook will be opened in read-only mode.

4. To save the workbook, click the Save As button that appears at the top of the sheet. The Save As dialog box will open so that you can save the workbook.

Sending an Excel File as an Attachment

You can email your workbook right from Excel. Excel will open a new message window, attach the workbook, and give you a chance to enter the To and Subject lines and the message body.

Email a Workbook

When emailing a workbook, keep in mind the size of the workbook because different email servers have different size limitations on attachments.

1. Click File to open Backstage view.

2. On the Share page, select Email.

3. Select Send as Attachment.

4. Fill in the message fields of the email message and click Send.

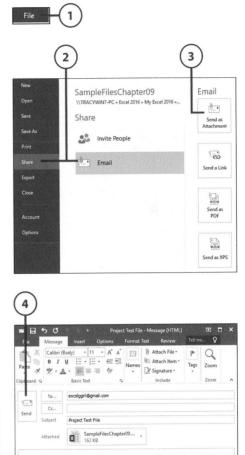

It's Not All Good

Opening Workbooks in Outlook

Outlook gives you the option to open workbooks from within emails. When you do this, a temporary copy of the workbook is created. Because some functionality in Excel requires a properly saved file, you may get errors when you try to work with the workbook. A safe practice is to always save a workbook to your desktop or another location on your hard drive before opening it.

Sharing a File Online

You don't need to email a file or save it to a network to share it with others. Microsoft offers space on OneDrive, a place online where you can save a file and allow others access.

Save to OneDrive

OneDrive is a free service by Microsoft for storing and sharing files. All you need to use it is a valid Microsoft account. For more information on setting up a OneDrive account and working with online workbooks, see Chapter 17, "Introducing the Excel Web App."

1. Click File to open Backstage view.

2. On the Save As page, select OneDrive.

3. If you aren't signed in to OneDrive, click Sign In. Follow the prompts to sign in to your account. Once signed in, you will be returned to the Save As page. Click OneDrive again.

4. Select a folder on your OneDrive.

5. Enter a filename, choose a Save As type, and click Save. The file will be saved to your local OneDrive folder and synchronized to the online account.

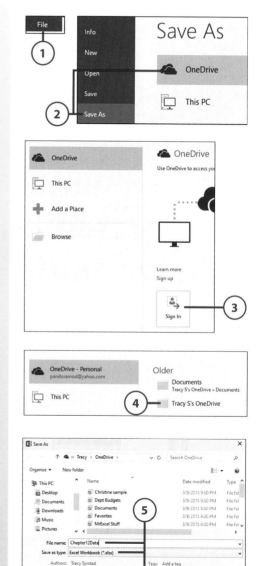

6. Return to Backstage view and click Share.

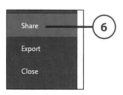

7. If it's not already highlighted, select Share with People.

8. Click the Share with People button to send an email to those with which you want to share the file. You'll be returned to your sheet, with the Share task pane open.

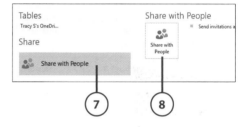

9. In the Share task pane, fill in the recipients' email addresses. Use a semicolon (;) to separate multiple addresses.

10. Select whether the recipients can edit the workbook or only view it.

11. Enter a message to the recipients.

12. Click Share to send the message. Note that the message is not sent through your local email application but via OneDrive's online system.

Share a Link

You can also share the workbook by providing a link. Click the Get a Sharing Link in the Share task pane to get a link that you can share any way you please: via email, blog, and so on.

Share a link to your workbook

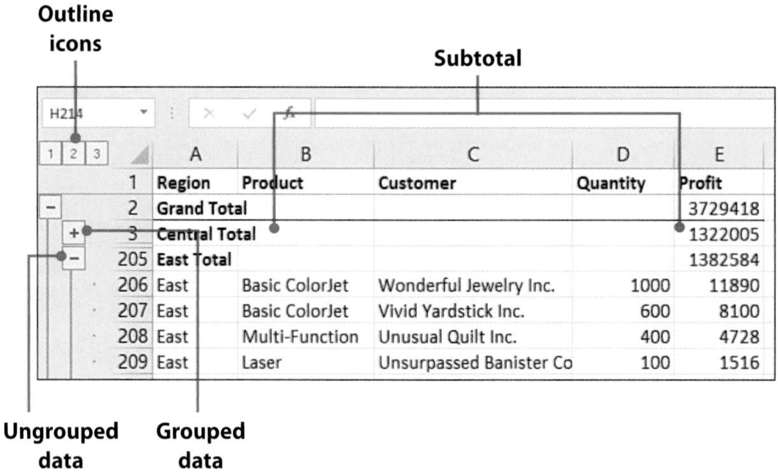

Outline icons

Subtotal

		A	B	C	D	E
	1	Region	Product	Customer	Quantity	Profit
−	2	Grand Total				3729418
+	3	Central Total				1322005
−	205	East Total				1382584
	206	East	Basic ColorJet	Wonderful Jewelry Inc.	1000	11890
	207	East	Basic ColorJet	Vivid Yardstick Inc.	600	8100
	208	East	Multi-Function	Unusual Quilt Inc.	400	4728
	209	East	Laser	Unsurpassed Banister Co	100	1516

H214

1 2 3

Ungrouped data   **Grouped data**

This chapter shows you how data can be summarized and grouped together using Excel's Subtotal and grouping tools. Topics include the following:

→ Manually entering subtotal rows using the SUBTOTAL function

→ Automatically summarizing data using the Subtotal tool

→ Copying just the subtotals to a new sheet

→ Grouping information so you can quickly show or hide data

Inserting Subtotals and Grouping Data

The ability to group and subtotal data allows you to summarize a long sheet of data into fewer rows. The individual records are still there, so you can unhide them if you need to investigate a subtotal in detail.

Using the SUBTOTAL Function

The SUBTOTAL function ignores the values of other SUBTOTALs within the assigned range, which means your calculated value won't get doubled. It also calculates the range of numbers based on a code used in the function. With the correct code, SUBTOTAL can calculate averages, counts, sums, and more. It can also ignore hidden rows when the 100 version (101, 102, and so on) of the code is used. The syntax of the SUBTOTAL function is as follows:

SUBTOTAL(function_num, ref1,[ref2],…)

Calculate Visible Rows

Most functions will calculate all values in its range, whether they are visible or not. If you want to ignore the hidden values, use the SUBTOTAL function with the 100 version of the desired calculation code.

1. Select the cell for the formula.

2. Type =**SUBTOTAL(**.

3. A drop-down of the various codes appears. The first 11 are like their corresponding functions. For example, 9 - SUM will sum all values. Scroll down to see the 100 codes that calculate only the visible cells. Select the desired code and press Tab, or double-click it.

4. Type a comma to move over to the next argument and then select the range to calculate.

5. Type the closing parenthesis and press Enter or Tab to calculate the formula.

6. Hide some rows in the range. The value will update to reflect the visible cells only.

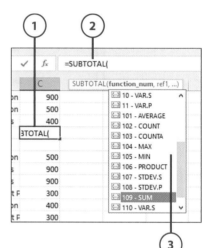

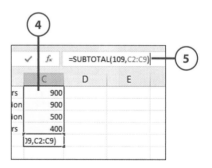

Hidden rows

Summarizing Data Using the Subtotal Tool

The SUBTOTAL function is useful, but if you have a large dataset, it can be time consuming to insert all the total rows. When your dataset is large, use the Subtotal tool on the Data tab. This tool groups the sorted data, applying the selected function.

The Table Limitation

You cannot use the Subtotal tool on a range that has been converted to a table.

Apply a Subtotal

Applying subtotals to a dataset is quick and easy when using the Subtotal dialog box. Because Excel will group the subtotals based on the changing data in the column you select, you need to sort the data in that column first.

Refer to Chapter 10, "Sorting Data," for more information on sorting.

1. Sort the data by the column on which the summary should be based.

2. Select a cell in the dataset.

3. On the Data tab, click Subtotal.

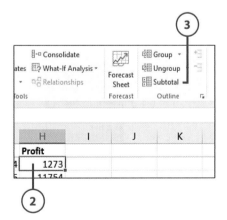

4. Select the column by which to summarize the data—the same column you sorted the data by in step 1.

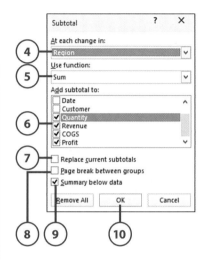

5. Select the function by which the subtotals will be calculated.

6. Select the column(s) to which the subtotals should be added.

7. Check Replace Current Subtotals if subtotals are already in the dataset and you want to replace them.

8. Check Page Break Between Groups if you want to print each subtotaled group on its own page.

9. Select Summary Below Data to place the totals below each group. Uncheck the box if you want the totals above the group.

10. Click OK. The data is grouped and subtotaled, with a grand total at the very bottom (or top, if that's what you configured).

Subtotal by Multiple Columns

To subtotal by multiple columns—for example, to sum the quantity of each product within a region—sort the dataset by the desired columns and then apply the subtotals, making sure Replace Current Subtotals is not selected. The sort and subtotals should be applied in order of highest level (Region) to lowest level (Product).

Expand and Collapse Subtotals

Use the outline symbols to the left of the data to expand and collapse the subtotaled data. The numbers represent the subtotal levels in the dataset.

1. Click 1 to view only the Grand Total.

2. Click 2 to view the first level of subtotals.

3. Click the last number in the set (in this case, 3) to view the data.

4. Click a + icon to expand a grouping.

5. Click a − icon to collapse a grouping.

Remove Subtotals or Groups

You can remove all the subtotals and groups or choose to remove only outline buttons, leaving the subtotals in place.

1. Select a cell in the grouped data.

2. On the Data tab, click Subtotal.

3. Click Remove All to remove all the subtotals and groups.

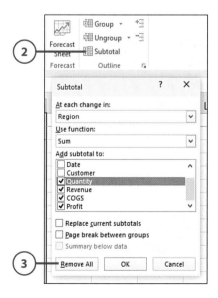

Clear Outline But Retain Subtotals

On the Data tab, click the Ungroup drop-down and then click Clear Outline to remove only the group and outline buttons, leaving the subtotal rows intact.

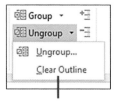

Clear the outline but retain the subtotals

Toggling the Outline Buttons

Press Ctrl+8 to toggle the visibility of the outline buttons.

Undoing Clear Outline

You cannot undo Clear Outline. If you accidentally select the option, click a cell in the table, bring up the Subtotal dialog box, and click OK. The symbols will be replaced.

Sort Subtotals

If you try to sort a subtotaled data-set while viewing all the data, Excel informs you that to do so will remove all the subtotals. You have to sort each grouped dataset individually.

1. Select the cells you want to sort, ensuring no column headers or total rows are included in the range.

2. On the Data tab, click Sort.

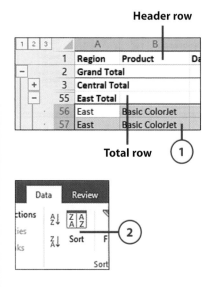

Header row

Total row (1)

(2)

3. Unselect the My Data Has Headers box.

4. Select the column by which to sort.

5. Select the sort order.

6. Click OK. The selected data will be sorted.

Sort Total Rows Only

If you just want to sort the total rows, not the data itself, collapse the dataset so you only see the totals, select a cell in the column with the Total text, and then apply the desired sort.

It's Not All Good

The Sort Dialog Box Option Changes Stick

If you follow instructions for sorting a dataset and then try to sort the subtotals, you may find your data all messed up. That's because the changes made in the Sort dialog box, specifically unchecking the My Data Has Headers box, are still in effect. If you are in doubt of what sort settings are in effect, open the Sort dialog box and check.

Copying the Subtotals to a New Location

With a few clicks of the mouse, you can copy and paste just the subtotals to a new location.

Copy Subtotals

Instead of providing all the individual
records used to calculate the subtotals,
copy and paste just the calculated totals.

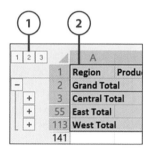

1. Click the Outline icon so that only
   the rows you want to copy are
   visible.

2. Select the entire dataset. If the
   headers are to be included, this
   can be quickly done by selecting
   a single cell in the dataset and
   pressing Ctrl+A.

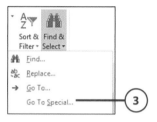

3. On the Home tab, click Go To
   Special from the Find & Select
   drop-down.

4. Select Visible Cells Only, and then
   click OK.

Select Visible Cells Keyboard Shortcut

Instead of using the Go To Special dialog
box, press Alt+; (semicolon) to select
only the visible cells.

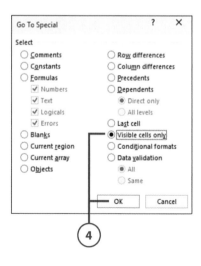

5. On the Home tab, click Copy.

6. Select the top-left cell where the data is to be pasted.

7. On the Home tab, click the Paste button.

8. The selection is pasted to the new location, and the SUBTOTAL formulas are converted into values.

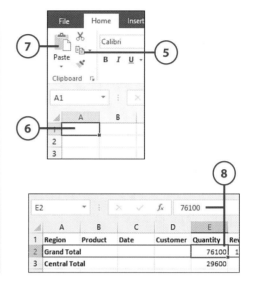

Formatting the Subtotals

Use steps 1–4 to select the dataset; then, instead of copying the data, apply the desired formatting.

Applying Different Subtotal Function Types

A dataset can have more than one type of subtotal applied to it—for example, a sum subtotal of one column and a count subtotal of another. Because you can only select one function at a time, you will have to use the Subtotal dialog box multiple times.

Create Multiple Subtotal Results on Multiple Rows

You can calculate multiple subtotals to a dataset by using the Subtotal dialog box for each calculation type.

1. Sort the data by the column on which the summary should be based.

2. Select a cell in the dataset.

3. On the Data tab, click Subtotal.

4. Select the column by which to summarize the data—the same column you sorted the data by in step 1.

5. Select the function by which the subtotals should be calculated.

6. Select the column(s) to which the subtotals should be added.

7. Click OK.

8. On the Data tab, click Subtotal.

9. Uncheck the Replace Current Subtotals box.

10. Select the function by which the subtotals should be calculated.

11. Select the column(s) to which the subtotals should be added.

12. Click OK.

13. The dataset reflects two subtotals, each on its own row.

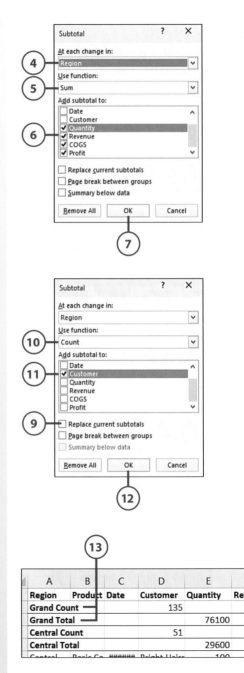

A	B	C	D	E	
Region	**Product**	**Date**	**Customer**	**Quantity**	**Re**
Grand Count			135		
Grand Total				76100	
Central Count			51		
Central Total				29600	
Central	Basic Co	#######	Bright Hair	100	

Combine Multiple Subtotal Results to One Row

When you're applying multiple function types, Excel places each subtotal on its own row. There is no built-in option to have the subtotals appear on the same row. However, you can manipulate Excel to make this happen by including all the desired columns when setting up the first subtotal. Then, you manually change the formulas to use the subtotal code actually needed.

1. Sort the data by the column on which the summary should be based.

2. Select a cell in the dataset.

3. On the Data tab, click Subtotal.

4. Select the column by which to summarize the data—the same column you sorted the data by in step 1.

5. Select the function by which most of the subtotals will be calculated.

6. Select the column(s) to which the subtotals should be added. Include the column to which the second subtotal function would apply. For example, if you're first applying a sum to Revenue and then applying a count to Customer, include the Customer column now.

7. Click OK.

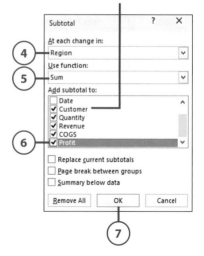

8. Click the "2" icon to collapse the dataset to show only the total rows.

9. Select the data in the column where the second function type should be.

10. Press Alt+; (semicolon) to select the visible cells.

11. In the formula bar, change the current subtotal code to the one you want. For example, to get a count instead of a sum, change the 9 to a 3. Press Ctrl+Enter to apply the change to the selected range.

12. The dataset reflects different types of subtotals on the same row.

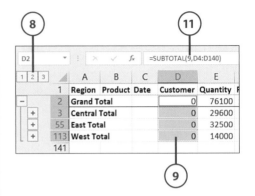

Adding Space Between Subtotaled Groups

When subtotals are inserted into a dataset, only subtotal rows are added between the groups. You have two ways to insert extra space into a sub-totaled report.

Separate Subtotaled Groups for Print

If the report is going to be printed, blank rows probably don't need to be inserted. Just the illusion needs to be created because the actual need is for more space between the subtotal and the next group.

1. Collapse the dataset so that only the subtotals are in view.

2. Select the entire dataset, except for the header row.

3. Press Alt+; (semicolon) to select the visible cells only.

4. On the Home tab, from the Format drop-down, select Row Height.

5. Enter a new value in the Row Height dialog box.

6. Click OK.

7. If the subtotal rows are below the data, then on the Home tab, select the Top Align button.

8. Expand the dataset.

9. Spacing now appears between each group.

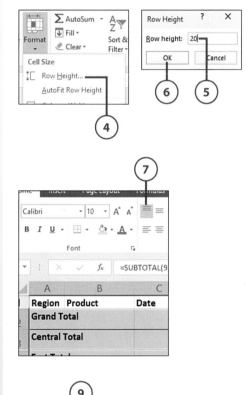

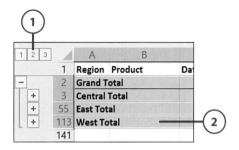

Separate Subtotaled Groups for Distributed Files

Although the method is a bit involved, a blank row can be inserted between groups in a file that you're going to distribute. The method involves using a temporary column to mark the space below where a blank row is needed.

It's Not All Good

Outline Icons Will No Longer Work

This method will disable Excel's capability to manipulate the subtotals in the dataset. The Total rows will remain, but the outline icons no longer work properly, and future subtotal changes will require the groupings and sub-totals to be manually removed first.

1. Collapse the dataset so only the subtotals are in view.

2. In a blank column to the right of the dataset, select a range as long as the dataset.

3. Press Alt+; (semicolon) to select the visible cells only.

4. Type **1** and press Ctrl+Enter to enter the value in all visible cells.

5. Expand the dataset by clicking the outline icon with the largest number.

6. Select the cell above the first cell with a 1 in it.

7. On the Home tab, from the Insert drop-down, select Insert Cells.

8. Select Shift Cells Down and then click OK. This shifts all the 1's one row down.

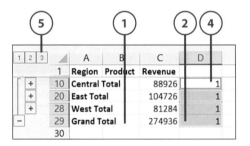

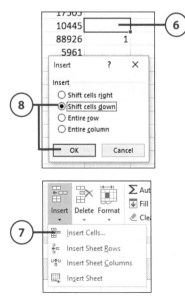

9. Select the column with the 1's in it.

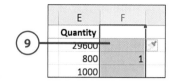

10. On the Home tab, from the Find & Select drop-down, select Go To Special.

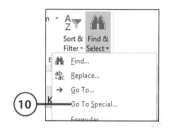

11. From the Go To Special dialog box, select Constants and click OK. Only the 1s are selected.

12. On the Home tab, from the Insert drop-down, select Insert Sheet Rows.

13. A blank row is inserted above each row containing a 1.

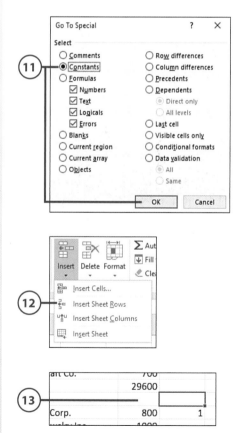

14. Right-click over the temporary column and select Delete.

15. Select a cell in the dataset. Then, on the Data tab, from the Ungroup drop-down, select Clear Outline to get rid of the outline icons.

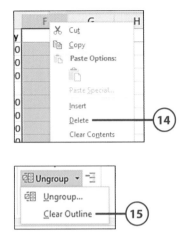

Grouping and Outlining Rows and Columns

You can manually group rows and columns together with or without subtotals. Once the data is grouped, an Expand/Collapse button will be placed below the last row in the selection or to the right of the last column in the selection. An outline can only have up to eight levels.

Selected rows and columns can be grouped together manually using the options in Data, Outline, Group. This is helpful if you have a sheet designed for multiple users and you want to only show rows and/or columns specific to them.

Apply Auto Outline

If the data to be grouped includes a calculated Total row or column between the groups, you can use the Auto Outline option found in the Group drop-down. This option creates groups based on whether the formulas calculate rows or columns. If there are both types of formulas, you'll get both types of groupings.

1. Select a cell in the dataset.

2. On the Data tab, from the Group drop-down, select Auto Outline.

3. The data will be grouped, placing the outline icon on the row or column used to estimate the group.

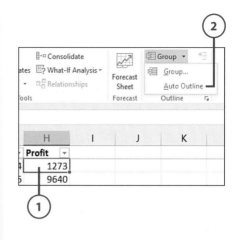

Group Data Manually

Use the Group option for absolute control over how the rows or columns are grouped.

1. Select a cell in the dataset.

2. On the Data tab, click Subtotal.

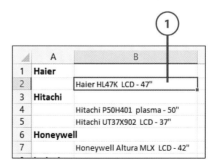

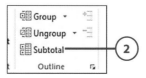

3. A message may appear that Excel cannot determine which row has column labels. Click OK.

4. If you want the outline icons above the data rows they control, ensure Summary Below Data is unchecked. Click OK.

5. Excel inserts subtotal rows in the data. Click the Undo button to remove the rows. Although it may appear that you've just undone all the previous steps, these steps are required to configure where the outline icon will appear.

6. Select the first set of rows to group together. Do not include the set's header. If you have just one row, then select just the one row.

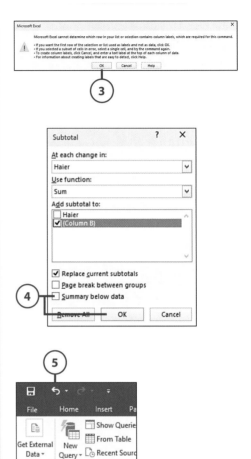

7. On the Data tab, click the Group button.

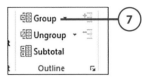

8. The data will be grouped, with an outline icon appearing across from the header.

9. Select the next group of rows and press F4. As long as you don't perform another command, pressing F4 will repeat the previous action, grouping the selected rows.

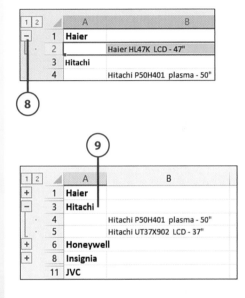

Remove the Groupings

To undo all the groupings, select one cell in the group and then from the Ungroup drop-down, select Clear Outline.

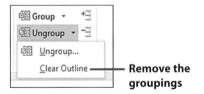

Remove the groupings

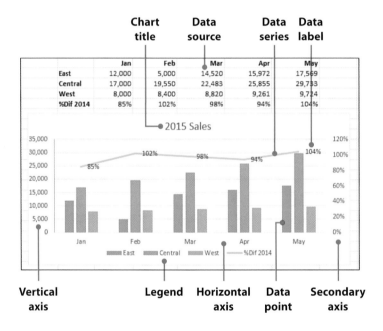

Chart title

Data source

Data series

Data label

	Jan	Feb	Mar	Apr	May
East	12,000	5,000	14,520	15,972	17,569
Central	17,000	19,550	22,483	25,855	29,733
West	8,000	8,400	8,820	9,261	9,724
%Dif 2014	85%	102%	98%	94%	104%

2015 Sales

Vertical axis

Legend

Horizontal axis

Data point

Secondary axis

This chapter will show you how easy it is to add and customize a chart. Topics in this chapter include the following:

→ Quickly adding a chart to a sheet

→ Creating a chart mixing bars and lines

→ Resizing and editing charts

→ Making a pie chart easier to read

→ Inserting sparklines into a report

14

Creating Charts and Sparklines

Using charts is a great way to graphically portray data. They provide a quick and simple way to emphasize trends in data. Some people prefer to look at charts instead of trying to make sense of rows and columns of numbers. Excel offers two methods for charting data—charts and sparklines. Charts, which you are most likely familiar with, are large graphics with a title and numbers and/or text along the left and bottom. Sparklines are miniature charts in cells with only markers to represent the data. This chapter provides you with the tools to create simple, but useful, charts.

Adding a Chart

A chart can make it easier to interpret a lot of numbers at a glance—for example, by showing a trend by how a line moves across time or how two values compare by the heights of the columns in the chart.

Add a Chart with the Quick Analysis Tool

Using the Quick Analysis tool is a fast way to insert a chart based on the selected data. You can choose one of Excel's recommendations based on its interpretation of the data.

1. Select the data you want to create a chart from, including any column headers and row labels.

2. On the Quick Analysis tool, select Charts.

3. Select a recommended chart.

Preview Charts

As you move your pointer over the recommended charts, a preview appears, showing how the data would look in the selected chart type.

4. The selected chart is added to the sheet.

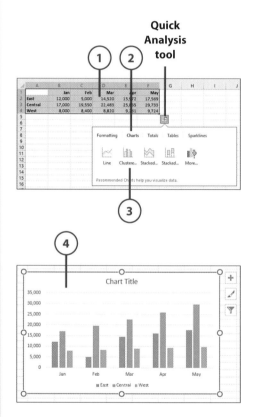

>>>Go Further

MANUALLY ADD A CHART

If you know what chart you want and don't need Excel's recommendations, choose the chart type directly from the ribbon.

1. Select a cell in the dataset.

2. Select a specific chart from the drop-down of the desired chart type on the Insert tab.

3. The chart is added to the sheet.

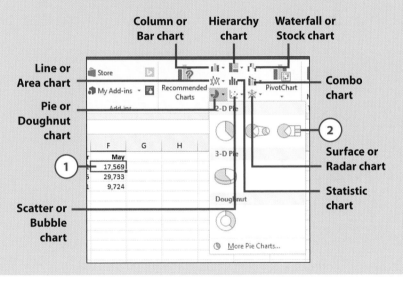

Preview All Charts

You can easily preview your data in all possible chart configurations through the All Charts tab on the Insert Chart dialog box.

1. Select a cell in the dataset.

2. On the Insert tab, select Recommended Charts.

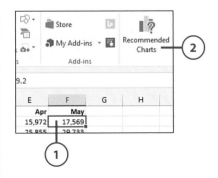

3. Click the All Charts tab.

4. Choose a chart type.

5. Click a chart subtype.

6. The preview frame will update to show how the data would look with the selected chart. If there are multiple previews, select the one you want.

7. Click OK when you find the desired chart, and it will be added to the sheet.

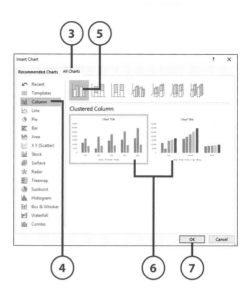

Switch Rows and Columns

You can switch what range is used for a series and what range is used for the category labels in an existing chart.

1. Select the chart.

2. On the Chart Tools, Design tab, click the Switch Row/Column button.

3. Excel switches the range used for the series and the range used for the category labels.

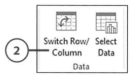

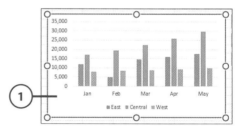

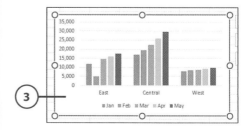

Apply Chart Styles or Colors

Once you've inserted a chart, you may want to move the chart title, move the legend, add a background, change the color of the series, or apply any number of changes to make the chart more attention getting. You can apply each change yourself, or you can see what chart styles and color palettes Excel has available.

1. Select the chart.

2. Click the Chart Styles button.

3. Select a chart style, and it will be applied to the chart.

4. Select the Color tab.

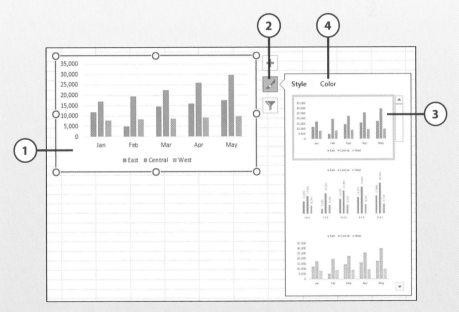

5. Select a color palette, and it will be applied to the chart.

6. Click the Chart Style button again to close it.

See More Styles at a Time

You can also access the list of styles by selecting your chart and opening the Chart Styles drop-down on the Chart Tools, Design tab.

Apply Chart Layouts

Chart layouts are predefined layouts offering different combinations of the chart elements: legend, chart title, axis title, data labels, and data table.

1. Select the chart.

2. On the Chart Tools, Design tab, select the Quick Layout drop-down.

3. Click the desired chart layout, and the chart will update.

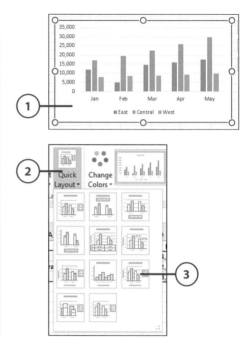

Resizing or Moving a Chart

The default location for a chart is the same sheet as the data. If you create your chart using the Quick Analysis tool or the Recommended Charts options, you have no control over where the chart is initially placed. However, a chart can be moved to another location on the same sheet, to a new sheet, or to its own chart sheet.

Resize a Chart

Use the resize handles around a chart to change its size.

1. Select the chart.

2. Place the pointer over any of the circles along the frame. When the pointer changes to a double-headed arrow, click and drag the chart to the desired size.

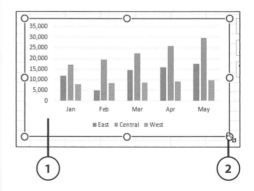

Move to a New Location on the Same Sheet

You can drag a chart to any location on a sheet.

1. Select the chart.

2. Place the pointer along any edge. When the pointer changes to a four-headed arrow, click and drag the chart to the new location.

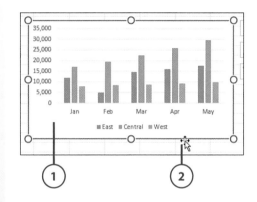

Relocate to Another Sheet

A chart can be moved to another existing sheet or turned into a chart sheet. A chart sheet is a special type of sheet in Excel used to display only charts. It doesn't have cells like the other sheets, and you can't add any information to it, other than the chart components.

1. Select the chart.

2. On the Chart Tools, Design tab, select Move Chart.

3. Select New Sheet to move the chart to a chart sheet. Enter a new name for the chart sheet.

Select an Existing Sheet

You can also select an existing sheet from the Object In drop-down.

4. Click OK, and the chart will be moved to the new location.

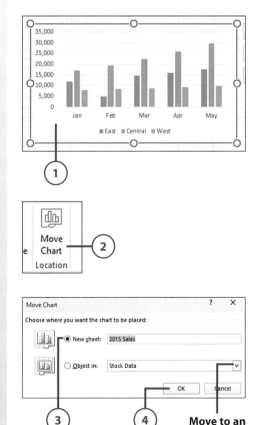

Move to an existing sheet

Editing Chart Elements

Depending on the selected element, different settings are available that you can configure as needed. From the task pane, you can make changes to the element's formatting, such as the color, 3D design, and alignment.

Use the Format Task Pane

The Format task pane allows you to format the various chart elements. Formatting options include colors, borders, size, location, and configuration options.

1. Select the chart.

2. Click the Chart Elements icon.

3. Selected elements are active on the chart. Unselected elements are inactive.

4. Place your pointer over an element and click the menu arrow that appears.

5. Select More Options to open the Format task pane.

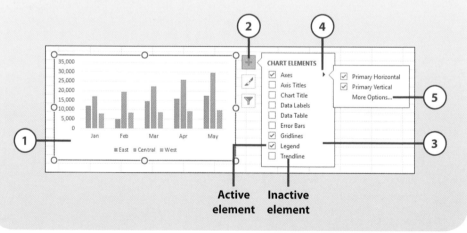

Active element   Inactive element

6. To edit a different element, select it from the Element drop-down.

7. Select Text Options to view text-formatting options for the selected element.

8. To view the various options available for an element, select *Element Name* Options. Not all elements have access to the same options.

9. Click an option icon to view the available settings. The chart updates as changes are made.

10. Click the X to close the pane.

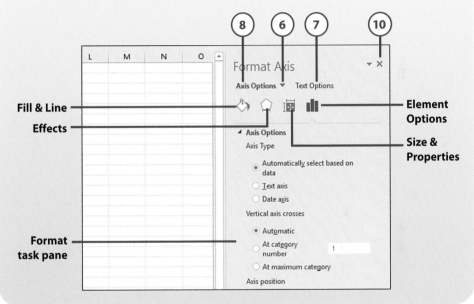

Fill & Line

Effects

Format task pane

Element Options

Size & Properties

Edit the Chart or Axis Titles

Edit the chart or axis titles to clarify the purpose of the chart.

1. Select the frame of the title you want to change.

2. As you type the new title, the text appears in the formula bar. Press Enter when done.

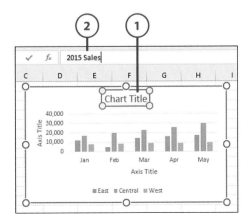

Changing Part of a Title

To change a specific word in a title, select the title then double-click the word you want to change. Press Esc or click a cell on the sheet when you are done with your changes.

>>>Go Further
DYNAMIC TITLES

Excel doesn't have the built-in ability, but with a little work, you can create a dynamic chart or axis title linked to a cell.

1. Click once on the title, ensuring the selection frame is solid, not dashed.

2. Place the cursor in the formula bar, type an equal sign (=), and then click the cell containing the title text.

3. Press Enter, and the title updates to reflect the cell's text. As the text in the cell changes, the chart title also updates.

If you decide to make the title static again, right-click the title, select Edit Text, and then clear the formula in the formula bar. You can also toggle the title on and off to reset the title.

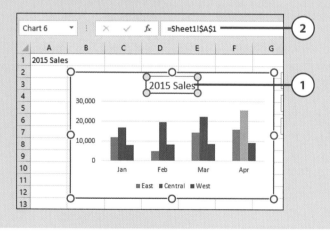

Change the Display Units in an Axis

Excel bases the units shown in an axis off the data. You can change the display units, reducing the amount of space used and making the axis easier to read.

1. Right-click the axis and select Format Axis.

2. Click the Axis Options icon.

3. Select the desired units from the Display Units drop-down.

4. The axis will update, including a label showing the applied unit base.

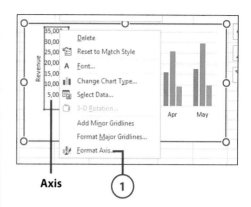

Axis ①

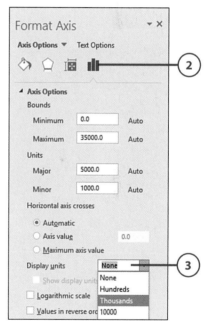

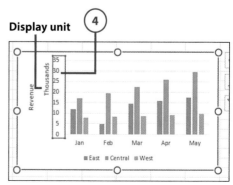

Display unit ④

Customize a Series Color

You can change the color of a single series on a chart without affecting the other series.

1. Click once on the series you want to change. All points of that series will be selected. If only the one point is selected, you clicked the point twice. Click elsewhere on the sheet and try again.

2. Right-click over the series and select Format Data Series.

3. Click the Fill & Line icon in the Format task pane.

4. Expand the Fill category and select Solid Fill.

5. Select a color from the palette drop-down.

6. The selected series will update to reflect the new color.

Change Only One Point in a Series

If you click twice (two single clicks, not a double-click) on a specific data point in a series so that only it, not the entire series, is selected, you can apply a color to just that data point.

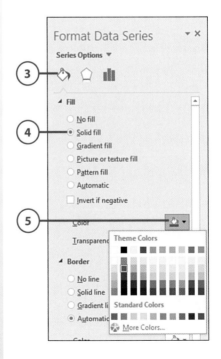

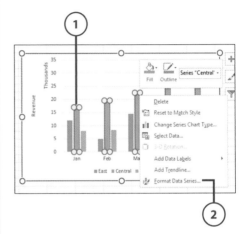

Changing an Existing Chart's Type

You don't have to re-create a chart from scratch if you want to change the chart type.

Change the Chart Type

It's easy to change a chart's type, finding the perfect chart to represent your data.

1. Select the chart.

2. On the Chart Tools, Design tab, select Change Chart Type.

3. Select the new chart type.

4. Click OK, and the chart will change to the new type.

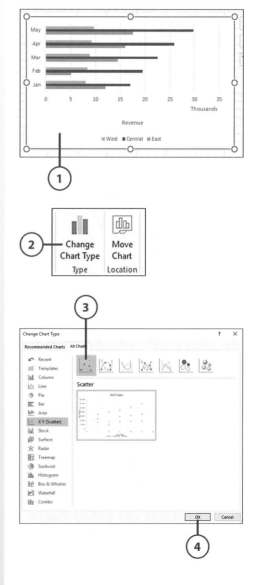

Creating a Chart with Multiple Chart Types

You can use some of the chart types together in a single chart by selecting Combo as the chart type.

Insert a Multiple Type Chart

Each series in a chart can have a different chart type.

1. Select a cell in the dataset.

2. Select Combo on the Insert tab.

3. Select Create Custom Combo Chart.

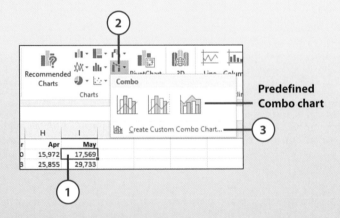

Choose Predefined Combo Chart

You don't have to create a custom combo chart. The Combo drop-down has several predefined combo charts you can choose from. If you see the one you want, click it and the chart will be added to your sheet.

4. Select a chart type for each series.

5. Select Secondary Axis for a series if the series needs to be shown on a secondary axis.

6. Click OK, and the chart will be created.

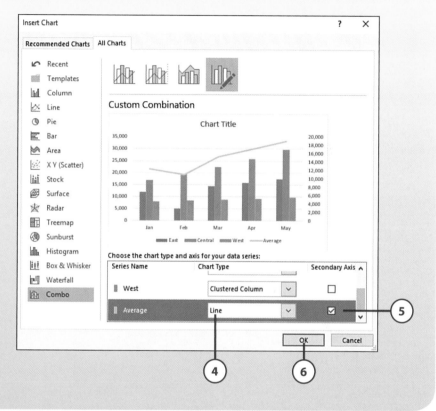

Add a Secondary Axis

A *secondary axis* is an axis that appears on the right side of the chart. It is often used for charting data of a different scale. For example, if you're plotting units sold, with values in the hundreds, and revenue generated, with values in the millions, you won't be able to clearly see the units sold. Adding a secondary axis allows the use of two different scales.

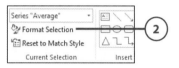

1. Click the series you want to chart on the secondary axis.

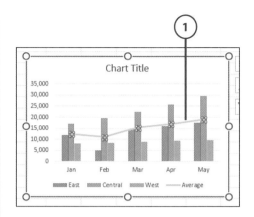

Another Way to Select a Series

Click the chart and then select the series from the Chart Elements drop-down on the Chart Tools, Format tab.

2. On the Chart Tools, Format tab, select Format Selection.

3. From the Format Data Series task pane, select Secondary Axis, and the chart will update.

Updating Chart Data

Unless the source data is a dynamic range, such as a table, the chart won't automatically update as new rows or columns are added to the dataset. You'll need to update the data source range to include the new data.

Change the Data Source

Change the data source to include new data to reference a completely new dataset.

1. Select the chart.

2. From the Chart Tools, Design tab, click Select Data.

3. With the current range in the Chart Data Range field highlighted, click the range selector tool.

4. Select the updated range.

5. Select the range selector tool to return to the dialog box.

6. Click OK, and the chart will update to reflect the new data.

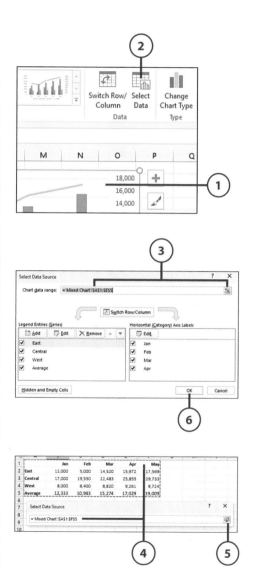

UPDATE MANUALLY

When a chart is selected, the data source is highlighted with a colored border. You can click and drag the fill handle on the border to include new data, thus changing the source range.

1. Place the pointer in the corner of the range, thus getting a double-headed arrow.

2. Click and drag to include new rows and/or columns. The chart will update to reflect the new data.

	Jan	Feb	Mar	Apr	May
1					
2 East	12,000	5,000	14,520	15,972	17,569
3 Central	17,000	19,550	22,483	25,855	29,733
4 West	8,000	8,400	8,820	9,261	9,724
5 Average	12,333	10,983	15,274	17,029	19,009

(1)

Adding Special Charts

Stock charts and bubble charts are two chart types that require a specific setup to chart the data properly.

Create a Stock Chart

You can create four types of stock charts using historical stock data. Each type has specific requirements for included columns and their order. If the order of the data is not met, the chart will not be created.

- **High-Low-Close**—Requires four columns of data: Date, High, Low, Close

- **Open-High-Low-Close**—Requires five columns of data: Date, Open, High, Low, Close

- **Volume-High-Low-Close**—Requires five columns of data: Date, Volume, High, Low, Close

- **Volume-Open-High-Low-Close**—Requires six columns of data: Date, Volume, Open, High, Low, Close

1. Make sure the data columns are adjacent and in the required order, which is reflected in the chart's subtype name.

2. Select a cell in the dataset.

3. On the Insert tab, from the Waterfall or Stock drop-down, select the specific stock chart matching the column configuration on the sheet. The chart will be inserted onto the sheet.

Stock chart sub type name

Create a Bubble Chart

A bubble chart displays a relationship among three variables. The x,y-coordinate represents two variables and the size of the bubble is the third.

- The first column of data is used for the horizontal axis, the x-coordinate.

- The second column of data is used for the vertical axis, the y-coordinate.

- The third column of data is used for the size of the bubble.

1. Select a cell in the dataset.

2. Select a Bubble chart from the Scatter or Bubble drop-down on the Insert tab.

3. The chart is added to the sheet.

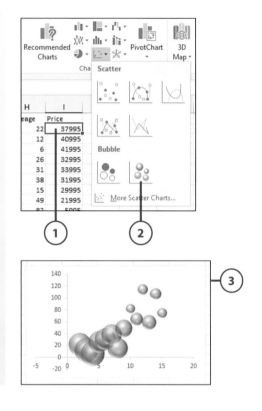

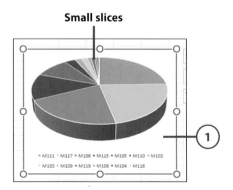

Pie Chart Issue: Small Slices

When creating a pie chart, you may end up with slices that are very difficult to see. Two possible ways of dealing with this are to rotate the pie or to create a "bar of pie" chart.

Rotate the Pie

Rotating the pie works best if the chart is 3D. By rotating the chart so the smaller slices are toward the front, you can make the slices easier to see.

1. Select the chart.

2. On the Chart Tools, Format tab, from the Chart Elements drop-down, select the series.

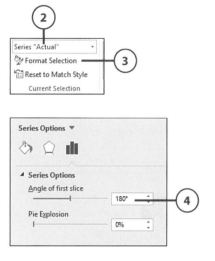

3. Select Format Selection on the Chart Tools, Format tab.

4. Increase the Angle of First Slice setting on the Format task pane. The chart updates when you let go of the mouse button, so you can see how far you need to move the slider.

5. Rotate the pie so the smaller slices are to the front.

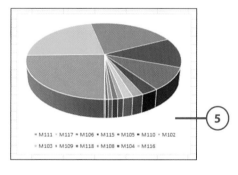

Create a Bar of Pie Chart

Bar of Pie is used to explode out the smaller pie slices into a stacked bar chart, making the smaller slices more visible. Excel creates a new slice called Other, which is a grouping of the slices now in the bar.

1. Select the pie chart.

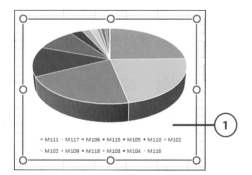

2. Select Change Chart Type on the Chart Tools, Design tab.

3. Select Bar of Pie from the Pie options.

4. Click OK. The chart changes to a bar of pie chart.

5. With the chart still selected, go to Chart Tools, Format, Current Selection, and select the series from the Chart Elements drop-down.

6. Click Format Selection. The Format Data Series task pane opens.

7. Click the Series Options icon. Change the number of slices in the bar chart by updating the Values In Second Plot field. As the value is changed using the spin buttons, the chart updates.

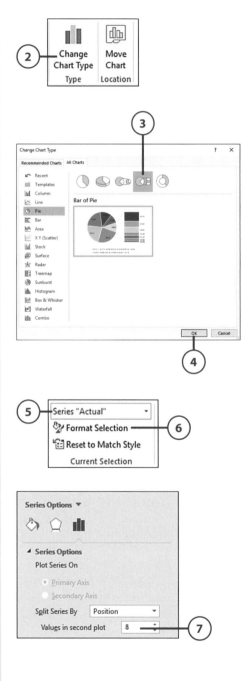

Using a User-Created Template

If you have a chart design you want to apply to multiple charts, you can save the design as a template. All the settings for colors, fonts, effects, and chart elements are saved and can be applied to other charts. Because the template is saved as an external file, you can share it with other users.

Save a Chart Template

Once the chart elements are configured as you want them, save the chart as a template.

1. Right-click the chart and select Save as Template.

2. Give the template a name and then click Save.

3. The template is now available in the Templates option of the Insert Chart dialog box and can be applied just like the Excel-defined charts.

Required Save Location
You must use the default location in the Save Chart Template dialog box for saving charts so the chart template will appear in the Insert Chart dialog box.

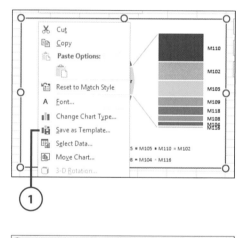

Use a Chart Template

If you're provided with a chart template, you'll need to save it to the correct location on your PC before you can use it.

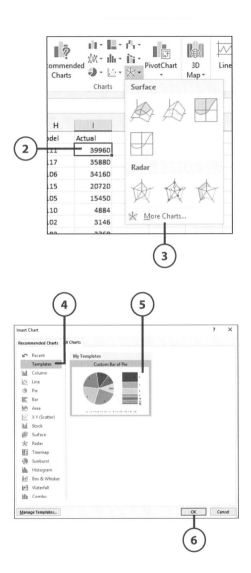

1. Save the chart template to the following location:

   C:\Users*username*\Appdata\ Roaming\Microsoft\Templates\ Charts

2. Select a cell in the dataset.

3. Select the More Charts option of any chart type's drop-down on the Insert tab.

4. From the Insert Chart dialog box, select Templates.

5. Select a chart.

6. Click OK.

Adding Sparklines to Data

A *sparkline* is a chart inside of a single cell. The data source is a single row or column of data. The sparkline can be placed right next to the data it's charting or on another sheet. Because the sparkline is in the background of the cell, you can still enter text in that cell.

Insert a Sparkline

Use a sparkline to show a trend in your data without losing valuable space to a chart.

1. Select the cell that will hold the sparkline.

2. On the Insert tab, select the sparkline type. The Create Sparklines dialog box will open.

3. Select the data range.

4. Verify the address for the sparkline.

5. Click OK, and the sparkline is added to the cell.

6. On the Sparkline Tools, Design tab, select a color style from the Style drop-down.

Select the Data Range First

If you prefer, you can select the data range first instead of the cell for the sparkline.

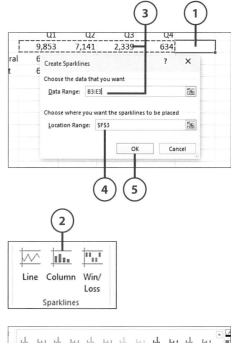

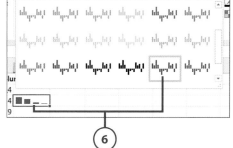

Emphasize Points on a Sparkline

After you've created a sparkline, you can choose to show the high point, low point, negative points, first point, last point, and markers (line charts only). Each point can have its own color.

1. Select the sparkline cells.

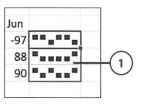

2. From the Marker Color drop-down on the Sparkline Tools, Design tab, select the desired point option, such as Negative Points, and then choose a color.

3. The sparkline will update, with the selected point(s) having a different color from the other data points.

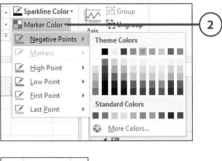

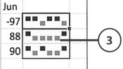

Pointer Color Not Applied

By default, when changing a point color, Excel will toggle the point on. But if the point has been turned off at some point, Excel will not turn it on. In that case, select the point yourself from the Sparkline Tools, Design tab.

**Toggle which points
are shown**

Space Markers by Date

The markers in a sparkline can be spaced out in respect to the dates of the dataset. The date range must include real dates.

1. Select the sparkline cell(s).

2. On the Sparkline Tools, Design tab, from the Axis drop-down, select Date Axis Type.

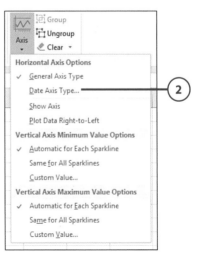

3. Select the date range.

4. Click OK.

5. The sparkline updates to accommodate the spacing in the selected date range.

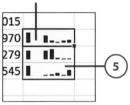

Missing dates ③

Space for missing dates

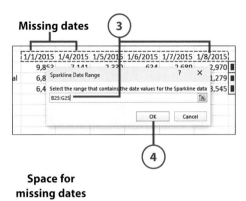

Delete Sparklines

You cannot simply highlight a sparkline and delete it.

1. Select the cell(s) with the sparkline(s).

2. If Excel is grouping your sparklines together and you only want to delete the sparkline from the cell you selected, on the Sparkline Tools, Design tab, from the Clear drop-down, select Clear Selected Sparklines.

3. If you have multiple sparklines grouped together and want to clear them all, on the Sparkline Tools, Design tab, from the Clear drop-down, select Clear Selected Sparkline Groups.

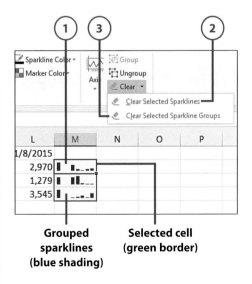

Grouped sparklines (blue shading) **Selected cell (green border)**

Row labels **Report filter** **Column labels** **PivotTable field list**

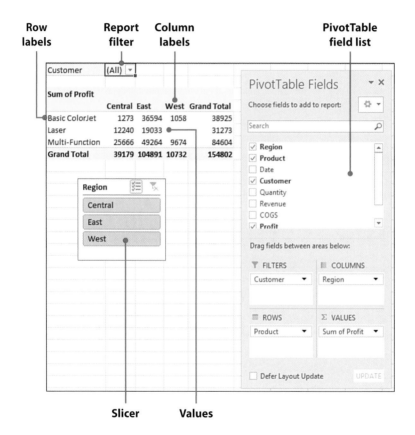

Slicer **Values**

In this chapter, you'll learn how to use a PivotTable to quickly summarize data. This chapter covers the following topics:

→ Creating a PivotTable

→ Sorting and filtering a PivotTable

→ Grouping dates in a PivotTable

→ Inserting slicers to help users filter a PivotTable

15

Summarizing Data with PivotTables

You can use a PivotTable to summarize a million rows with five clicks of the mouse button. For example, if you have sales data broken up by company and product, you can quickly summarize the sales by company, then product, or, with a few clicks, you can reverse the report and summarize by product, then company. Suppose you're in charge of all the local kids' soccer leagues and you want to create a report showing the number of boys versus girls, grouped by age. A PivotTable can do all this, and more.

They're so powerful with so many options that this chapter cannot cover them all. This chapter provides you with the tools to create straightforward, but useful PivotTables. For even more details, refer to *Excel 2016 Pivot Table Data Crunching* (ISBN 978-0-7897-5629-9) by Bill Jelen and Michael Alexander.

PowerPivot

There is an advanced version of PivotTables called PowerPivot that this book does not review. PowerPivot is a powerful data analysis tool for working with very large amounts of data.

Creating a PivotTable

The dataset must be set up correctly to get the most out of a PivotTable. The column headers will become the fields you use to set the row labels, column labels, and report filters. This means the column headers can't be a unique item, such as a date or specific product. Instead, you should have a column labeled Dates or Products with the unique items arranged below it. Here are the other requirements:

- There can't be any blank rows or columns in the dataset.

- Every column must have a unique header.

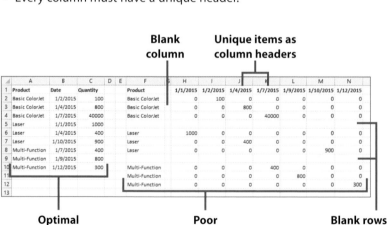

Blank column

Unique items as column headers

Optimal dataset

Poor dataset

Blank rows

Use the Quick Analysis Tool

The Quick Analysis tool provides a quick way to create a PivotTable.

1. Select the dataset, ensuring there are no blank rows or columns, and each column has a unique header.

2. From the Quick Analysis Tool, select Tables.

3. Excel will recommend some PivotTable configurations. Move your pointer over each one to see a preview. When you find the one you want, click its icon. If Excel doesn't have any PivotTable recommendations, refer to the section "Create a PivotTable from Scratch."

4. The selected PivotTable will be created on a new sheet.

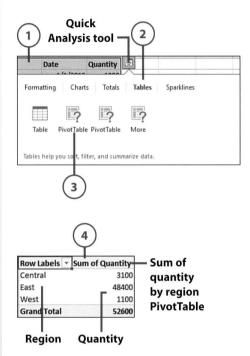

Create a PivotTable from Scratch

Once you've told Excel what the data source is, you can quickly create a PivotTable by moving the desired fields in the field list to the correct PivotTable area.

The following example will create a region report summing the quantity and profit for each product, grouped by customer.

1. Select a cell in the dataset. Ensure there are no blank rows or columns, and each column has a unique header.

2. On the Insert tab, select PivotTable.

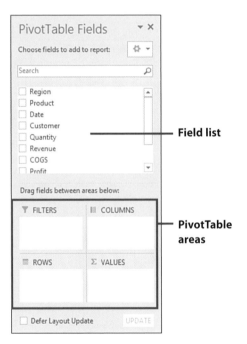

Field list

PivotTable areas

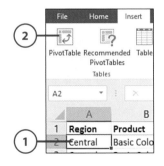

3. Verify the range shown. If it's incorrect, inspect the dataset for blank rows or columns and start over.

4. Select New Worksheet to put the PivotTable on a new sheet.

Place a PivotTable on the Current Sheet

To place the PivotTable on the data sheet, select Existing Worksheet and select a location on the current sheet. If you choose this option, select a location for the PivotTable below the dataset so that as the report is pivoted, it doesn't affect the data.

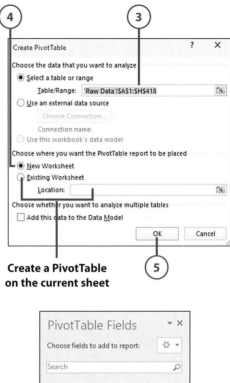

Create a PivotTable on the current sheet

5. Click OK. The PivotTable template and field list appear on a new sheet (or on an existing sheet, if that is what you selected).

6. Click and drag Customer from the field list to the Rows area.

7. Click and drag Product from the field list to the Rows area.

Adding a Date Field

If you add a date field, Excel will recognize it as such and automatically group the dates into months, quarters, or years. To ungroup them, right-click over a grouped date in the PivotTable and select Ungroup.

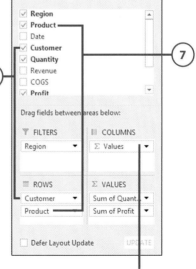

Automatically added by Excel

8. Click and drag Quantity from the field list to the Values area.

9. Click and drag Profit from the field list to the Values area. When you select two or more fields to summarize, Excel adds a Values field to the Columns area.

10. Click and drag the Region field from the list to the Filters area.

11. The report is complete. If you don't like the order of the fields, you can click and drag them where you want from the PivotTable field list areas.

Remove a Field

To remove a field from a PivotTable, deselect it from the field list or click it in the area and select Remove Field. You can also click and drag the field from the area to the sheet until an X appears by the pointer. When the X appears, release the mouse button.

Use the Columns Area

Instead of placing the Product field in the Rows area, you could place it in the Columns area. You would then have a set of Quantity and Profit columns for each product.

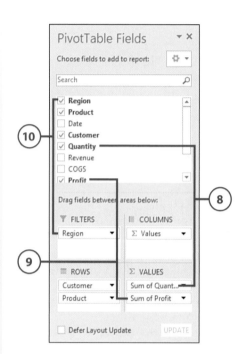

Region	(All)	
Row Labels	**Sum of Quantity**	**Sum of Profit**
⊟ Alluring Shoe Co.	18400	215654
Basic ColorJet	5200	65225
Laser	6100	74372
Multi-Function	7100	76057
⊟ Appealing Calculator Corp.	19300	226313

Change the Calculation Type of a Field Value

When creating a PivotTable, if Excel identifies a Values field as numeric, it automatically sums the data. If it cannot identify the field as numeric, it will count the data. There are many other calculation options you can also choose from.

1. Select the field in the Values area of the PivotTable Fields task pane.

2. Select Value Field Settings.

3. Choose the desired calculation type. For example, if the data is numeric, you can perform calculations, such as sum or average. If the data is not numeric, you can only count it.

4. Click OK.

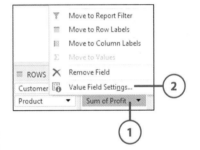

A Numeric Column Was Counted

If you have a column of numbers but Excel returns a count instead, check the column. Either there are words in the column (other than the header) or the numbers are being treated as text.

Format Values

If you use the numeric formatting tools on the Home tab or Format Cells dialog box, next time you refresh the PivotTable, the formatting will be lost. Use the PivotTable's formatting options to set the numeric format the fields should use.

1. Right-click a calculated value in the PivotTable.

2. Select Value Field Settings.

3. Click Number Format.

4. Select the desired number format from the Format Cells dialog box and click OK.

5. Click OK on the Value Field Settings dialog box.

More About Number Formats

Refer to "Applying Number Formats" in Chapter 6, "Formatting Sheets and Cells," for more information on the different number formats.

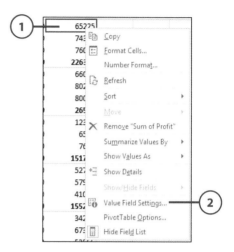

Changing the PivotTable Layout

The default layout of a PivotTable is the compact form, where the row labels are stacked, sharing the same column. Two other layouts are available, providing each row label with its own column. You can also repeat the labels using these other layouts.

- **Compact**—This is the default configuration. All the fields in the row labels area share the same column. The total appears in the same row as the field.

Compact form

	A	B	C
Region	(All)		
Row Labels		Sum of Quantity	Sum of Profit
Alluring Shoe Co.		18400	$215,654.00
Basic ColorJet		5200	$65,225.00
Laser		6100	$74,372.00
Multi-Function		7100	$76,057.00
Appealing Calculator Corp.		19300	$226,313.00
Basic ColorJet		5600	$66,043.00
Laser		6400	$80,249.00
Multi-Function		7300	$80,021.00

- **Outline**—The fields in the row labels area each have their own column. The total appears in the same row as the field.

Outline form

	A	B	C	D
Region	(All)			
Customer	Product		Sum of Quantity	Sum of Profit
Alluring Shoe Co.			18400	$215,654.00
	Basic ColorJet		5200	$65,225.00
	Laser		6100	$74,372.00
	Multi-Function		7100	$76,057.00
Appealing Calculator Corp.			19300	$226,313.00
	Basic ColorJet		5600	$66,043.00
	Laser		6400	$80,249.00
	Multi-Function		7300	$80,021.00

- **Tabular**—The fields in the row labels area each have their own column. The total appears in its own row beneath its group.

Tabular form

	A	B	C	D
Region		(All)		
Customer		Product	Sum of Quantity	Sum of Profit
Alluring Shoe Co.		Basic ColorJet	5200	$65,225.00
		Laser	6100	$74,372.00
		Multi-Function	7100	$76,057.00
Alluring Shoe Co. Total			18400	$215,654.00
Appealing Calculator Corp.		Basic ColorJet	5600	$66,043.00
		Laser	6400	$80,249.00
		Multi-Function	7300	$80,021.00
Appealing Calculator Corp. Total			19300	$226,313.00

Choose a New Layout

You can replace the default Compact Form with a different layout. If you choose Outline or Tabular, you can also repeat the item labels.

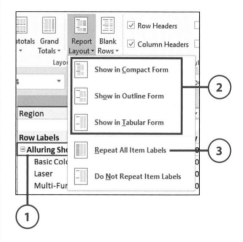

1. Select a cell in the PivotTable.

2. On the PivotTable Tools, Design tab, from the Report Layout drop-down, select a different layout, such as Outline Form or Tabular Form.

3. On the PivotTable Tools, Design tab, from the Report Layout drop-down, select Repeat All Item Labels to fill the cells beneath a label.

PivotTable Sorting

Excel automatically sorts text data alphabetically when building a PivotTable. You can click and drag the fields to a new location or use the standard sorting tools to re-sort it.

Click and Drag

Any row label, column label, or record can be dragged to a new location.

1. Select the row or column label you want to move.

2. Place the pointer on the edge of the selection. When it turns into a four-headed arrow, hold down the mouse button and drag it to a new location.

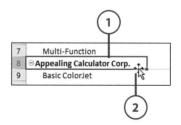

Reset the Table

To reset the table back to its default state, remove the affected field from the area, refresh the table, and then put the field back.

Use Quick Sort

The quick sort buttons offer one-click access to sorting cell values.

1. Select a cell in the column to sort by.

2. On the Data tab, select AZ to sort lowest to highest or ZA to sort highest to lowest.

Sorting Data

There are other ways to sort data, including the following:

Right-click the cell and select Sort, Sort A to Z or Sort Z to A if your data is text; select Sort Smallest to Largest or Sort Largest to Smallest if the data is numerical; select Sort Oldest to Newest or Sort Newest to Oldest if the data is a date.

From the filter drop-down of a row or column field, select Sort A to Z or Sort Z to A. If you're using the compact report layout, select the field to sort from the pivot label field drop-down. The sort descriptions change based on whether the label is text, numeric, or date.

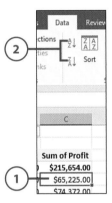

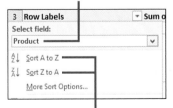

Sort options in the right-click menu

Field selection for compact layout only

Sort options in the filter drop-down

Expanding and Collapsing Fields

If the rows area contains multiple fields, row labels appear in groups that can be quickly expanded and collapsed by clicking the + and – icons.

Expand and Collapse a Field

Expand a field to view more details; collapse it to hide the details.

1. Click the – icon to collapse a single group.

2. Click the + icon to expand a single group.

3. Right-click and from the Expand/ Collapse submenu, select Expand Entire Field to expand all the groups in the field.

4. Right-click and from the Expand/ Collapse submenu, select Collapse Entire Field to collapse all the groups in the field.

5. Right-click and from the Expand/ Collapse submenu, choose Collapse to "*Fieldname*" to collapse a specific field by name.

6. Right-click and from the Expand/ Collapse submenu, choose Expand to "*Fieldname*" to expand a specific field by name.

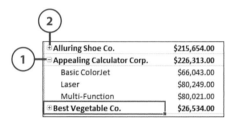

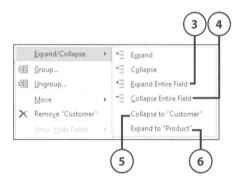

Grouping Dates

Excel will automatically group dates into month, years, or quarters, but if you don't want those groupings, you can ungroup what Excel has provided and create your own group.

Grouping and Multiple Reports

If you have multiple reports based on the same data source, grouping a label on one report will group the labels on the others. To prevent this, unlink the reports you don't want the same grouping on. See the section "Unlinking PivotTables" for more information.

It's Not All Good

Cannot Group That Selection

A common issue with PivotTables occurs when someone tries to group a date field and receives the error "Cannot group that selection." The reason may be that the dates are not real dates, but instead text that looks like dates. If that's the case, see the "Fixing Numbers Stored as Text" section in Chapter 4, "Getting Data onto a Sheet," to convert the text dates to real dates (because real dates are numbers).

Group by Week

Use the Days option to group by week.

1. Right-click over a date in the PivotTable and select Group.

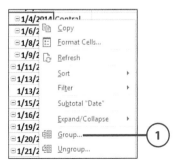

Dates Already Grouped

If you created a PivotTable and the dates are already grouped, but not how you need them to be, right-click and select Ungroup.

2. Select Days and unselect Months.

3. Enter **7** for Number of Days.

4. Excel will group the selected number of days based on the range in the dialog box, so if the weeks need to represent a normal week, such as Sunday to Saturday, change the starting date to be a Sunday that will include the first date in the dataset.

5. Click OK.

6. Excel will change the labels to show the days of week grouped together.

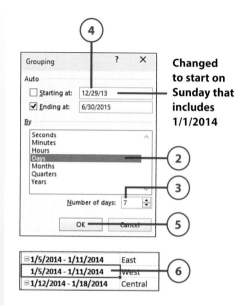

Changed to start on Sunday that includes 1/1/2014

Group by Month and Year

When you group by month and year, the days are still available within each month.

1. Right-click over a date in the PivotTable and select Group.

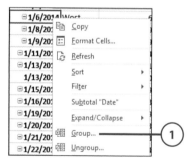

2. Select Months and Years from the list box.

3. Click OK.

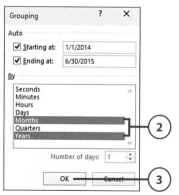

4. The data is grouped into months and years, and a Years field is added to the field list. You can move the Years field to a different area.

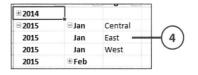

Filtering Data in a PivotTable

Filtering allows you to view only the data you want to see. Unlike Excel's AutoFilter (see Chapter 11, "Filtering and Consolidating Data"), filtering a PivotTable doesn't hide the rows. Instead, the rows are removed from the report.

Filter for Listed Items

The filter listing is probably the most obvious filter tool when you open the drop-down.

1. Click the drop-down arrow of the label you want to filter.

2. If using the compact report layout, select the field to filter from the pivot label field drop-down.

3. The selected items are the ones that will appear when the column is filtered. Unselect the items you want hidden.

4. Click OK.

5. The report will update, removing the rows of the items you unselected. An icon that looks like a funnel will replace the arrow on the labels that have a filter applied.

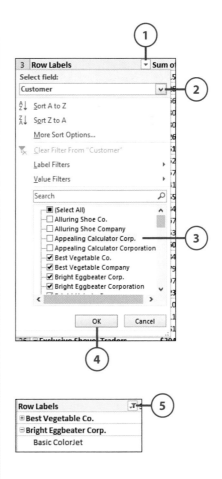

Clear a Filter

A filter can be cleared from a specific label or for the entire PivotTable.

1. To clear a specific label, open the label's drop-down.

2. If using the compact report layout, select the field to clear from the pivot label field drop-down.

3. Select the Clear Filter from "*FieldName*" option.

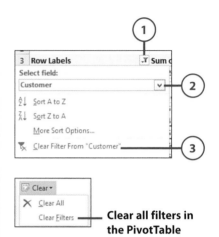

Clear All Filters

Select Clear Filters from the Clear drop-down on the PivotTable Tools, Analyze tab to clear all filters.

Clear all filters in the PivotTable

Creating a Calculated Field

A *calculated field* is a field you create by building a formula using existing fields and constants. Creating the formula isn't that different from building one in the formula bar, but instead of cell references, you use the field names.

Add a Calculated Field

In the following example, the dataset has fields for revenue and quantity, but not for the price of the items sold. You could create a formula outside the PivotTable report, but when the table is updated, the formula may be overwritten. Instead, create a calculated field to calculate the average price.

1. Select a cell in the PivotTable.

2. Select Calculated Field from the Fields, Items & Sets drop-down on the PivotTable Tools, Analyze tab.

3. Enter a name for the new field, such as **Average Price**.

4. Select Revenue and then click Insert Field.

5. Type **/** (a slash) in the Formula field.

6. Select Quantity and then click Insert Field.

7. Click OK. If you have more calculated fields to add, click Add instead.

8. The calculated field is added as the last value, but you can move it as needed. You can also change the calculation type, as you would a regular field.

Sum of Revenue	Sum of Quantity	Sum of Average Price
1624635	73600	22.07384511
1523178	79500	19.1594717
1781814	77400	23.02085271
4929627	230500	21.38666811

Edit or Delete a Calculated Field

To edit a calculated field, return to the Insert Calculated Field dialog box. Select the field from the Name field drop-down and then make the desired change.

To delete a calculated field, return to the Insert Calculated Field dialog box. Select the field from the Name field drop-down and then click Delete.

Hiding Totals

By default, subtotals and grand totals are automatically added to the PivotTable.

Sum of Quantity		Region				
Product	Customer	Central	East	West	Grand Total	
Basic ColorJet	Bright Hairpin Co.	100		100	200	Grand total for columns
Basic ColorJet	Cool Jewelry Corp.		800		800	
Basic ColorJet	Remarkable Meter Corp.		700		700	
Basic ColorJet	Safe Flagpole Supply		300		300	
Basic ColorJet	Wonderful Jewelry InCo.		40000		40000	
Basic ColorJet Total		100	41800	100	42000	Subtotal
Laser		900	1500		2400	
Multi-Function		2100	4500	1000	7600	
Grand Total		3100	47800	1100	52000	

Grand total for rows

Hide Totals

You can choose which totals in your PivotTable will be shown.

1. To hide all totals, select Off for Rows and Columns from the Grand Totals drop-down on the PivotTable Tools, Design tab.

2. To show only column totals, select On for Columns Only from the Grand Totals drop-down on the PivotTable Tools, Design tab.

3. To show only row totals, select On for Rows Only from the Grand Totals drop-down on the PivotTable Tools, Design tab.

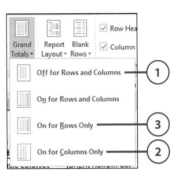

Show Grand Totals

To show all grand totals, select On for Rows and Columns from the Grand Totals drop-down on the PivotTable Tools, Design tab.

Hide Subtotals

You can choose to hide specific subtotals or all subtotals in your PivotTable.

1. To hide a specific subtotal, right-click over its label and select Subtotal "*Fieldname*", thus removing the check mark by the option.

2. To hide all subtotals, select Do Not Show Subtotals from the Subtotals drop-down on the PivotTable Tools, Design tab.

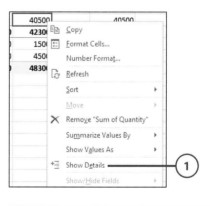

Show Subtotals

To show a specific subtotal, right-click over one of its labels and select Subtotal "*Fieldname*". To show all subtotals, select either Show All Subtotals at Bottom of Group or Show All Subtotals at Top of Group from the Subtotals drop-down on the PivotTable Tools, Design tab.

Viewing the Records Used to Calculate a Value

You can create a new report showing the records from which a specific value was derived. This is known as *drilling down* and can be useful if you notice a value in the PivotTable that stands out and you need to investigate it in more detail.

1. Right-click the value and select Show Details.

The Double-Click Method

You can also drill down by double-clicking on the value.

2. Excel inserts a new sheet with a table consisting of the records from the data source that were used to calculate the value.

Region	Product	Date	Customer	Quantity	Revenue	COGS	Profit
East	Basic Color	1/7/2015	Wonderful Je	500	21730	9840	11890
East	Basic Color	1/7/2015	Wonderful Je	40000	21730	9840	11890

Questionable quantity ②

Correcting the Data

The new table is not linked to the original data or the PivotTable. If you need to make corrections to the data, make them to the original source and refresh the PivotTable. You can then delete the sheet that was created for the drill down.

Unlinking PivotTables

PivotTables created from the same data source share the same data cache. The data cache not only holds the records used by the PivotTable, but also configurations, such as grouped dates and calculated fields. This means if you group the dates on one report, all the linked reports will have grouped dates. You'll need to assign the reports different data caches if you want to have different configurations on the different reports.

Unlink a PivotTable Report

The PivotTable Wizard isn't available on the ribbon. You'll have to use a keyboard shortcut to open it.

1. Select a cell in the report in which you want to break the link.

2. Press Alt+D and then P to open the PivotTable Wizard.

3. Since the wizard opens on its 3rd step, click Back to go to step 2.

4. Change the range so that it uses one less row.

5. Click Next.

6. Select Existing Worksheet.

7. Make sure the range is the same as the report.

8. Click Finish. The report now has a separate, different cache.

9. Press Alt+D and then P to open the PivotTable Wizard.

10. Click Back.

11. Change the Range field so that it includes the full range.

12. Click Next.

13. Select Existing Worksheet.

14. Make sure the range is the same as the report.

15. Click Finish.

⑥

PivotTable and PivotChart Wizard - Step 3 of 3   ?   ✕

Where do you want to put the PivotTable report?

○ New worksheet

● Existing worksheet

Sheet1!$A$3

Click Finish to create your PivotTable report.

Layout...   Options...   Cancel   < Back   Next >   Finish

⑦   ⑧

⑪

PivotTable and PivotChart Wizard - Step 2 of 3   ?   ✕

Where is the data that you want to use?

Range: Book2!$A$1:$H$418   Browse...

Cancel   < Back   Next >   Finish

⑫

Don't Use Change Data Source

If you ever need to update the data source, you will have to do so through the PivotTable Wizard. Using the Change Data Source button will relink it with the other reports.

Planning Ahead

If you know you're going to be creating multiple PivotTables from the same data source and don't want them linked, start the reports with different data ranges. Then use the PivotTable Wizard to update the data source.

Refreshing the PivotTable

PivotTables don't automatically refresh as the data source is changed. You have to manually update the PivotTables. You can configure the data to update when the workbook is opened, though this does not update the data source.

Refresh on Open

You can manually set a PivotTable to refresh the data when the file is opened. This will affect all reports created from the same data source.

1. Select a cell in the PivotTable.

2. Select Options from the PivotTables Tools, Analyze tab.

3. Select Refresh Data When Opening the File from the Data tab.

4. Click OK.

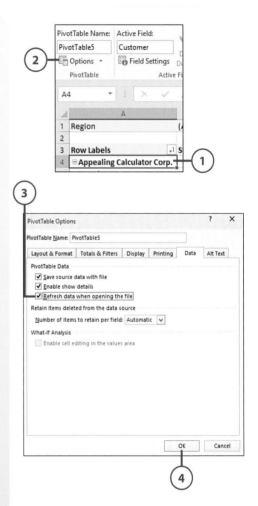

Refresh After Adding New Data

Unless you use a formatted table as the data source, you'll need to update the data source range when new rows or columns are added it.

1. Select a cell in the PivotTable.

2. Select Change Data Source from the PivotTables Tools, Analyze tab.

3. With the current range in the field highlighted, click the range selector tool.

4. Select the updated range.

5. Select the range selector tool to return to the dialog box.

6. Click OK.

7. Right-click over the PivotTable and select Refresh.

Unlinked Reports

If you have multiple reports using the same data source and you followed the instructions in "Unlinking PivotTables" to separate their caches, you can't use this method to update the data source because it will relink the reports. Instead, use the PivotTable Wizard to update the data range.

③

Change PivotTable Data Source   ?   ×

Choose the data that you want to analyze

⦿ Select a table or range

    Table/Range: 'Raw Data'!$A$1:$H$418

○ Use an external data source

    Choose Connection...

    Connection name:

○ Use this workbook's data model

OK   Cancel

⑥

Move PivotTable   ?   ×

'Raw Data'!$A$1:$H$420

④   ⑤

▤ Copy
▦ Format Cells...
↺ Refresh ——————— ⑦
   Sort   ▸

Refresh After Editing the Data Source

You have to refresh the PivotTable if you change a value in the data source.

1. To refresh a specific PivotTable, right-click over the report and select Refresh.

2. To refresh all the PivotTables in the workbook, select Refresh All from the Refresh drop-down on the PivotTables Tools, Analyze tab.

▤ Copy
▦ Format Cells...
↺ Refresh ——————— ①
   Sort   ▸

                    🗷 Clear ▾
                    🗏 Select ▾
Refresh Change Data   🡒 Move P
  ▾   Source ▾
↺ Refresh
↺ Refresh All ——————— ②

Working with Slicers

Slicers allow you to filter a PivotTable. Unlike the lists in filter drop-downs, slicer lists are always visible and you can change the dimensions of the slicer to better fit your sheet design.

Create a Slicer

Once inserted, a slicer can be sized and placed as needed.

1. Select a cell in the PivotTable.

2. On the PivotTable Tools, Analyze tab, select Insert Slicer.

3. Select the field you want a slicer for. It does not have to be a field shown in the report.

4. Click OK. The slicer is added to the sheet.

5. Place the pointer on the slicer's edge so it turns into a four-headed arrow. Click and drag the slicer to a new location.

6. Place the pointer over one of the circles on the slicer's edge so it turns into a two-headed arrow. Click and drag to resize the slicer.

Hide Filter Drop-Downs

If you set up slicers, you can hide the filter drop-downs by going to the Display tab of the PivotTable Options dialog box and unselecting Display Field Captions and Filter Drop Downs.

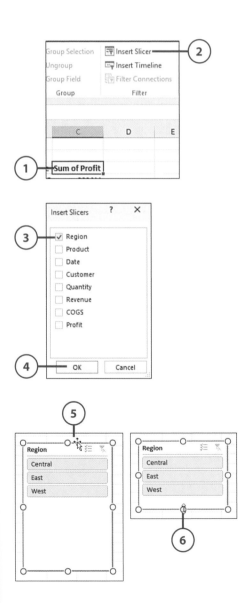

Use a Slicer

Use the slicer to filter the PivotTable.

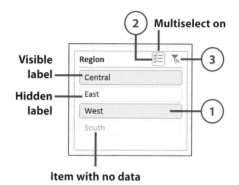

1. Toggle a label to have it visible or hidden in the PivotTable. Colored labels are visible. White labels are hidden.

2. Toggle the multiselect option. When the button has a border, the option is active, allowing the user to select multiple labels.

3. Clear the filter, making all labels visible.

It's Not All Good

Faded Slicers

By default, a slicer will show labels that were once used by the slicer, even if those records no longer exist in the PivotTable. Even when there are no filters in effect, these old labels are greyed out but still selectable. You can hide them by unselecting Show Items Deleted from the Data Source from the Slicer Settings on the Slicer Tools, Options tab.

Slicer Settings

Source Name: Region
Name to use in formulas: Slicer_Region
Name: Region
Header
☑ Display header
Caption: Region
Item Sorting and Filtering
- ◉ Ascending (A to Z)
- ◯ Descending (Z to A)
- ☑ Use Custom Lists when sorting
- ☐ Hide items with no data
- ☑ Visually indicate items with no data
  - ☑ Show items with no data last
- Show items deleted from the data source

OK   Cancel

Unselect to hide deleted items.

Picture with effects

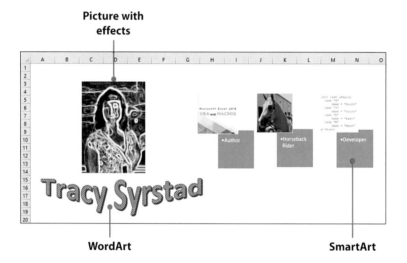

WordArt

SmartArt

In this chapter, you'll be introduced to Excel's image and graphic tools. Here are the topics covered in this chapter:

→ Inserting SmartArt

→ Designing a WordArt logo

→ Adding special effects to imported pictures

Inserting SmartArt, WordArt, and Pictures

You can add a little pizzazz to your workbooks by using graphic text and images. This chapter introduces you to SmartArt, which combines graphics and text to depict ideas. You'll also learn about WordArt, which can be used to twist colorful text, and the Picture tools you can use to manipulate imported images.

Working with SmartArt

SmartArt is a collection of similar shapes, arranged to imply a process, a relationship, or a hierarchy. You can add text to SmartArt shapes, and for some shapes, you can include a small picture or logo. For example, you could use SmartArt to create an organization's hierarchy chart with pictures of the employees.

SmartArt and the Web App

SmartArt graphics are removed when you open a workbook in the Excel Web App.

Insert a SmartArt Graphic

When you select a specific SmartArt graphic, Excel provides information about it and its more common uses.

1. On the Insert tab, select SmartArt.

No SmartArt Button

If you don't see the SmartArt button on the Insert ribbon tab, look under the Illustrations drop-down.

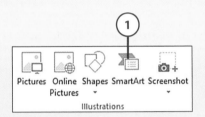

2. Select a SmartArt category.

3. Select a specific SmartArt design.

4. Click OK.

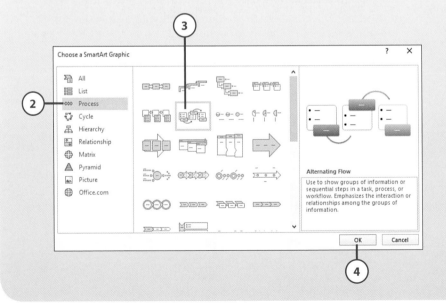

5. Select a bulleted item in the Text pane and enter the desired text.

Enter Text in Shape

You can enter text directly in a shape instead of through the Text pane. To do this, select the text in the shape and enter the desired text.

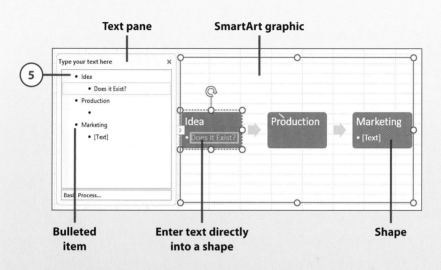

Text pane   **SmartArt graphic**

Bulleted   **Enter text directly**   **Shape**
item   **into a shape**

6. Press Enter to add a new item below the currently selected item.

7. To delete an item, remove all the text and then press Delete one more time to delete the bullet.

8. Select a cell on the sheet when you're done editing the graphic.

Missing Text Pane

Do not click the X in the upper-right corner of the Text Pane to close it; otherwise, the next time you place SmartArt, the Text Pane will not automatically appear. If this happens, you can manually open the Text Pane by selecting Text Pane from the SmartArt Tools, Design tab.

Insert Images into SmartArt

Some SmartArt layouts, such as the Hexagon Cluster, include image placeholders.

1. Insert a SmartArt graphic that includes image placeholders.

2. Click the image placeholder in the Text Pane.

   Or

3. Click the image placeholder in the graphic.

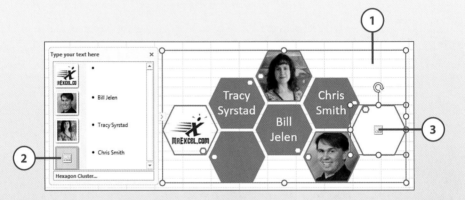

4. Select a location to browse.

5. Select the desired image and click Insert.

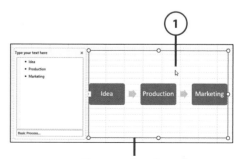

Edit or Change a Picture

The Picture Tools are available once a picture is selected. To change the image, select Change Picture from the Picture Tools, Format tab. Use the options on the Picture Tools, Format tab to make any required changes to the image. See the section "Inserting Pictures" for more information on tools for modifying pictures.

Move and Resize SmartArt

Selecting a SmartArt component must be done carefully. If you have the incorrect frame selected, you will move that shape instead of the entire SmartArt frame. When moving or resizing the graphic, you'll see that the Text Pane momentarily disappears.

1. Click near the graphic, but without clicking a shape, to select the graphic. Only the frame around the SmartArt graphic will be visible. Also, nothing will be selected in the Text Pane.

Frame only selected

2. To move the graphic, place the pointer on the frame until it turns into a four-headed arrow; then click and drag the graphic to a new location.

3. To resize the graphic, place the pointer over any resize handle on the frame. When it turns into a double-headed arrow, click and drag the graphic to a new size.

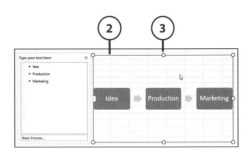

4. Click a shape to select it, and the frame around it becomes visible.

5. To move a shape, place the pointer within the shape so that the pointer turns into a four-headed arrow. Click and drag the shape to a new location.

6. To resize a shape, place the pointer over any resize handle on the frame. When it turns into a double-headed arrow, click and drag the graphic to a new size.

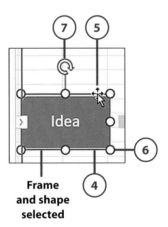

Frame and shape selected

7. To rotate a shape, place the pointer over the rotation handle. When the pointer turns into a circular arrow, hold the mouse button down and drag to rotate the shape.

8. To undo all size and movement changes to a shape, right-click over the shape and select Reset Shape.

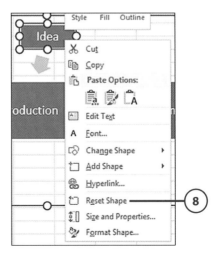

It's Not All Good

Resizing Shapes

When you resize a shape by moving one edge of it, the opposite edge will also move. For example, if you pull the bottom edge of a square down, the top edge of the square will move up, increasing the shape in both directions.

Reorder Placeholders

A placeholder can be moved up and down within its level, promoted up a level or demoted down a level.

1. Select the graphic so the Text Pane appears. If it does not appear, on the SmartArt Tools, Design tab, select Text Pane.

2. Select the text to be moved.

Moving Items with Children

Each item can be moved individually, with a sublevel moving with its parent level. If you're moving an entire shape, select level 1.

3. On the SmartArt Tools, Design tab, select Move Up or Move Down. Move Up and Move Down refer to the order of the items as shown in the Text Pane, not their actual position in the graphic.

4. Select Promote to increase the level of the selected item. The item will move to the left in the Text Pane.

5. Select Demote to decrease the level of the selected item. The item will move to the right in the Text Pane.

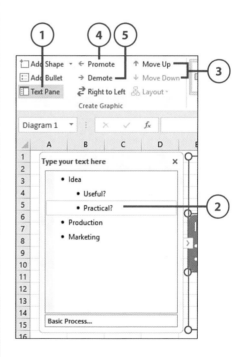

Move an Item to a New Level

An item can be moved only within its level; it cannot be moved into another group level. To get around this, promote the item, move it under the group level you want it in, and then demote it.

Change the Layout

Existing levels and text will transfer over to the new layout.

1. Select the graphic.

2. On the SmartArt Tools, Design tab, select a new layout from the Layouts gallery.

   Or

3. Select More Layouts to choose a completely new category.

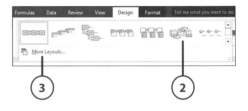

Change an Individual Shape

SmartArt doesn't have to be all squares or all circles. Once you've placed the initial shapes, you can change them to different shapes.

1. Select the shape to change.

2. On the SmartArt Tools, Format drop-down, select a new shape from the Change Shape drop-down.

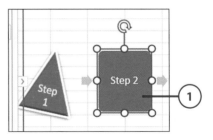

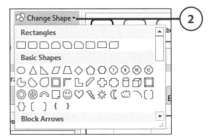

3. The selected shape will change.

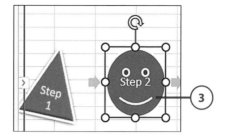

Working with WordArt

WordArt allows you to design text beyond the capabilities of the normal font settings on the Home tab. WordArt is a graphic you insert onto a sheet and then modify using various tools.

WordArt and the Web App
WordArt is removed when you open a workbook in the Excel Web App.

Insert WordArt

Designing your own WordArt is easy. Once inserted, you can place it wherever you want on the sheet.

1. On the Insert tab, select a text style from the WordArt drop-down.

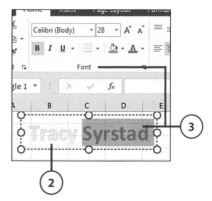

No WordArt Button
If you don't see the WordArt button on the Insert tab, look in the Text drop-down.

2. Select the default text in the WordArt and then type your own text.

3. To change the WordArt's font, select the WordArt frame or the desired text. Then, on the Home tab, make selections from the Font group.

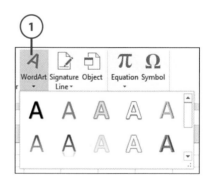

4. On the Drawing Tools, Format tab, select an effect from the Text Effects drop-down.

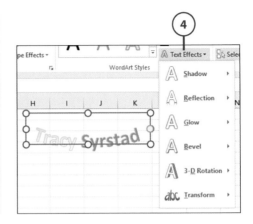

Inserting Pictures

Excel includes tools for modifying a picture, including picture correction, cropping, and special effects.

Insert a Picture

You can insert your own pictures or downloaded images onto a sheet. Once inserted, you can place the picture anywhere on the sheet.

1. Select the cell where you want the upper-left corner of the picture to be. This is the initial position of the image.

2. On the Insert tab, click Pictures to select a local picture or click Online Pictures to download an image.

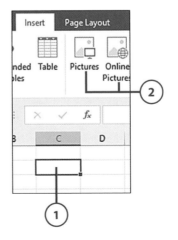

No Picture Button
If you don't see the Picture button on the Insert ribbon tab, look under the Illustrations drop-down.

---

3. Select the desired image and click Insert.

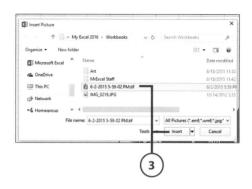

③

Resize and Crop a Picture

When you import a picture, it comes in its true size. That is, if the image is 8×10, then it will be 8×10 on the sheet. If you want only a part of the imported picture, you can crop it, removing what you don't need.

Cropped Images and the Web App

Cropped images are removed when you open a workbook in the Excel Web App. If the image is not cropped, it will remain in the workbook.

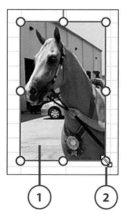

1. Select the picture.

2. To resize the picture, place the pointer over any circle on the frame. When the pointer turns into a double-headed arrow, click and drag the graphic to a new size.

① ②

Change the Aspect Ratio

By default, the aspect ratio is locked when using the corner resize handles on an image. To unlock them, right-click over the picture and select Size & Properties to open the Format Picture task pane. Unselect Lock Aspect Ratio underneath the Size properties.

Enter Specific Dimensions

You can enter the exact size of an image. On the Picture Tools, Format tab, enter specific dimensions in the size fields.

3. On the Picture Tools, Format tab, select the Crop button.

4. Click and drag the crop handles to frame the area you want to keep.

5. Click Crop again to trim away the shaded excess.

6. Select Reset Picture & Size from the Reset Picture drop-down to return the image to its original size. This will also undo any cropping, as long as the cropped areas haven't been permanently deleted to reduce the file size.

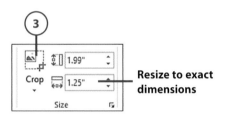

Resize to exact dimensions

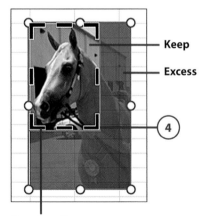

Keep

Excess

Crop handle

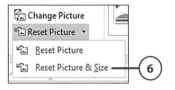

>>>Go Further

CROP TO A SHAPE

Select Crop to Shape from the Crop drop-down to crop the image to one of the shapes available in the drop-down. The image will be recut to the selected shape.

To nudge the image within the shape, right-click the image and select Format Picture. In the task pane, select the Picture icon. Underneath the Crop category, change the values in the Offset X and Offset Y fields. Adjusting the Offset X value moves the image left or right in the shape; adjusting the Offset Y value moves the image up or down in the shape.

Apply Corrections, Color, and Artistic Effects

You can correct the brightness and contrast, change a color image to a black-and-white image, or apply artistic effects to the selected image through the options in the Adjust group of the Picture Tools, Format tab.

As you move your pointer over an option in a drop-down, the image automatically adjusts, providing a preview of the option. Click the option to accept the change to the selected picture.

1. Select the picture.

2. Select Picture Corrections Options to open the Format Picture task pane.

Preset corrections

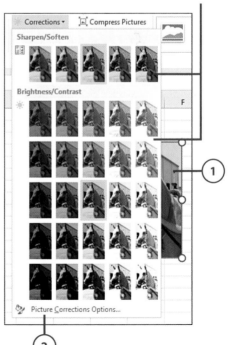

Choose From Preset Corrections

You can apply a number of preset corrections to your image. From the Corrections drop-down on the Picture Tools, Format tab, select an option to sharpen/soften the image or change the brightness/contrast.

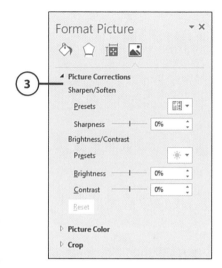

3. Adjust the settings for Sharpness, Brightness, and Contrast.

4. From the Color drop-down, modify the color saturation or tone, or apply a recolor option.

5. From the Artistic Effects drop-down, select an effect, such as Glow Edges, Film Grain, Light Screen, or any other effect that will change the way the image looks.

Reduce a File's Size

Importing a picture into a workbook can dramatically increase the file size. Compress the picture to reduce the file size.

1. Select the picture.

2. On the Picture Tools, Format tab, select Compress Pictures.

3. Unselect Apply Only to This Picture to compress all pictures in the workbook.

4. To further reduce the file size, select Delete Cropped Areas of Pictures to remove any picture parts that have been cropped. If you do this, you will not be able to reset the image.

5. If the picture is of high enough resolution, additional Target Output options will be available.

6. Click OK.

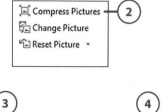

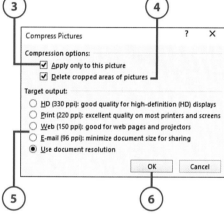

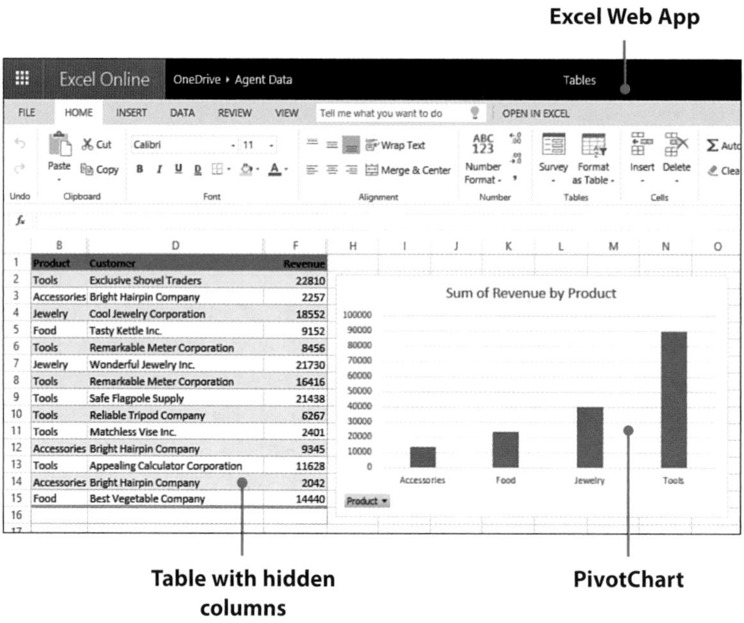
Excel Web App
Excel Online
OneDrive ▸ Agent Data
Tables
FILE HOME INSERT DATA REVIEW VIEW
Tell me what you want to do
OPEN IN EXCEL
Product Customer Revenue
Tools Exclusive Shovel Traders 22810
Accessories Bright Hairpin Company 2257
Jewelry Cool Jewelry Corporation 18552
Food Tasty Kettle Inc. 9152
Tools Remarkable Meter Corporation 8456
Jewelry Wonderful Jewelry Inc. 21730
Tools Remarkable Meter Corporation 16416
Tools Safe Flagpole Supply 21438
Tools Reliable Tripod Company 6267
Tools Matchless Vise Inc. 2401
Accessories Bright Hairpin Company 9345
Tools Appealing Calculator Corporation 11628
Accessories Bright Hairpin Company 2042
Food Best Vegetable Company 14440
Sum of Revenue by Product
Accessories
Food
Jewelry
Tools
Product
Table with hidden columns
PivotChart

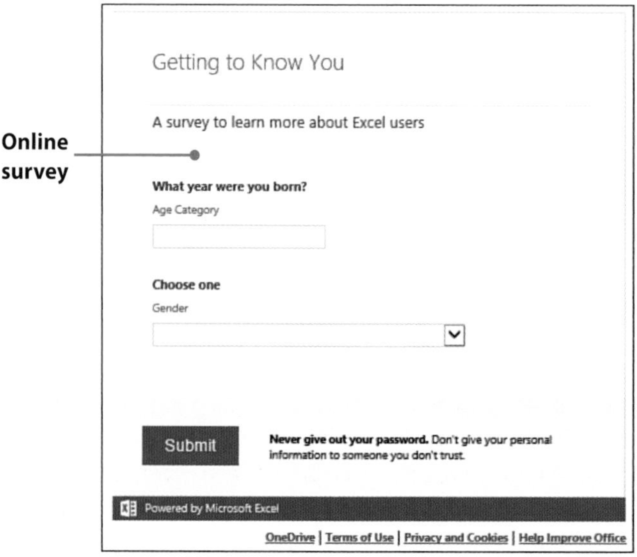
Online survey
Getting to Know You
A survey to learn more about Excel users
What year were you born?
Age Category
Choose one
Gender
Submit
Never give out your password. Don't give your personal information to someone you don't trust.
Powered by Microsoft Excel
OneDrive | Terms of Use | Privacy and Cookies | Help Improve Office

The Excel Web App allows multiple users anywhere with Internet access to enter data in the same workbook. Topics in this chapter cover the following:

→ Sharing a workbook online

→ Creating an online form to help users fill in a sheet and print the results

→ Creating a survey that can be filled out anonymously by others

Introducing the Excel Web App

The Excel Web App is a browser-based version of Excel that allows users to enter new data and formulas in an Excel workbook while online. Those users do not need to have Excel installed on their computers to use the app. Advanced functionality, such as creating PivotTables, is not present, but if you insert the PivotTable on the desktop version, it can be pivoted in the Web App.

All you need to get started is a Microsoft account, a current web browser, and an Internet connection.

Acquiring a Microsoft Account

With a Microsoft account, you can access the OneDrive online storage, where you can store, view, edit, and share your Excel workbooks. You don't need a Microsoft account if you are accessing a public file on someone else's OneDrive. But if you want to upload your own files or access a OneDrive requiring sign in, you will need a Microsoft account.

Other Microsoft-Owned Sites

A Microsoft account enables you to sign in to a variety of websites, such as Skype, Office Online, Outlook.com, and Xbox Live, using one account. If you already signed in to a Microsoft-owned site, it is possible you already have a Microsoft account. Before creating a new account, try signing in to onedrive.com with your existing credentials.

Create an Account

You can create the account using an existing email address, or you can obtain a new email address through the outlook.com or hotmail.com domain.

1. Use your web browser to navigate to signup.live.com.

2. Fill in the fields and click Create Account.

3. Follow the Microsoft instructions for verifying your email address.

Call us overprotective, but we need to verify that excelggirl@gmail.com is yours

Before you can continue, you need to check your inbox for a message from the Microsoft account team. Follow the instructions in the mail to finish setting up your account. Use a different email address as your Microsoft account

Resend email

4. You'll be signed in to your OneDrive account.

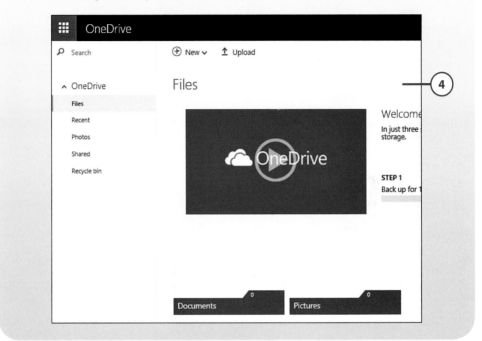

Uploading a Workbook

After you've signed in to your Microsoft account, you can upload your own workbooks or create new ones for viewing, editing, and sharing.

Upload Through OneDrive

You don't have to go through Excel to upload a workbook to OneDrive.

1. Select the folder to which you want to add your workbook.

2. Select Upload.

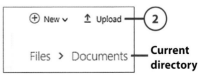

3. Select the file and click Open.

Unprotect the Workbook

Only unprotected workbooks can be opened online.

4. The file will be uploaded to your OneDrive. When the upload is complete, the page will update with an icon for the file.

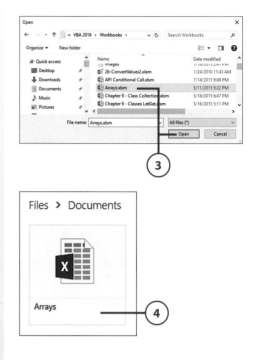

Save from Excel

You can save the workbook you're working on in the desktop version directly to the OneDrive.

1. Click File to open Backstage view.

2. Select Save As.

3. Select the OneDrive icon and then select a specific folder to save to.

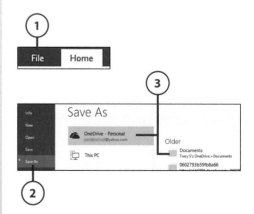

4. Enter a filename.

5. Select a file type.

Uploading Workbooks with Macros

You can upload a workbook with macros, but the macros will not work online.

New Folder link

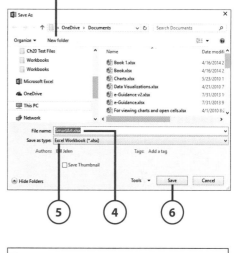

6. Click Save.

Create New Folder

If you need to create a new folder on your OneDrive, select any visible folder to open the Save As dialog box and use the New Folder link there to create the new folder. The folder will be created in your local OneDrive folder and online.

7. The file will be saved locally and then uploaded. You can watch the status of the upload in the status bar.

Delete a File from OneDrive

Delete files from your OneDrive when you no longer need them.

1. Right-click over the file and select Delete.

   Or

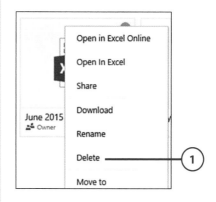

2. Place your cursor over the file, but do not click it yet.

3. Check the box that appears in the upper-right corner. It will change color to show it is selected. Repeat for any other files.

4. Select Delete.

Undoing Deletions

When you delete a file, a message box appears, for a few seconds, in the upper-right corner of the page, giving you the chance to undo the deletion. If you miss that chance, click the Recycle Bin on the left side of the page and restore it from there.

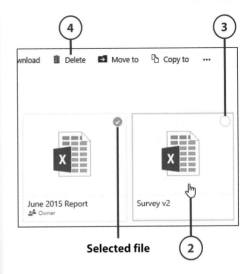

Selected file

Opening a Workbook Online or Locally

If don't see a ribbon when you open a workbook in the Web App, the workbook is in Reading View, which is view-only.

View-only workbook

Editable workbook

Open a Workbook

You can open an online workbook using the Web App or with the locally installed version of Excel.

1. Click the File icon to open the file in the Web App.

2. Right-click and select Open in Excel to open the file in the desktop version of Excel.

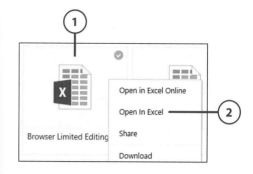

Download a Workbook

Eventually, you will want to work on a workbook saved locally. This can be done in several ways.

1. Right-click over the file and select Download. Follow your browser's prompts to save the file.

   Or

2. Place your cursor over the file, but do not click it yet.

3. Check the box that appears in the upper-right corner. It will change color to show it is selected. Repeat this step for any other files.

4. Select Download. Follow your browser's prompts to save the file.

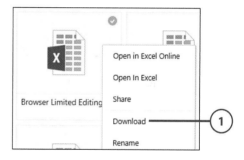

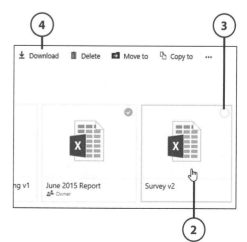

Download an Open Workbook

There are two ways to download a workbook you already have open in the Web App:

- With the file open in Reading View, select Edit in Excel from the Edit Workbook drop-down.

- With the file open normally, select Open in Excel.

In either case, Microsoft will warn about viruses. Click Yes if you trust the file.

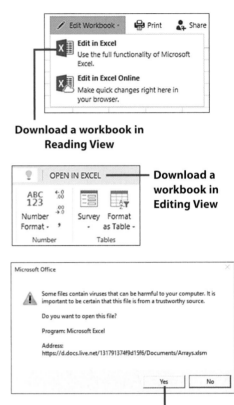

Download a workbook in Reading View

Download a workbook in Editing View

Click to download the file

Creating a New Workbook Online

You aren't limited to workbooks created previously in the desktop version of Excel. You can create a new workbook online and download it when you return to the office.

Create a Workbook

Excel will automatically save a new file online, using the default workbook naming convention (Book1.xlsx, Book2.xlsx, and so on).

1. From your OneDrive account, select Excel Workbook from the New drop-down.

2. The workbook is opened in the Web App.

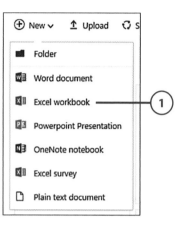

Rename the New Workbook

Because the Web App will automatically save the workbook you create online using the default naming convention, you have the option of renaming the file or saving a new copy of it.

1. Select File.

2. Select Save As.

3. If you want to leave the file in its current location but give it a new name, select Rename.

4. Enter a new name and then click OK.

5. If you want to save a copy of the file in a new location, select Save As.

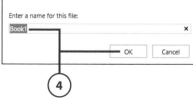

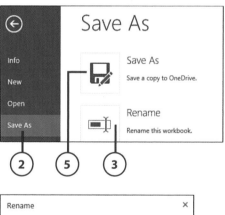

6. Select the folder you want to save the file in and click Save.

Create a New Folder
You don't have to go back out to the OneDrive main page to create a new folder. If you find you need a new folder while doing a Save As, click the New Folder button and follow the prompts.

7. Enter a filename and then click Save.

Don't Include the Extension
Do not include an extension when saving a file. The Web App will automatically include the extension, which is xlsx for new files. If you need to change from one file format to another (for example, from *.xlsx to *.xlsm), you will need to do this in the desktop version of Excel.

☁ OneDrive

✓ ☁ Tracy Syrstad's OneDrive
　■ Agent Data
　> ■ Client Records
　> ■ Documents
　　■ Pictures
　> ■ Purchasing Reports

You're not sharing this folder.

Save　Cancel　New folder

6

Create a new folder

Save to OneDrive　✕

Destination folder: 'Agent Data'

Enter a name for this copy:
June Reports　✕

Save　Cancel

7

Sharing a Folder or Workbook

OneDrive doesn't just provide you with the convenience of being able to work with your workbooks wherever you are. It also helps you share your workbooks and the folders you create with other people.

Create a View-Only Folder

If you set up a view-only folder, by default, any new files created in the folder will also be view-only.

1. Select Folder from the New drop-down.

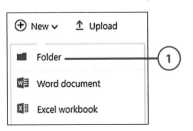

⊕ New ⌄　⬆ Upload

■ Folder ──── 1

W▤ Word document

X▤ Excel workbook

2. Enter a name for the folder and then click Create.

3. Place your cursor over the new folder, but do not click it yet.

4. Check the box that appears in the upper-right corner. It will change color to show it is selected.

5. Click the details icon to view the properties of the folder.

6. Select the Share link.

7. Select Get a Link.

8. Select View Only from the drop-down

9. Select Create Link.

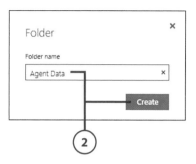

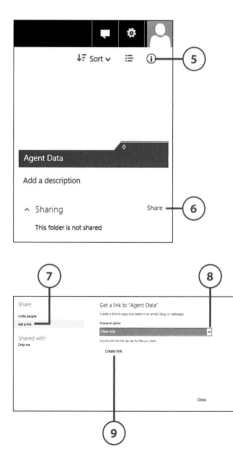

10. Copy the link if you wish to share it now. Click Close.

>>>Go Further

ALLOW SOME USERS TO EDIT THE FOLDER

If you want to allow some users to edit the folder, use the Invite People option. This option allows you to control permissions for each person, thus allowing a user to edit the folder. You can even set up whether the recipient does or does not require a Microsoft account to access the folder and its files.

Remove Sharing

If you've shared a link to your workbook but no longer want others to access it, you can remove their access.

1. Right-click over the folder and select Details.

2. Select the Share link.

3. Select the link to remove.

4. Select Remove Link.

No Remove Link Button

If a folder gets its sharing setting from its parent folder, the Remove Link Button will not be available. You will have to remove the sharing from the parent folder.

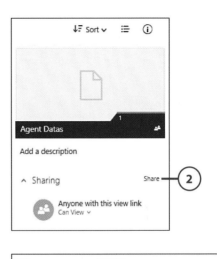

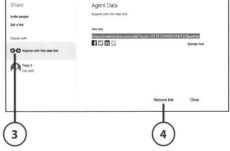

>>>Go Further

REMOVE A CO-OWNER

A user who creates a file in a folder becomes co-owner of the folder. This means if you delete the shared link previously sent to users, the co-owner will have access to any new workbooks added to the folder until the co-owner permission is also removed from the Sharing list.

To remove a co-owner, go into the Share properties of the file or folder, select the person's name, and then select Stop Sharing from the drop-down.

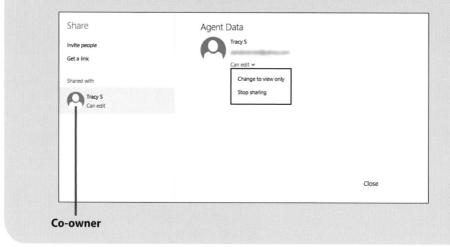

Co-owner

Edit Simultaneously

If you're allowing others to edit your workbook, eventually you will be editing the workbook at the same time as another person. You'll be able to see changes as they happen. The latest entry always has priority.

1. Click the drop-down to get details on who else has the workbook open.

2. The cells being edited will be highlighted with the user's corresponding color.

3. Place the cursor over an edited cell to get a user name tag.

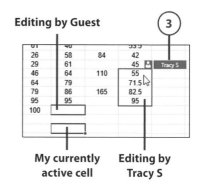

4. A cell is shaded when another
user is actively editing it.

55.5
42
45
100
200
82.5
95

④

Configuring Browser View Options

You can control which sheets are visible in the Web App from the desktop
version of Excel. You can also configure specific ranges on the sheet for data
entry, whether the user has View or Edit privileges. All of this is done via the
Browser View Options available through the Save As dialog box in Excel.

Create an Online Form

You may not want users to see all your
sheets or be able to edit any cell they
wish. You can choose sheets to hide
and configure parameters, limiting
user entry.

1. In the desktop version of Excel,
apply a name to each cell you
want the user to edit. Note
that only single cells, including
merged cells, can be configured
for user entry. Use short names
that will make sense to users as
they fill in the form.

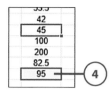

More Information on Named Ranges

For more information on created
named ranges, see "Using Names to
Simplify References" in Chapter 8,
"Using Formulas."

2. Click File to open Backstage view.

3. Select Save As.

4. Select your OneDrive and then the specific folder.

5. Enter a filename.

6. Select a file extension.

7. Select Browser View Options.

8. To hide specific sheets, select Sheets from the drop-down on the Show tab.

9. Unselect the sheets you don't want users to see. They'll still be uploaded, just hidden.

10. On the Parameters tab is a list of all permissible names.

11. Select a name and click Delete to remove it from the list.

12. Click OK.

13. Click Save. The file will be uploaded to your OneDrive.

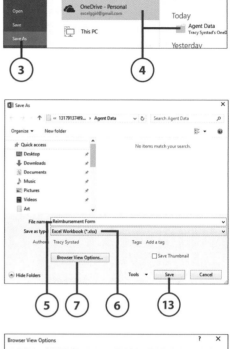

14. To view the file as another user would, open the file in the Web App and select Reading View from the View tab.

15. Users can place data into the allowable fields by entering the data in the Parameters task pane.

>>>Go Further
LIMITATIONS FOR THE BROWSER VIEW OPTIONS

When you add parameters to a sheet, a few of the Web App sharing rules change:

- Recipients with View and Edit links can only enter information in the parameters. The rest of the workbook is protected.

- Workbooks with data entry parameters are not shared. Each user opens a unique copy.

- Entries are not automatically saved. The user must save his or her own copy.

- Parameters only affect the online sheet. Once the sheet is downloaded, the data entry limitations are removed.

Designing a Survey Through the Web App

You could design a survey on a sheet and share the workbook. Or, you can use the Web App tools to create a survey that looks nothing like a sheet. Users can fill it out anonymously and the results will be saved to an online workbook.

Create a Survey

Create an online survey from within the Web App and provide a link to others to fill it out.

1. Select Excel Survey from the New drop-down in the OneDrive Web App.

2. Fill in the title and description of the survey.

3. Select the first question field.

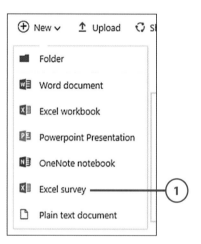

4. Fill in the fields in the Edit Question dialog box.

5. Select Done.

6. Select Add New Question for each additional survey question and fill in the required information.

7. To edit a question, select it, and the Edit dialog box will open. If it doesn't, click the Settings icon for the selected question.

8. Click Save and View to see what the survey will look like.

9. Click Share Survey to generate a link to distribute the survey.

10. As users fill out the survey, their results are added to the workbook. To view the survey results, open the workbook.

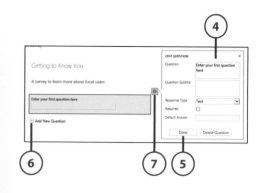

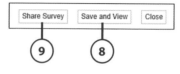

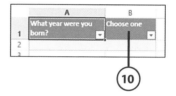

Edit an Existing Survey

To edit an existing survey, open the workbook in the Web App and select Edit Survey from the Survey drop-down on the Insert tab.

Index

Symbols

A

C

D

E

F

M

O

Q

T

X-Y-Z

More Best-Selling **My** Books!

Learning to use your smartphone, tablet, camera, game, or software has never been easier with the full-color My Series. You'll find simple, step-by-step instructions from our team of experienced authors. The organized, task-based format allows you to quickly and easily find exactly what you want to achieve.

Visit quepublishing.com/mybooks to learn more.